Date Due

SAFARI OF DISCOVERY

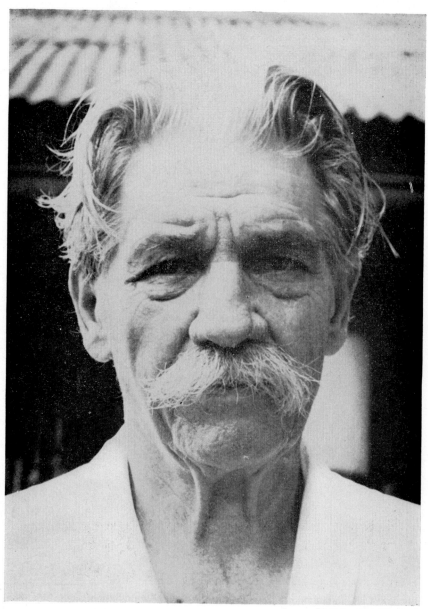

Photo by Clara Urquhart.

This recent picture of Dr. Schweitzer shows lines chiselled by excessive work, continuous exposure to the elements, and a cosmic concern for man in his period of unprecedented peril.

SAFARI
OF
DISCOVERY

THE UNIVERSE OF ALBERT SCHWEITZER

by Herbert M. Phillips

TWAYNE PUBLISHERS
NEW YORK

Acknowledgments

Although my travels have personally acquainted me with many of the authors of the growing number of books about Dr. Schweitzer, I would like first of all to thank those writers in this field whom I have not yet met. The books by these authors unknown to me have been counsellors, comforters, and lively companions. My hearty debates and silent disagreements with absent and unknown authors have not lessened my sense of fellowship with these strangers. Let me say that these authors, unknown to me in face-to-face friendships, are remembered individually and collectively with gratitude.

I heartily contest the truth of most views expressed by the late Oskar Kraus in his book, *Albert Schweitzer: His Work and His Philosophy.* Nevertheless I appreciate the fundamental questions he put to Dr. Schweitzer—questions so precisely stated that they drew answers from Dr. Schweitzer which have been more definitive than many chapters of exposition.

I could not disagree more completely than I do with John Middleton Murry's convictions expressed in *Love, Freedom, and Society.* But his attacks on Dr. Schweitzer show clearly many of the cleavage lines most worthy of continuous debate.

I want to thank especially the inquiring and penetrating E. N. Mozley for *Theology of Albert Schweitzer for Christian Enquirers.* This book helped me to see the important meaning Dr. Schweitzer has as a symbol for conventional religious people in the Western world.

I wholeheartedly state my general concurrence with the perceptive, apocalyptic interpretation given by Mrs. C. E. Russell in *The Path to Reconstruction.*

Albert Schweitzer: An Anthology, skillfully compiled by Charles R. Joy, has been my constant traveling companion on three continents. The volume, *The Africa of Albert Schweitzer,* which Mr. Joy and Melvin Arnold collaborated to produce, was an invaluable source book in preparing for my own pilgrimage. Likewise Hermann Hagedorn's *Prophet in the Wilderness* was a dramatic guide to my explorations in Africa.

To Eugene Exman I give my thanks, not only for the encyclopedia of facts he skillfully condensed into the text of *The World of Albert Schweitzer,* but for the more capricious spiritual qualities he managed to capture in his prose. I have invariably given this book to newcomers wishing to drink vicariously at the spiritual oasis in Lambaréné.

Except for its almost complete neglect of Dr. Schweitzer's *Philosophy of Civilization,* I consider Robert Payne's *The Three Worlds of Albert Schweitzer* the most readable, realistic, and refreshing of recent biographies.

And now a toast to the gifts of friendship. I wish to acknowledge with personal affection the scattered penmen and coterie of interpreters with whom I became well acquainted while immersed in my own research.

I must mention with gratitude Erica Anderson, the determined Austrian-born photographer from New York City, who became one of Dr. Schweitzer's closest friends. She succeeded, where big producers had failed, in making an "Oscar"-winning documentary movie covering Dr. Schweitzer's life. Also, in collaboration with Eugene Exman, she published from her own collection of arresting photographs a most revealing book of pictures entitled *The World of Albert Schweitzer,* mentioned earlier.

I am similarly indebted to Clara Urquhart from London. This charming author, photographer, and voluntary co-worker at Lambaréné is responsible for the delightful book, *With Dr. Schweitzer at Lambaréné,* featuring the too-often neglected personnel upon whose services the Lambaréné hospital depends.

It is a pleasure to acknowledge a most profitable and enjoyable visit I had with Dr. Max Tau of Oslo, author of *Albert Schweitzer and the Road to Yourself,* and editor of the *Library of Peace.* In my judgment this German-born and now favored foster son of Norway has one of the finest minds in the world of ethics.

Among those whose written works in my library remind me of friendships and personal correspondence, there are eight whom I wish to thank for their willingness to read my book in typescript. Their generosity exceeded the call of friendship.

Precision reading for the purpose of critical judgment, even as a labor of love in the interest of Dr. Schweitzer's good name, involves hours of tedious mental exertion. I must admit it was gratifying to me that—save one—the reports sent to me by the author-readers were preponderantly favorable.

In the category of authors whose reactions in preview were preponderantly favorable, I wish to mention the following European writers with grateful appreciation: the Very Reverend George Seaver, Dean of the Church of Ireland and Albert Schweitzer's first and most prolific biographer and earliest exponent in the English language; Dr. Fritz Buri, minister of the Cathedral at Basel, Switzerland, and Professor of Systematic Theology at the University of Basel; Emil Mettler, Swiss-born resident of London, who has known Gandhi, Toyohiko Kagawa, and Einstein personally and who has been Dr. Schweitzer's confidant for thirty-five years and was his host when he received the Order of Merit in England; Dr. Hans Casparis, President of the Albert Schweitzer College of Churwalden, Switzerland.

On the American scene, I want to express thanks to my very dear friend Dr. Ernest Cadman Colwell, who as President of the University of Chicago presided when Dr. Schweitzer received his honorary degree in 1949. Because of Dr. Colwell's eminence as a theological scholar and author, I was heartened to know that in his judgment I had faithfully presented the image of Jesus revered by Albert Schweitzer, even though Dr. Colwell reminded me that his own interpretation of Jesus is still less orthodox. I am indebted also to Norman Cousins, editor of the *Saturday Review* and author of numerous articles about

Albert Schweitzer, for his sympathetic perusal of my manuscript and the insights he has contributed to my understanding of Dr. Schweitzer.

I should mention here one man who is not yet an author but whose claim to competence as a judge of Dr. Schweitzer's views and activities arises from seven years of service as chief surgeon at Lambaréné. Dr. Emerick Percy examined the book in great detail. His help in checking statements pertaining to medical matters was invaluable. His over-all commendation gave me comfort and considerable confidence as I proceeded toward publication.

It would be far from the truth to say that these learned readers who favored my interpretation of Dr. Schweitzer on major issues did not challenge minor propositions. I scrutinized these contested points very carefully. It was fortunate for all concerned that my attention was directed to some weaker premises in time for me to repent and rewrite. Where I could not yield to a critic, I buttressed my assertions with more evidence and quotations from Dr. Schweitzer's own writings.

I do not suppose I would have endured the pains and tedium of double-checking my central propositions if Dr. Johann B. Hygen from the Department of Ethics, Theology and Philosophy in the University of Oslo, Norway, had not disagreed with me on almost every major issue. He questioned my interpretation of Dr. Schweitzer as a prophet and his complex views of God, Jesus, Paul, Christianity, religion in general, the meaning of civilization, Hegel, Marx, the nature of education, as well as the equating of "will-to-live" with freedom. With absolute candor and as an admirer of Dr. Schweitzer, Dr. Hygen openly confessed his own prejudice and fairly admitted basic differences with much of Dr. Schweitzer's theological scholarship. Nevertheless, Dr. Hygen's lengthy, more orthodox challenge provoked in me a session of careful self-searching and a tedious review. Thanks to his questioning of my central convictions, my book now can be sent forth with renewed agreement between my mind and my manuscript. In this period of re-examination I cured myself of the last vestige of any indecision on the big issues.

On the affirmative side of the ledger, I hasten to state that I owe much to literally hundreds of authors who have attempted to find and express the core of Dr. Schweitzer's message in pamphlets, in journals, and articles appearing in mass media. In this category I tender my special thanks to those I met and with whom I exchanged ideas. I recall with gratitude my visit with Mr. Gunnar Jahn, chairman of the Nobel Peace Prize Committee, from Norway; Mr. Waldemar Ahlen, organist from Stockholm, and the Rev. Harald Tigerstrom, pastor from Linkoping, Sweden.

I owe more than I can express to my neighbor, Dr. Homer Jack, editor of editions of Gandhi and the weekly pamphlet called *Disarmament,* and pastor of the Unitarian Church of Evanston.

There is a small group of specialists whose help I wish to acknowledge with gratitude. These people are little acquainted with Dr. Schweitzer's writings. Nevertheless they formed a semi-professional group of critical readers, particularly in the field of education. They are: Dr. Everett Olson, head of the Geology Department at the University of Chicago; Mrs. Harry M. Mulberry, member of the Chicago Board of Education; and Mr. and Mrs. Louis Cheskin, experts in art, color, and motivation research.

From the category of lay readers I must thank Mrs. Patrick Adduci, Mrs. Fergus Irvine, Dr. and Mrs. J. W. Stocks, and Mrs. Jack Boozer, and some who read fragments of my manuscript with an eye to stamping out sins of syntax.

In this group Mrs. John Mansnerus merits special thanks. She generously has given many hours to careful critical reading. More than this, she transcribed the first chapters into braille in order that Richard Kinney, a deaf and sightless scholar-poet, could read and criticize my efforts. I give my thanks to both, and I must add that Mr. Kinney's soaring, creative spirit was a most stimulating inspiration.

There are many who are not authors of writings dealing with Dr. Schweitzer and many who did not read my manuscript, who nevertheless contributed one way or another to my adventure and therefore to my book.

I am grateful to that renowned circle of "Schweitzer-philes" that includes individuals like Mrs. Julian Rogers, organizer of a weekly radio show on Albert Schweitzer in Boston; Rev. Duncan Littlefair, of the Fountain Street Church, Grand Rapids, Michigan; Rev. Preston Bradley of the People's Church of Chicago; Governor Adlai Stevenson; Harold Fey, editor of the *Christian Century;* Dr. Paul Schilpp, philosophy professor at Northwestern University; and Dr. and Mrs. Larimer Mellon, founders and operators of the Albert Schweitzer Hospital in Haiti. These people by friendship and deeds have in diverse ways helped me in understanding the contagious spirit of Albert Schweitzer.

I am more than grateful to Mme. Hanna Oberman, Ali Silver, Mathilde Kottmann, Dr. Jan Van Stolk, and "Doctoress" Van der Kreek, and all others who supplemented the gracious hospitality extended to me at Lambaréné with unforgettable gestures of personal kindness. Each servant at Lambaréné is a creative personality when known at close range.

In connection with the educational theme that runs through the book I must acknowledge the advice, cooperation and counsel I received from: Emory Ross, treasurer of the Albert Schweitzer Fellowship in the United States; Douglas Steere, chairman of the Philosophy Department at Haverford College and present head of the Department of Geography at the University of Chicago; Gilbert White, former president of Haverford College; James Luther Adams, Professor of Ethics at Harvard; Howard C. Rice, librarian at Princeton University; Payson Wild, Vice-President and Dean of the Faculties at Northwestern University; Percival Brundage, former director of the

United States Budget and head of fund-raising in America for the Albert Schweitzer College of Churwalden, Switzerland; Harold Stassen, recently advisor to President Eisenhower on disarmament; Gen. Millard Young, former head of psychological warfare under the Joint Chiefs of Staff; and Joseph Lohman, scholar sheriff of Cook County (Chicago), Illinois.

How can one ever thank the really great men in the field of ethics? Intrusions into their consecrated hours burden their allotment of time and their sensitive energies, straining to answer the demands of destiny. May I just humbly thank Toyohiko Kagawa, Rabindranath Tagore, Mahatma Gandhi, and Albert Einstein? Their gifts of brief moments are treasures of great magnitude to me.

I am grateful to Arnold Toynbee, to whose books and personal counsel I owe the means I used to "discover" Dr. Schweitzer for myself and the courage to present him as the overdue, much needed Prophet of the divided Western world. On a recent personal visit I made to London, Dr. Toynbee agreed that the Prophet theme of my book and the theme of Freedom merited a reasonable expectation of being worthy of public consideration.

The aid I received from friends in Dr. Schweitzer's orbit does not lessen my own responsibility for the residual inadequacies in this book. These are mine alone.

My fondest hope is that some readers will as a result of this book see for themselves fires worthy of fanning for freedom's sake. It will be perhaps an appetizer for some, tempting them to devour Dr. Schweitzer's deeper and more difficult books in translation or—better—in the original French and German.

I would be less than honest if I kept from the reader the truth that most of all I am grateful for having been an eye witness to the vast wonderment of good will that is spontaneously generated by Dr. Schweitzer among those who know him. Actually most of the surprising eagerness and warmth shown me and my project were tributes to the distant magnetic man.

And now before closing, I would like to state my gratitude
to the unnamed German-speaking barber in Switzerland who
saw fit as a secret gesture of veneration to close his shop to
escort the "lost" English-speaking traveler to the home of Albert
Schweitzer's daughter. This deed was a beginning in a chain
of wonderful events very important to me. The barber represents hosts of helpers including many young students whose
names have escaped my recall but whose charitable deeds and
probing questions arise to delight my periods of reminiscence.

Frustrating though my first meeting with Dr. Schweitzer was,
I am thankful to Madame Rhena Eckert for arranging my
initial encounter with her illustrious father. Less auspicious
but not less charming were later hours spent with her and her
family. I thank her most for letting me peel potatoes in her
kitchen like kinfolk or like a family friend.

I would like to close with a modest corsage of well-picked
words for my closest companion and the silent accomplice who
has made possible through forbearance as well as indispensable
technical assistance all that I have done. The indignities my
sweet co-conspirator has borne in the name of adventure in the
hottest corners of the dusty earth would have exhausted the
virtue of a lesser angel. But one cannot thank a wife for the
inexhaustible patience needed to tolerate a roving spirit. In
boundless gratitude all I can do is thank Providence for such
a wife.

                                                         H. M. P.

Table of Contents

Entrance to a Forest
Cathedral of Ideas

Three ebony lepers—one minus fingers and toes—paddled me in a dugout tree-trunk up the swift Ogowe River through the great forest of French Equatorial Africa toward Albert Schweitzer's famous—in the view of some, "notorious"—jungle hospital.

The main motive for my trip to Lambaréné was probably plain curiosity. I had long admired Dr. Schweitzer's voluminous writings. But what, I had often asked myself, was this famous scholar of ethics hoping to do in his unique medical mission hospital in one of the darkest recesses of the black continent?

From the beginning, back in my library, I saw Dr. Schweitzer through the mists of my ethical ignorance as a new model of a free man presenting in words and deeds a gospel of freedom so much needed by the free individuals of the world in their collisions with tyranny. This big hypothesis, I had learned in my early, too-precipitous inquiry at Gunsbach, really needed long, patient, painstaking examination, clarification, and testing by reading and cross-references.

My deeper motives for this safari were modestly masked by a fine, respectable mission. The ostensible object of my visit was to request the renowned and eccentric man of learning to lend his spirit of scholarship to higher education in America by allowing university "chairs" or "distinguished professorships" to be created in his name.

Of course, I considered my ostensible mission valid and valuable. This may have become my primary purpose. Had I not set forth zestfully on this pilgrimage from Chicago, assured by several of Dr. Schweitzer's friends and each of six major universities consulted that the educational plan was wholly worth while?

Now that I was approaching my destination, affected by the strangeness of the inscrutable Africans paddling their primitive craft along this sullen jungle highway, I felt a creeping uncertainty about the merit of my mission. If Dr. Schweitzer agreed—and what man would not? —I wondered: would the educational impact on our American youth and universities generally, whether great or small, be wholesome? Selfishly, I wondered most how his influence would affect my own sons if they were exposed to his compelling wisdom and charm.

A chilling doubt within me whispered: The issues involved in Dr. Schweitzer's ethics are explosive, and you are a frail and wavering reed on a God-sized errand.

Lost in self-searching, I recalled that over four decades ago this unorthodox Alsatian scholar had been requested to pledge to the Paris Missionary Society that he would be "mute as a fish" in matters of his theology before they grudgingly accepted him and provided for his medical needs an abandoned, decaying, filthy, windowless henhouse in their mission station at Lambaréné. Rumors testify that German missions turned him down without a hearing.

Unlike the evangelists in this Paris Missionary Society, the young doctor had to provide from his own resources all of the actual expenses for his entire undertaking. He committed his earnings from organ concerts, university lectures and sermons, as well as the royalties from his popular book on Johann Sebastian Bach. He accomplished this feat of free enterprise while earning his third doctorate degree and learning tropical medicine.

I wondered if Dr. Schweitzer suspected before going to Africa what the missionary society failed to realize, namely, that the jungle doctor's unique and silent service would prove so deafeningly eloquent and spiritually disturbing to many throughout the world. Surely no one else guessed that his remote, quiet

deeds of love performed in secret would have the popularity
of parables and would start controversies in many circles in the
Western world.

My chanting paddlers kept close to the edge of the forest
that projected into the water. The unfamiliar trees buttressed
by a network of roots, and the labyrinth of creepers that choked
the giants and kept the dead and decaying trees from falling,
helped to hold my thoughts on the storms of controversy and
the paradoxes surrounding Schweitzer-land. Recent visitors have
reconnoitered and returned with allegations of shocking defects.

Dr. Schweitzer is censured by some for saving bodies, not
souls. Some of his mission practices and many of his personal
convictions have been judged un-Christian.

There is considerable evidence that the British Broadcasting
Corporation's religious advisory committee for a time timidly
banned discussions of Albert Schweitzer on the air because his
views are not in the main stream of the Christian tradition. One
whole book purported to prove that Dr. Schweitzer is perniciously
un-Christian. Another whole book vindicated his Christianity
but even more, his fundamental religiousness.

Some attack Dr. Schweitzer's hospital for its alleged lack of
sanitation. John Gunther spoke of the sanitary arrangements
as "picturesque." He condemned the hospital as "filthy beyond
description" and "the most unkempt place of its kind . . ." In
its magazine, the Free Church of Scotland attacked the sanitary conditions, stating that "animals with serious infections
mingle with the staff and patients and deposit their filth everywhere, including the operating rooms."

Many American missionaries accuse Dr. Schweitzer of colonial
sympathies and segregation practices. Many label him authoritarian, dictatorial, pedantic, prejudiced in race relations. Some
say he is Teutonic, irascible and paternalistic, preaching to
Africans that "father knows best." Some say his interest in
animals supersedes his concern for man, and man rather than

men. Liberals have claimed his colonial policy is not only naive but a "fundamental defect in Schweitzer's outlook."

In his writings Albert Schweitzer has taken issue with the direction in which science is impelling the modern world. In recent years Dr. Schweitzer has called on the conscience of all scientists to acquaint the public with the horrors of hydrogen weapons. One release split the world of science by pleading for a ban on hydrogen bomb tests. This historic argument, like his previous arguments, could have been ignored were it not for the fact that it somehow mobilized public opinion of the world behind its claim to wisdom, challenging the leadership of science.

Perhaps the most disquieting issue, or perhaps the most de-basing manifestation of slander, has grown out of the clash between Schweitzer and many men classified as scientists. Many who disagree have hinted in veiled ways and openly in national publications that Albert Schweitzer gives aid and comfort to the Commies and is himself either a Red sympathizer or at best a naive dupe. Naturally I was inclined to discount the charge but was determined nevertheless to make my own judgment.

On the other hand, Dr. Schweitzer has idolaters who go the limit in eulogy. Some believe him to be Jesus incarnate. Among the disciples of this cult, their Lord can do no wrong.

One with my kind of curiosity is pressed to ask: Why do these wide differences of interpretation occur? What are the facts? Are these differing reports like those of the blind men describing the elephant? Do some open eyes see not at all while others half-shut see overmuch? Was there in Dr. Schweitzer and his hospital some undiscovered order, a coordinating consistency in the paradoxes, that would explain the conflicting opinions?

I was confident that my surgical background would help to clarify the cold, scientific, clinical issues for me; but would my predispositions favoring antisepsis hermetically seal my mind to ethereal undercurrents and overtones? Something more than a scientific yardstick and professional understanding—perhaps a new kind of objectivity—might be needed to stalk truth in Dr. Schweitzer's strange cathedral built of ideas.

Though the merit of my ostensible mission was in doubt for the moment, my free curiosity was intrigued and challenged. I found myself pondering about Albert Schweitzer's role in human history and about the abiding mysticism that surrounds the man and his strange ethic of Reverence for Life.

Paradoxically enough, through my uneasiness I held fast to the conceit that somehow I would find the wisdom to interpret and evaluate the stubborn old heretic and his silent deeds of gentle violence.

I did not realize then in the dugout canoe on the Ogowe River that this free curiosity was to lead me to a glimpse of a wholly new modern power in man. Fully realized, his vision of the universe, life and goodness might cause history to change its wavering course.

Even before the lepers beached my canoe at Dr. Schweitzer's hospital, I was surprised by haunting music that ran out over the water to meet me. On the bank Mlle. Mathilde Kottman greeted me warmly. When the music stopped, Dr. Schweitzer came out of his room. He gave me a hearty welcome—alas, in French!

Albert Schweitzer, past eighty-one, the aging yet seemingly ageless peasant before me in baggy pants, beat-up shoes, and open-throated white shirt with short sleeves, surmounted with a cork helmet, gesticulated his greeting. He kept his parchment-crinkled face mobile with smiles that said unmistakably, "Welcome, friend, to my African home and hospital."

Depressed by my language limitations, I followed Mlle. Mathilde down a long veranda, passing a tier of identical cells inhabited by doctors and co-workers, to a long, narrow chamber that already held my bags. Mlle. Mathilde, whom I had pre-

viously met in Dr. Schweitzer's home in Gunsbach, Alsace, in
1954, deserves a special service halo for decades of devotion to
Dr. Schweitzer. She speaks, however, only French. Soon, as
with the doctor, due to my own lack of language fluency,
communications stuck on dead center.

Left alone, I examined my room. I confess that first of all
I checked the narrow iron cot and found it made up with a
tidy blanket and rough, clean sheets. The bed looked inviting
enough. I found none of the specimens of tiny man-eating
wildlife in my bed that I had known too well in France, India,
China, Afghanistan, and even in California. I had come armed
with insect repellents, fearing that "Reverence for Life" might
be carried at Lambaréné to the point of reverence for lice and
other nocturnal companions. I saw none of the "fine" black
spiders and "splendid" flying cockroaches Dr. Schweitzer speaks
of ejecting mercifully from his rooms. While looking for snakes
about the floor, I found a "potty" discreetly placed behind a
curtain.

My homemade stall I saw at a glance lacked air-conditioning,
radio, electric lights, telephone, tub, shower, and hot water. I
reminded myself that the room did contain the simple comforts
that I had found temporarily charming during holidays in
Wisconsin, Michigan, Yellowstone National Park, and Canada.

There was in my screened-in quarters, for example, "running
water"—that is to say, water that could be made to flow out
of two large tin pitchers plainly labelled Rain Water. A separate flask contained boiled drinking water. A rough homemade
desk and two chairs congested the far end of the small room
that looked down on some of the other forty-odd earthy but
sturdy hovels composing the settlement. The windows were
screened but lacked glass. Simple drapes assured privacy. An
old-fashioned kerosene lamp stood on the desk. A lantern was
provided for night prowling. (The unpleasantly fly-infested
wooden outhouse was a block away.) I unpacked with my
spirits rising.

After setting my watch to Dr. Schweitzer's time, twenty minutes slower than standard time, I went on a get-acquainted walk. In the freedom of a private, unguided stroll about the settlement, I encountered many Africans and Europeans. The sick and the strong among the human inhabitants mingled with multitudes of animals. I investigated most of the scattered corrugated iron-roofed buildings and witnessed certain shocking images and events that explained the controversial evaluations pilgrims bring back concerning the hospital settlement.

The yards between the scattered wooden buildings built on piles, though cleared of jungle, were unlandscaped, raw, dusty terrain, cluttered by dead leaves, old tenacious roots, twigs, and general disorder. As on many a proper farm, a spotty mantle of animal excrement blended with the good earth. But on Lambaréné's dirty face it seemed as natural as smudges on the face of a coal miner.

The reality struck me with clarity: Albert Schweitzer's so-called hospital was designed essentially as an African forest village to suit his "clients." All the daytime functions that occur between birth and death in African villages—gathering firewood, hunting food, fetching water, cooking in soot-blackened utensils, unceremonial eating of staples like bananas, manioc, imported rice, and river fish, desultory working, resting, mending, and baby sitting—were here occurring in complete candor. Most garbage, but not all, gets incinerated. Latrines, not too well concealed, are conspicuous by their smell. Pregnancy is prevalent.

The African community, I noticed, huddled in separate clusters. The encampment, though designed as a village, is composed of many tribal groups hailing from ten separate language areas. Each convalescent patient is tended by his wife (or wives), members of his family, or his friends, who also must tend to their own simple creature wants under the pall of smoke from many fires. Tribal taboos, superstitions, and customs that give order, honor, and homogeneity in the separated pockets of people in the forest, add variety in this strange, ragged congregation. Tribal enemies, many of them ex-cannibals and head-hunters, are here separated only by a language barrier. They cook separately, lest their food be poisoned by a hostile stranger. Cases of actual poisoning are occasionally treated in the clinic.

Though African villages commonly swarm with animals, Dr. Schweitzer's reservation appears to be a veritable zoo. To the disgust of some visitors, to the delight of others, and to the awe of all, Dr. Schweitzer, the lover of life, lives in the midst of a varied menagerie of his own choosing. He has been a veterinary, friend, and host to monkeys, apes, chimpanzees, dogs, fawns, chickens, ducks, storks, goats, lizards, porcupines, parrots, pelicans, and wild pigs.

The state of nature which Kant, Locke, and Rousseau had to imagine is written in the activities of daily life for Albert Schweitzer. He can read the unwritten codes of the jungle and its rules of justice from the living archives about him. He can witness natural rights, human rights, self-evident truths, anarchy, and democracy in their primordial nakedness. Though reasoned ethics are absent among animals, fraternity, equality, and liberty are the unwritten, natural commandments that flow from the primeval forest into Dr. Schweitzer's own front yard. The spiritual unreason and unfreedom of lawless anarchy is everywhere apparent.

On my rounds I wandered down toward the river, through the fenced-in vegetable garden planted by the late Mlle. Emma Haussknecht. I knew from my reading that this cultivation represented a great triumph for Albert Schweitzer the Planter and Sower of Seeds. Enormous labor had led to the hospital's virtual independence in matters of vegetable foods for the staff. Admittedly the terraces were not artistic like those of a Japanese garden, but the planting was orderly and the fruits of labor were flourishing.

The physical scheme of Schweitzer-land, with so much in common with African villages, would seem to deny that it is a Western Christian mission. The staff, in fact, are not typical missionaries. If this settlement is evangelistic, its message must be unique.

In nosing about the settlement with my inadequate French and German, I found that many religious faiths and several philosophies are represented in the Lambaréné brotherhood. I saw no church, chapel, monastery, or missionary school, no denominational insignia. There were no priestly robes, no vestments, no garments to signify religious orders. The conglomerate white congregation, so congenial and hospitable to the black indigenous tribal animists of the forest, were strangely un-Christian in their liberality. I was told that tribesmen who bring several wives and non-Western customs to the hospital are never made to feel adulterous, sinful, or profane. Dr. Schweitzer reasons that, as it was among the pre-Christian Israelites, polygamy will be replaced by monogamy through cultural and economic evolution. Far more deadening is Africa's fear of fetishes, and even heretics could help in abolishing superstition.

It is Dr. Schweitzer's view that Africans of that region are savage and primitive in skills and objective knowledge though equal to Europeans in ethics, particularly when discussing fundamental relations to one another, to mankind, and to the universe.

As I strolled about the hospital that is not a hospital, the native village that is more than a village, the community that is among other things a zoo, and the mission station that is not a Christian mission, I groped for hidden wisdom, buried motives, the sources of influence, and centers of magnetism.

Is Schweitzer-land unkempt because the man's reach exceeded his grasp? And is his heaven therefore so earthy? I could not believe that Albert Schweitzer the Scholar ever intended this Lambaréné experiment in ethics as a final design for social destiny, a mirror image of perfect human relations, a valid total

portrait of Reverence for Life in action. If not, is it con-
sciously or unconsciously contrived as an affront to the pre-
conceptions of good and evil that Westerners like myself bring
to this hospital—Westerners who have forgotten about the goodness of nature, the oneness of life, and the beauty of simplicity
under the virtues of intimate mercy and direct love? Could
Dr. Schweitzer's Lambaréné be general headquarters for soldiers
in a moral global war?

In making the rounds of the buildings I noticed that the
small permanent European population and large transient
African population were housed separately. Eating customs
were utterly different and independent. I saw boss Schweitzer
and the other Europeans starting off with a small crew of slow-
moving natives. Ogowe tribesmen work only for immediate
goals, not long-term benefits. I had heard often that Dr.
Schweitzer encourages the able-bodied Africans among the
patients and all healthy members of the patient's family to
give labor as token payment for medical services. Echoes of
Dr. Schweitzer's booming voice could be heard at a great
distance cajoling, scolding, and directing the jungle dwellers.
Superficially at least it would seem that the charges of autocrat
and segregationist were valid.

However, I noticed that Dr. Schweitzer also scolded and
cajoled the European workers. The palefaces were divided,
not into paid and unpaid volunteers, but into permanent unpaid
staff and transients and unpaid guest helpers. Unlike the
Africans, these white people were not even indebted to Dr.
Schweitzer for medical services. Theirs is a labor of love. The
Europeans toil for Africans as their servants in the hospital.
They manage as bosses in work projects. Dr. Schweitzer is
"Chairman of the Board" and the hardest working servant.

In the absence of institutional connections, Dr. Schweitzer has
nothing but force of personality to attract funds and helpers
and to impose minimum working order on all individuals in
the hospital. No one is told what to think. All Europeans are

work volunteers. All patients come voluntarily. Dr. Schweitzer treats whites and blacks with respectful courtesy owed to infants and novices in ethics. He is everybody's brother, the elder brother of all at Lambaréné. Many Western doctors are inclined to be professional dictators and expert authoritarians. All hospitals are slightly autocratic. Some swank hospitals unnecessarily practice vicious double standards in segregation. In this primitive African jungle setting, "going native" completely would not be wise democracy. It would be dangerous, as these hardy people live with diseases that would be devastating to the less immune Europeans. It is said native immunity is so great that many Africans can drink polluted river water that would be lethal for most Europeans.

The local effect of Dr. Schweitzer's activities seems superficially like real segregation and autocracy, but these twin evils are mortal enemies of the whole message of Reverence for Life. Albert Schweitzer has worked for forty-four years for black people. He has done the most loathsome jobs himself. He has crossed every human barrier between man and man. He married into a Jewish family. He attracts and works with all denominations and nationalities. His open life of love is observed by all the world. It became quite apparent to me that the critics who call him autocrat and segregationist usually do so because they abhor his freedom in theology and stand guilty of their own special histories of discrimination, provincialism, hostilities, and hatreds.

In my reading I had learned that the climate of this fetid, humid, unhealthful area on the equator is a trial because there is no easy escape for whites and no possible escape for blacks. Mosquitoes and malaria are constant companions of the black forest dwellers in their villages. Men live unprotected from the dread tsetse fly. They endure the destructive work of termites and the horror of marching columns of traveler ants.

Inland peoples endure also the attacks of red ants and the destruction of wild pigs and herds of elephants in their banana plantations. They are kept in bondage by seasons too wet and too dry and by climate too hot and always enervating. Many drag about on painful, bleeding feet kept sore by ulcers and bites of chiggers. In the timber sites natives get rich enough to buy wives, tobacco and rum, or a Western shirt or pants. But new strains often defeat the gains. Detribalization in timber sites is a spiritually painful process, and jobs do not always last. At times there is no place where starvation is easier than in game-filled, luxuriant jungles. Many hopeless, helpless peoples sit in their huts overwhelmed by adversity and await death simply because it is famine time.

The hundreds of ragged black people at the Schweitzer hospital haven live, when in their home villages, with all these threatening terrors of the jungle. Many are isolated from medical help by vast papyrus swamps and impenetrable bush. The network of rivers and natural waterways inhabited by hippopotami and crocodiles is the only interconnecting highway system for five hundred square miles around Lambaréné. As I looked at sores, splints, and bandaged wounds, I wondered how one could measure how much one man has meant to so many.

I did not see hippos and crocodiles in the river here. I was shocked, however, to see an indigenous African clinging to two big, bloody stumps with claws. They might have been dinosaur limbs. Actually the man had purchased these crocodile legs for meat at the river's edge and he was complaining bitterly to a nurse that prices were outrageously high these days. I was told that indigenous folk enjoy all manner of flesh, including boa constrictor, monkey, and hippo.

No meat is butchered at the Schweitzer menage, though it would be compatible with Dr. Schweitzer's "doctrine of necessity" if the need were urgent. Canned meats arrive by launch every two weeks. The Africans have a tiny store where supplies may be purchased.

I wandered into the main hospital buildings, the outpatient department, and the living quarters of the European staff. The terraced arrangement of these buildings on hardwood stilts allows the torrential rainwater to collect in streamlets and pour into the river according to a drainage plan, thus defeating the mosquitoes by reducing their breeding sites.

Though these home-designed, handmade buildings were built by Dr. Schweitzer without benefit of any power-driven tools, they are sturdy. They are not prepossessing in appearance. Many now have termite-proof cement footings and rustproof corrugated iron roofs. The double floor and roof construction aids ventilation and therefore gives protection from oppressive heat. There are screens on the windows in many buildings, but there are no glass windows. Mosquito netting is provided some, if not all, patients. Although Dr. Schweitzer loves animals, the "hospital" for sick and injured animals does not provide the above comforts. Those who say the Doctor cares more for animals than people must be either fractious, capricious, or malicious. The kinship of all life is sacred to him.

At lunch, while we were all eating together, the river turned up an interesting "emergency." Dr. Schweitzer received a note during the noon meal. He left in mid-course, and all in the dining hall trooped after him. An African five-piece orchestra had come by river to serenade the Doctor. They were dressed in Western clothes and played Western music. It was bizarre to see the classical musical scholar auditioning with patience and gratitude some brassy modern swing tunes. The fawns outside of Dr. Schweitzer's room, accustomed to Bach, pranced around startled by the strains of blues and jive. Dr. Schweitzer, in high spirits, mimicked and mocked the antics of the fawns for the amusement of all. He thanked his serenaders with warm sincerity. Then he asked the orchestra to go through the hospital and play for the patients, and afterwards stay for lunch.

In a conversation with one of Dr. Schweitzer's loveliest apostles, Miss Ali Silver, I discovered that the enigmatic Doctor was planning to work in the leper village during the afternoon

of my first day as guest at Lambaréné. "May I go with him?"
I asked. "Certainly," she replied promptly.

My inability to speak in French, German, Hebrew, Greek,
Aramaic, or Latin, any of which my host would have understood, made me dread the trip without an interpreter. I was
anxious to see what manner of man Dr. Schweitzer is when
working, so I went with him to the strange village. As it turned
out, there was no talk during the walk over "Philosopher's
Trail," and my apprehension faded into the forest.

I simply hustled after the big figure who set a fast pace with
his deliberate stride. The narrow, elevated, and ascending path
progressed through a damp, swampy area that nourished dense
tropical tangles of green undergrowth topped by tall trees.

I must confess that even this so-called new leper village
did not strike me as exactly the place that the pampered
American would choose for treatment. I did see 180 leprous
jungle folk using these primitive yet new and tidy cubicles,
if not with gratitude at least with uncoerced willingess. Dr.
Schweitzer's Nobel Peace Prize money that purchased and partially lined and roofed the leper wards with corrugated iron
sheeting seems to have been well spent. Crude as it is, this
new leper village is higher, drier, cooler, and freer from mosquitoes than the now abandoned "sanitarium" down by the
river's edge. It occurred to me that it must take courage-plus
in one's autumn years to re-build and move a whole jungle
village of lepers. Fifteen of the twenty buildings designed are
now completed.

The new leprosarium overlooks a spectacle of frustration.
Below it lies an orchard in the process of losing a desperate
battle with the jungle. The fruit trees are surrendering in their
struggle for existence before this inexorable luxuriance. Nature's
tropical splendor is mingled with decay. Proud arboreal giants
are strangulated by dense vines lusting for life. This tragedy
is evidence to support Dr. Schweitzer's contention that the
universe was not designed with special regard for our tiny

planet, for life on earth, or for puny man. His conviction that man must accept his destiny as the sole builder of reasoned ethics is understandable in this ghastly and glorious laboratory where "fitness," not "goodness," means liberty to live. Yet this fitness is not physical. Fitness viewed universally is freedom. The same freedom in man is furthered by reason into patterns of goodness. The will-to-live is the will-to-be-free.

Reason does not yet order the behavior, even in Lambaréné. The forest folk used to steal the fruits and vegetables. Then they would sell these back to Dr. Schweitzer in the vegetable market at the hospital.

While wandering about to get my bearings in the leper village, I discovered a young blond girl clothed in a nurse's garb. The young girl merrily cheered the blighted blacks in her rough-hewn dispensary while washing wounds and bandaging stumps. She passed out smiles with pills. I actually felt a saintly aura about her.

A dark-skinned three-year-old with laughing eyes, a son of a leprous family, watched her with adoration on his countenance. She told me in German-tinctured English that her young companion had amused her by saying, "Jesus loves me and he loves you because he loves everyone, especially children." She asked him, "Where is Jesus?" He answered, "He is busy making sure that God is good." We agreed that Jesus transfigured by tribal traditions must reach the young mind in wondrous images. Some adult natives insist they see God walking in the forest, and they often identify Jesus with tribal heroes.

I found this nurse (who introduced herself as "Miss Trudy") a Pied Piper personality with the children. She was also wonderfully self-giving with patients of all ages and stages of infirmity. Because of a recent injury to her foot, she had to be carried in an improvised chair-car to and from the leper village twice a day.

While I was at the leper village, one badly mutilated and incurably crippled leper told his indefatigable nurse in a sur-

prisingly Western but non-Christian metaphor that he felt like
"an old, useless bottle with a hole in the bottom." "Why," he
asked her, "do you keep filling a leaky bottle you know is
broken and can never be mended?" I thought I glimpsed in
this living parable a measure of support for Dr. Schweitzer's
theory of Reverence for Life. It seemed to me a dramatic
expression of the core idea breathed into the forest long ago
by a younger Dr. Schweitzer. He had whispered in effect:
"Send me your diseased and doomed, man or beast, and we will
love the living and keep them breathing till the precious privilege
of life is spent or till they are free to roam without pain in
their native haunts."

As I wandered about among the desultory groups of lepers
sprawled in various postures, I chanced upon another European
woman disciple in white. I learned that this widowed volunteer
was Mme. Oberman from Holland. To my great joy, she spoke
lilting English coherently, if not with fluency. Through her
extravagant praises of the Doctor, his work, and the beauties of
Schweitzer-land, I heard a new kind of contagious spiritual
music. I deliberately stiffened my endeavor to be strictly objective.

The Dutch lady pattered about after Dr. Schweitzer, who
was carrying and fetching, measuring and nailing wood and
galvanized iron sheetings. Madame Hanna Oberman told me
that "through his way of living, the far-off Jesus becomes visible
among us; we get better understanding of Him."

Able-bodied, if not whole-bodied, male lepers worked under
the booming directions of Schweitzer the Carpenter, as a confused mass of salvage wood was brought from a wrecked
building. My efforts to help in arranging this debris were hopeless, for Dr. Schweitzer seemed loath to systematize orders; and
every move of every helper centered on the Doctor's seemingly
arbitrary dictates. I had thought I could pile wood as well as
anyone, yet I was rebuked for faulty sorting. I bristled at the
criticism. In my judgment the good Doctor was spending far

too much time sorting and piling these miserable scraps of lumber in a storehouse.

When I spoke a word half-critical of the old gentleman for husbanding this "termite fodder," Mme. Oberman said: "Dr. Schweitzer gets a little money from poor widows; and you will see he wastes nothing, even though they can't watch him using their contributions." I could not but recall the gospel story of the widow who gave from want and received the fullest benediction of Jesus.

Strangely enough, my reaction changed from "What folly!" to "How tireless, how detailed, how intimate, how inseparably personal is this modern Jefferson in disposing of the little gifts of widows for the needs of the poor leprous jungle dwellers!"

Still, something was wrong, for philosophers are known more for lofty *thoughts* than thoughtful *deeds*. My mind explored the comparison of Albert Schweitzer with Christ. Jesus, unlike philosophers, walked in coarse garments with the multitude. He spat in the dust to make a mud pack for the eyes of an unknown man afflicted with blindness. He spat on the tongue of one, thus curing his speech defect. And he did not delegate to others the task of washing the feet of his disciples. Dr. Schweitzer's manual toil with lepers for lepers' dwellings may be inefficient and uneconomic in modern terms. Yet, through its intimacy, how would one prove this is not the personification of the pattern and spirit of Jesus today? How would one show there is a better way to answer the call, "Follow thou me"? I did not fail to observe untidiness in the new leper village. Still, despite everything, it seemed of far less consequence than the Doctor's personal touch and presence.

Our walk back from the leper village to the main cluster of buildings of the settlement at six o'clock was again practically wordless. Our progress was interrupted twice by unexpected duties. While we walked toward home, the big "farmer" continually fed the eager chicks and chickens en route, from a bag of rice. He did not "converse" with this poultry

parade, but he was, with his handouts, the center of excitement.
At one point he noticed that a chick was missing. He would
not proceed until the tiny ball of fluff was found. This modern
man of love looked for the chick because all life is kith and kin
to be loved and cherished.

The old planner stopped to pace off the site for a new
dwelling next to the small ward for the insane. While we
paused, I carefully inspected the tiny cubicle and thought,
"What a mockery here masquerades as an asylum for the
insane!" It was disgracefully inadequate. But it occurred to
me that few missions I have visited about the world provide
any space at all for mentally deranged natives. Many maniacal
patients have been delivered bound tight in wiry vines and cords
of bash which make them wilder and weaker. Usually the
tribes turn the "bewitched" into the forest to die or drown
them in the river. Are not even the state institutions in America
occasionally described as scandalously filthy "snake pits" staffed
by heartless mercenaries? Dr. Schweitzer, I had been told,
took some pleasure in the truth that this "asylum" was a mite
bigger and a little better than the first one he built. I found
there are many case histories of complete rehabilitation from the
ranks of the mentally ill at Lambaréné.

I discovered that the disoriented souls, under Dr. Schweitzer's
instructions, were fed, bathed, and exercised daily by nurses.
Though they were deprived of their wits, their will-to-live was
still treated as a treasure not to be squandered. Dr. Schweitzer
has never pretended to know either miracle methods or all the
modern psychiatric techniques of casting out devils and demons.
He treats the demented to the limit of his ability and cares for
their creature wants. I reasoned that Dr. Schweitzer, as a man
of uncommon mercy, must have his *deep rational roots* in the
same subterranean power channels known *intuitively* to Jesus.
I had often heard that Albert Schweitzer has followed the pattern and spirit of Jesus for forty years. But it seems to me rather
that the modern scholar has paralleled that which he feels is

eternally true in the person of Jesus. Thus he feeds his pets while he toils as a healer and teacher. He labors for the glory of the infinite will in all life with his hands, his head, and his heart.

In the parable where Jesus meets two possessed of fierce devils, a divergence between these two healers separated by 1,950 years can be illustrated. Jesus sent the demons into a herd of swine who ran violently into the sea and perished. If he could, Schweitzer would lock the violent devils in a cell where he would wash and feed them till they died naturally, curing the possessed, sparing the swine, and saving the living demons if possible.

Our dinner the first night of my stay in Lambaréné consisted of soup, bread, cheese, cold cuts, jellies, and fruit juice. I wore my coat to the communal dining hall where the staff break bread together three times a day. Dr. Schweitzer, grinning from ear to ear, said, "We are happy to see how distinguished you look, but you will honor us if you take off your coat." I yielded to his smile.

Dr. Schweitzer ate his dinner in studied defiance of several rules of Emily Post. Trivial amenities are discouraged, but a natural courtesy pervades the hall. At the table Dr. Schweitzer fed his dog. After Bible reading the Doctor played the piano in the room for hymn singing. Following these "liberal" services, the lover of all life left the dining hall, taking scraps of food in his work-calloused hands to feed the other pets.

After supper I had coffee and a long visit with aging, genial Mme. Schweitzer, who complained, after proving that she remembered much, of her loss of memory. She complained, too, that she had no new work and could not perform her former tasks. Her English was superb, and I was charmed by tales of her struggles as a bride when brought to the bush by a wonderful madman. Dr. Schweitzer had been impulse-driven. He proclaims his path is reason. He is not an ascetic or a hero of renunciation. Mme. Schweitzer, on the other hand, gave

beyond the call of reason for deep and sacrificial feminine
motives. Without his internal fire, she was still a heroine of
sacrifice.

After coffee with Mme. Schweitzer, I cornered Mme. Oberman, my interpreter, and explained my mission. Though I had
many personal interests in visiting Dr. Schweitzer, I had one
legitimate objective. As explained earlier, I represented a number of Dr. Schweitzer's friends; and I was to ask the Doctor
to lend his spirit of scholarship to higher education in America
by allowing university "chairs" or "distinguished professorships"
to be created in his name.

I explained my objective in detail to Mme. Oberman. She
spontaneously endorsed the idea. I handed her a portfolio and
asked that she present the plan and the portfolio to Dr. Schweitzer for his consideration. The folder contained letters from six
major universities. Each letter wholeheartedly welcomed the
idea of Dr. Schweitzer's symbol of scholarship to their respective
campuses. Also in the folder were personal letters addressed to
Dr. Schweitzer from some of his closest American friends. These
letters pled the purpose of my mission. There was also a long
memorandum describing the preliminary groundwork. There
were several pledge cards that subscribed specific gifts which
would be made available to the Albert Schweitzer Education
Foundation if it became a reality. Some hoped that groups of
students might be inspired by the Schweitzer symbol to have a
deep and meaningful foreign service experience as an integral
part of their education.

Shortly after Dr. Schweitzer reviewed the contents of the
portfolio, I received through Mme. Oberman his unequivocal
refusal. Her brief message was: "Dr. Schweitzer appreciates
the gesture. The honor is far too great. The idea is utterly
impossible."

Perhaps fearing that I would jump into the Ogowe River,
Mme. Oberman said, "Please be assured that Dr. Schweitzer

is delighted to have you as a guest. He hopes you will enjoy your stay and will be comfortable in his jungle hospital."

While I was brooding over my apparently doomed mission at the end of my eventful day, two young doctors, Van Stolk and Margrietha D. Van der Kreek ("Doctoress" as she is called), approached me with a question: "Would you mind if we 'exploit' you while you are here? Will you teach us dentistry?" I was overwhelmed by their eagerness and was delighted to be "trapped" into working on tooth problems of the staff and native people. I rejoiced that my training was so basic that it was needed as a part of the health services in the jungle.

Actually a fourth of my flight baggage allowance was made up of syringes, anesthetics, and tools of my profession. The call to work was music to my ears. How could I hope to become better acquainted with Lambaréné antiseptic and hygienic practices than by actual experience in the inner sanctum of this "holy surgery"? I went to sleep confident that I would learn the sanitation and hygiene strengths and weaknesses of the surgery and more of its affirmative program for Africans.

I had already discovered at first-hand that Schweitzer-land is a unique, towering cathedral of contagious ideas in an antediluvian wilderness. The positive purpose of the mission is to arouse kindred spirits of the world to some action. Negatively, it is to shame with a shock treatment the rich, white, healthy, well-fed, literate, Christian nations of the Western world. The West, like Africa, is still diseased with taboos, idolatry, and savagery. Both the West and Africa lack most a coherent, reasonable ethic and a common theory of the universe, life, and goodness. Dr. Schweitzer is a standard bearer for a new concept of civilization and its obligations.

I was sure that the intimate view I was to have of the surgery during my days of drilling, filling, extracting, teaching dentistry, and learning about techniques in use here, would shed light on my quest. I hoped to learn more of the affirmative, mysterious mechanism of this unique mission.

In the Surgery

After a night of reading, dawn hours of sleeping, and a hearty breakfast in the community dining hall, I went with the two young doctors to the dental clinic to be "exploited."

Among the museum pieces which greeted me was a foot-engine with a flexible cable in which one tiny screw was missing. This loss, which had apparently occurred years ago, necessitated an extra assistant lending a hand to hold the handpiece in place during drilling.

Let me now tell about a letter I received after my safari through South Africa. In Johannesburg I found the proper parts and sent them back to Lambaréné. "Doctoress," the woman doctor from Holland, acknowledged the gift in a letter that contained these delightful sentences: "Thank you very much for the missing spare part and the extra cable arm. It is a large advantage to don't need an extra assistant."

I spent my second day and most of the remainder of my stay at the Lambaréné settlement in the primitive dental surgery. I demonstrated to the two eager physicians extractions, porcelain fillings, amalgam fillings, root canal fillings, cleanings, and gum surgery, as well as local anesthesia. My medical pupils could not pass a dental state board, but they were doing a creditable job and their ingenuity made up for deficiencies in dental training.

The dental chair was a rare article that could have accommodated a barber as readily as a dentist. The head-rest surmounting the back was adjustable, but the chair could neither tilt, revolve, nor go up and down. And the patient's feet rested or roved on the floor itself. There was no electrical gadget other than the surgical light brought in from the surgery.

The words "dental clinic" may convey too much. The operatory is an incompletely partitioned room. It is a part of a long, narrow structure that houses dispensary services, examination activities, laboratory and x-ray facilities, and the surgery knives and needles.

At first, crude conditions in the clinic occasioned some gnashing of teeth on my part; but it dawned on me that my equipment at home with its thousands of screws plus its gas and electrical connections and plumbing parts could be a great source of frustration here in the jungle without a corps of experts and suppliers to service it.

I was not a stranger to primitive dental devices and the countless needful professional services that can be accomplished without modern gadgets. I had cut my professional teeth, as it were, on a foot-engine and a detachable head-rest and chairs similar to these items in the dental clinic. As a matter of record, almost identical crude portable dental equipment had taken my wife and me on our earn-as-you-go honeymoon tour through twenty-six countries around the world. Memories of my dental days in the villages of India flooded my mind as I worked with Joseph, a brilliant, dark-skinned assistant. He reminded me of my assistant Chedy, who traveled with me as translator, trouble-solving magician, and professional apprentice throughout the whole subcontinent of India, eventually becoming a practicing dentist himself.

The barefooted Joseph in the Schweitzer clinic helped me manage the quaking patients, sterilize tools, and dispose of waste. With real skill he kept all things on the dental conveyor belt orderly. He translated for all of us. When I suggested paying Joseph for his extra work, I was told politely that he would much prefer the loud sport shirt I was wearing to cash. We consummated a bargain with mutual satisfaction.

Some workers at Lambaréné still speak of another colorful, now very old, Joseph who was Dr. Schweitzer's first surgical assistant more than four decades ago. Having previously been a cook for Europeans, Joseph the First described patients' ills in his own delightfully mixed vocabulary. "This patient," he might say, "has an ache in his leg of mutton," and "that woman has a pain in her cutlet or in her loin."

This first barefooted Joseph also had a weakness for Western fashion. Once he defied Dr. Schweitzer's counsel by spending some of his hard-earned money to buy a pair of rotting patent leather shoes displayed in a moth-eaten, moldy general store, the "Saks Fifth Avenue" of Lambaréné.

Local peoples in the Ogowe district, I discovered, think that sickness is due to evil spirits and magic. Pain in general is thought to be due to a worm that moves about inside the body. In the surgery, tribal people think they are killed during anesthesia, then cured, and finally resurrected. If pain is gone, the worm is gone.

How much anguish Dr. Schweitzer has relieved by dispelling psychoses can't be measured. Tribal fears of fetishes and spells are fantastic. Repeaters who return to the hospital have a degree of confidence in the Doctor and his medical methods that becomes terrifying.

I found to my amusement that new patients in the hospital, accustomed only to witch doctors, are often congealed by their fear of European medical men and perhaps more particularly of the newly arrived American master of dental horrors. One old woman, fresh from the bush and panicky as a fawn in a forest fire, removed herself from my dental chair four times before she worked up the courage to have an aching tooth removed. She would not stop crying and quaking, even when she and her offending tooth were parted. Much later she smiled her gratitude. The worm was gone.

My experience in the Schweitzer dental surgery attested to the razor-sharp distinction that is maintained between hygienic and aseptic procedures within the operating rooms and the lax liberties practiced by the human and animal communities out-

side its windows. In the dental surgery asepsis and antisepsis
were meticulously performed. Though ordinary kitchen hygiene
would have served for some items, everything touched was
thoroughly boiled. It seemed to me I was forever waiting for
freshly boiled syringes and instruments and even bib holders
to cool. And the women on their knees washing the rough floor
with soaps and antiseptics were almost a nuisance to the doctors
and nurses rushing about the surgery.

On the third day of my stay at Lambaréné I had a dramatic
opportunity to observe the Lambaréné community of servants
act out a real-life play in the surgical theater.

Dr. Schweitzer's hospital for the most part gets diseases and
disasters that baffle the tribal witch doctors, who are consulted
first in the tribal villages. The witch doctors take little time in
deciding which cases are the kind "le grand docteur" could
handle.

Four natives before us, who had hacked one another with
knives, fell into this category. The butchered boys came from
great distances, starting far upstream on tiny capillaries which
flowed into larger arteries and emptied into the river highway
passing Lambaréné. They had paddled in their dugout canoes
all night, bypassing other hospitals to get to the congenial
atmosphere of Dr. Schweitzer's hospital settlement.

These boys had wrapped their wounds in dirty rags. They
were a sad spectacle of filth and dried blood when they arrived
in the middle of my Sunday morning dental surgery. The two
doctors at my elbow responded like firemen to the peremptory
call to duty.

One boy's black back was so slashed that ribs and pleura
(lung covering) were clearly visible. A second boy carried his
completely severed thumb in a dirty bag. His cheek, nose and
upper lip were split wide. The third boy's hand was cut through
the tendons, and bone fragments glistened in the gaping wound.
The lacerated lower lip of the fourth dangled almost to his
chest, and his scalp had a straight but bloody parting. What

had provoked the hostilities was not made clear, but during the voyage the boys had become friends instead of enemies, and now, except for sullen glances, they were amicable enough toward one another.

First, narcotics were aimed at the pain. Then, with millions of microbes as the target, modern miracle drugs were administered.

The operating room was carefully prepared, even though the wounds to be treated were long contaminated. Considering the capricious cause of this thankless task, uncommon mercy, compassion, and charity were shown. The South African doctor, Van Stolk, observed the wounds of one patient and said: "This would have killed me." He looked into the smiling face of the boy and mused under his breath, "I'll bet this kid has an I.Q. of 140. What a waste of gifts!"

The raw wounds were cleansed and medicated under the kind oblivion of general and local anesthesia. Two operating tables with two teams were kept busy. Some of the housekeeping staff were mobilized and doubled as nurses. All wounds and grateful patients were doing well when I saw them last.

I did some surgical assisting but found I was not as versatile in the medical field as the young doctors proved to be in mine. However, the prologue to my assisting should interest some critics of the asepsis and hygiene procedures observed.

I volunteered to assist in suturing the wounds. I was allowed to do so only after the routine ritual of a clock-timed surgical scrub-up. I had previously been observing at some distance in a clean gown. I was now forced to don a sterile gown and to wear a sterile mask and sterile gloves. However, in the presence of the flying fingers of the deft surgeon, "Doctoress" Van der Kreek, I played a part that was mostly ornamental.

Many varieties of accident cases come to the hospital. There is one story with a comic twist. An African was injured when he fell from a tree while trying to steal honey from a bees' nest. Another, bent on robbing the same hive, decided to cut down the tree to get the honey. The tree fell on a flimsy hut, crushing the inmate. Both of the injured drifted to Dr. Schweitzer's hospital.

Many accidents occur in the timber camps. Old Man River provides his share, particularly when logs are made up into rafts to be coaxed downstream for milling and export. Gunshot wounds, accidental and intentional, are frequent. Victims of maulings by gorillas, gorings by wounded elephants or angered hippos, and bites by snakes drift into the medical encampment, adding variety and an element of surprise to the health services.

The average patient coming to Lambaréné presents one acute immediate problem and many chronic ills. For example, he may present a strangulated hernia. Preliminary examination almost always reveals one of the following ailments and sometimes a combination of them: malaria, intestinal parasites, amoebic and bacillary dysentery, venereal disease, heart complaints, rheumatism, osteomyelitis, nicotine and strophanthus poisoning, elephantiasis, tuberculosis, skin ulcers, phagedenic ulcers of the lower limbs, avitaminosis, malnutrition, and sometimes alcoholism. Cancer is comparatively infrequent. Appendicitis is non-existent. Stones are non-existent. Sleeping sickness, once widespread, is less prevalent and is now always referred to a government hospital. Dr. Schweitzer's spiritual courage is brought into shining relief by the bitter irony that comes in knowing that the cured will leave only to be reinfected by jungle pollution which in ignorance they ignore.

The ultimate impact of Lambaréné is probably directed in a preventive way at the chronic wounds of the world, the suppurating, ever-running sores of world society and the festering causes of war that reside in spiritually sick people. I had the feeling that the jungle is a better school for surgery than war. Surgery in the jungle illuminates the promise of divinity within humanity. In basic human relations cures may be found for the most stubborn social ills that to date remain incurable and threaten man's survival.

The administration of medicines at the hospital at Lambaréné
is laborious because, left to their own devices, patients would
devour a bottle of pills in a gulp, reasoning that if one tablet
is good, many are better. Quantities of ointment given to be
applied to the skin periodically may disappear in one generous
dosage or be eaten instead. Some who have been given powders
for specific sores become enthusiasts and rub the wonder dust
on the skin indiscriminately.

As a result of their propensities, the sick must queue up for
medication; and the action looks like feeding time at an aviary.
Pills go from bottle to mouths by forceps, untouched by human
hands.

All treatments and dressings are arranged individually. Patients who want only one specific painful condition treated will
sometimes try to conceal other ailments if they hear the cure
is objectionable, particularly if dreaded, lonely isolation is part
of the treatment. One man sick with elephantiasis insisted on
living with his only fellow tribesman in the clinic. His comrade
was isolated because he was suffering with severe contagious
dysentery. The determined patient with elephantiasis persisted,
saying he would rather die than be separated from his incontinent, contagious "brother."

I can testify that tooth disorders are probably the most
universal of all pathological conditions that plague the Africans.
I would venture to speculate that mouth afflictions are also
perhaps the most debilitating. I suspect millions of abscesses
go undetected because of the absence of X-ray machines. But
these oral ills are certainly the least lethal of the many ills
among the Africans. Dr. Schweitzer has extracted many teeth;
he tells of finding teeth so loose they can be plucked out with
fingers. Chronic pyorrhea caused by undisturbed tartar deposits
is almost universal. Tooth brushing seems to the Africans a
superstitious fetish practiced by the white tribal intruders in
Africa.

The rigors of life, ravages of disease, the high infant mortality rate (sixty per cent), and the natural hazards lowering life expectancy serve to weed out the less fit. The resulting distillate—a survival of the rugged—is in many ways hard and hardy. They possess resistance in depth.

One thing I thought I detected among the black community at the hospital was a total lack of the sullen insolence that glares forth from smoldering eyes in many places of subjugation in the Dark Continent, especially in the Union of South Africa. I saw much boisterous merriment, particularly among the children. The children do not seem to know that they should be unhappy. Even sick adults seemed uncommonly gay compared to some hypochondriacs I have known.

Although the operating equipment and rooms are kept surgically clean and operating lights are available when the only Diesel-driven generator is running, the average professional man and layman would look at the rude wooden structure minus marble floors and tile corridors and worry about conditions. Even records of surgical success would not relieve the concern of some. Perhaps a review of the history will give real insight on a matter of *relative* appearances. It will help to know the tribulations of the *first hospital* that was born in a filthy, rotten henhouse contributed as a makeshift hospital by the Paris Missionary Society in 1913. The henhouse eventually collapsed while in use.

As I looked about the present hospital—a shambles compared to Mayo—I remembered reading about the appalling conditions of indescribable congestion and confusion that occurred on the restricted, overcrowded grounds provided by the Paris Missionary Society. As the hospital services grew, the pressures to expand grew. Dr. Schweitzer built by hand, in hours stolen from medical duties, flimsy bamboo structures. Each new "ward" was erected over a mud floor. They were roofed over by leaky raffia leaves and represented a "relative" blessing. This sole haven of medical mercy for the desperately diseased folk in the area could not be challenged by comparisons, for no rival health dispensaries existed. Africans in the Ogowe were being served at the time by evangelists who ministered to bodily needs from a background of "good-will" and medical innocence.

At Dr. Schweitzer's first hospital there was no room provided to isolate the contagious sick and separate the patients according to their ailments. There was no place to segregate dysentery sufferers, tubercular patients, lepers, or the insane. The area was hot, low, and poorly ventilated. It had poor drainage. When chronic dysentery, almost endemic in the Ogowe district, flared into an epidemic plague, the influx produced chaos. Overcrowded by weakened, sick, incontinent inmates, the medical haven was reduced to a loathsome mire of stinking muck. The obstacles to raising standards would have been insuperable to many men with generous missionary backing. Dr. Schweitzer's self-imposed limits of financial aid, for the most part restricted to individual well-wishers, made expansion not feasible.

There were other difficulties. Aboriginals away from their tribal home can resist everything but temptation. Their first bamboo huts lacked sturdy doors and locks, and often the primitive "receivers" stole from the "givers" as well as from one another. They purloined valuable stores and personal belongings. They pilfered and burned valuable lumber to cook their food, although worthless wood for fires was plentiful in the forest only a step away. Gratitude toward strangers was then alien to their tribal thinking. The European was rich and somehow got richer—and this impression held even when they sized up mission doctors. One ungrateful man, when cured, demanded that Dr. Schweitzer buy him a wife. In the course of time, however, African patients have learned to appreciate the loving kindness that is showered upon them by a great spirit.

Dr. Schweitzer understands that peoples' ethics are as wide as their love and loyalty. Members of an unspoiled tribe pool their good fortunes and their misfortunes; but beyond their tribal brotherhood covetousness, avarice, murder, and plunder are normal manifestations as among animals in the carnival of killing, vandalism, and plunder of the jungle struggle.

Tribes to Dr. Schweitzer are communities of men who have pooled their prejudices and assume mutually binding "loyalty oaths." Humanitarian and universal brotherhood is still undreamed. While tribes in Africa go forth to war for planting areas, bark and bamboo supplies, and hunting grounds, tribe-like nations war for exclusive rights to oil, coal, gold deposits, and mining privileges.

It is the sway of ethics that determines where the militant ways of the jungle and nature will appear as "normal expectations." It is in this light that both tribal and national circles of loyalty are dwarfed as petty by Jesus, who said: " . . . and all ye are brethren." They are further dwarfed by Albert Schweitzer's wider ethic. In Reverence for Life, all life shares a sacred kinship. The domain of ethics is cosmic and universal.

Dr. Schweitzer describes without the faintest trace of egotism all his routine concurrent toils which were supplemented by new duties during the period he was joyously clearing the site for the new hospital. Heroic new labors were sandwiched into the routine of caring for the wretched sick in the old wards and patching the old decaying hospital hovels.

The transient able-bodied Africans, ignoring debts of gratitude, often would work only when rewarded with bonus food rations, special privileges, and presents. They thought it shameful the Doctor did jobs beneath tribal dignity. They mocked the Doctor especially for his silly mercies, such as transplanting trees merely to preserve their mute but precious lives.

The Doctor admits to bribing reluctant laborers. They never received from him, however, the most coveted currency in the area—gunpowder, tobacco, rum, or Western trinkets—which many receive as rewards for labor from white employers, especially timber merchants.

Dr. Schweitzer speaks out, citing the debt of Westerners to Africans. Certainly Dr. Schweitzer's hospital work has been infinitely harder because of the contagious venereal diseases brought to the Dark Continent by emissaries of Western "culture." Albert Schweitzer as a Westerner is not an example of renunciation, salvation, or benevolence, but of conscience, duty, and atonement.

The first site on the old mission grounds had no room for planting, and starvation was a ghastly spectre in periods of famine. In the new site there is room for orchards and gardens for a steady food supply.

Perhaps Dr. Schweitzer's greatest cross was his own freedom. He believed and practiced a man-to-man, person-to-person service. There were no national, institutional, or church ties. Therefore, in order to make the leap from the old to the new hospital, Dr. Schweitzer by choice assumed the burden of raising his own funds through the medium of letters to friends in Europe, pleas penned by hand and by lamplight.

In Europe he could earn money by concerts, lectures, and preaching. But he could not get home before the new hospital was built. He could and did borrow against future earnings in Europe. Most mission hospitals have had an army of preachers pleading with hosts of parishioners for support. In many missions, institutional support has often been supplemented by government grants, at least for the hospitals and schools. Not so in Albert Schweitzer's case, except for some land grants.

Dr. Schweitzer felt from the beginning that free individuals should carry their independent skills to needy individuals, no strings attached, without representing organized churches, institutions, or nations. When he cannot save the hopeless, he shows them the love of one who cares much and strives mightily to make their end easier.

Most Africans, of course, are far beyond Dr. Schweitzer's small range. Millions today are overwhelmed by insurmountable health hazards and succumb prematurely and painfully

in a cruel land that devours half its babies at birth. Many
Ogowe tribes are perishing, and some have become silently
extinct without disturbing the complacency of man's inhumanity
to man.

Albert Schweitzer has harassed himself with all the chores
of clearing, planting, maintenance, and pleading for funds.
He ordered his medical supplies and labored over his many
literary notes and manuscripts, which he slowly edited into
his books. Through it all, he kept up with his studies in medicine
and liberal arts, philosophy and theology. His musical skills
he refreshed daily by playing the special piano given him by the
Paris Bach Society. This piano, incidentally, had a precarious
delivery by dugout canoe.

It is said that Dr. Schweitzer felt unspeakable delight in the
new hospital. One plain-spoken native, legend claims, revealed
his deep pride in the new structures on the new site by saying:
"Grand Docteur, these are fine huts."

Though I knew the history of the first hospital and this
current one, still I wanted to assess the present settlement more
precisely, not in charity but in fairness. One thing was clear.
The chaos I was observing could not be called, according to
Western standards, a typical modern hospital.

I came out of the surgery that Sunday afternoon, feeling
that this village built by Dr. Schweitzer is a unique symbol of
mercy, compassion, love. It is an international haven of respect
for the liberty and worth of the poor, humble, and destitute
of this century.

It is obvious that the hospital and surgery are only instru-
mentalities of a more dynamic idea, and not ends in themselves.
Most of the co-workers are blind to the central idea, or at best
have only partial sight concerning it. They are naive followers
or dedicated disciples. Many do not even read Dr. Schweitzer's
books.

The common denominator among the workers is a disdain
for wealth and a love of service. A young doctor from South

Africa confided to me that he had no idea what his salary was or even if he had a salary. He was sure only that Dr. Schweitzer was generous, and that it was a privilege to have a tour of duty in his hospital.

Though Albert Schweitzer's core idea may be timeless, I had the feeling there was a physical impermanence about this settlement in Africa. I could see no provisions for a long life. Where would one look for a candidate to fill Dr. Schweitzer's shoes? Other physicians could undoubtedly "improve" the health service. The French government could convert the property to "good use." The uniqueness of Schweitzer-land is the pious rebel himself, and this spirit is not easily bequeathed to others.

Much that is imperishable is preserved in Albert Schweitzer's hand-penned library and in the consciousness of liberal, unorthodox, uncommitted sympathizers the world over who are looking for a practical, plausible pattern for living with ethics at the center. Schweitzer-land is already a treasured legend preserved where neither moths nor rust can corrupt, even if its sturdy buildings are one day consumed by the voracious jungle.

It crossed my mind that the physical Lambaréné could be preserved in the distant future as an integral part of the medical school that wished to provide a foreign service experience as a background for the mature professional ethics so fast disappearing in the West—a professional ethics that calls upon the whole man.

As I pondered the meaning of Lambaréné, it occurred to me that Jesus' way of life left no hospitals and no schools and no church buildings. He left his thought in people's minds. He was unorthodox in a Jewish world. His liberality brought with it persecution. Though his gospel, in the mind of Paul, became earthly and universal in scope for the elect and righteous, Jesus walked in a provincial area in rough garments with the poor, weak, and the meek. He forgave prostitutes and transgressors. He loved his weak and simple apostles who knew him imperfectly. He thought symbolically, spoke metaphorically, and lived influentially. All righteous men were his beloved neighbors; and he pitied his enemies, even his murderers.

All of these characteristics have some parallelism in Albert Schweitzer today. He gives not his wealth but himself, and this completely, not alone to people but to the stream of life.

I have learned that the sensitive Doctor suffers when he is misunderstood. But I have never seen a document in which Dr. Schweitzer has defended himself or his hospital village or his way of life.

Was this the answer: Albert Schweitzer is living in the pattern and spirit of Jesus, the half of Jesus he admires without limit? Is he at war with the other half? I know from his books that Dr. Schweitzer himself makes no claim of divinity or any special knowledge of the supernatural. This is to him imponderable and irrelevant. He expects no eternal reward. He has washed the wounds of lepers and in his day has bathed the bodies and scrubbed the sheets dirtied by incontinent African strangers. He built the village for black brothers with lovingkindness, nail by nail, board by board.

The specific addition of the Schweitzer ethic to the Christian ethic is to be seen in the hospitalized animals. Not only does he feed his pets, who are also his distant brothers, his current neighbors, his guests, and friends, but when necessary he splints subhuman fractures and bottle-feeds orphan cubs. His own will-to-live is sacred to him only if he cherishes the perishable freedom of individuals that compose the whole animate world. He toils tirelessly but claims he does so because it is reasonable to reverence life and to aid all life within his sphere. This doctrine is Darwinian in concept, completely alien to the Jesus ethic and cosmology and ideas of creation.

At this point I developed a new hypothesis to fit the facts of Dr. Schweitzer's Lambaréné settlement. It seemed clear that Albert Schweitzer was motivated in every thought and deed by a new personal religion. Perhaps the ethical community had never been intended by its builder to be a Christian mission hospital. Perhaps it has always been the outward manifestation of his own design for living. Perhaps the jungle doctor hoped from the start that his satisfying personal religion would one day motivate all men. Perhaps then the Lambaréné settlement was a conscious or unconscious instrument of this great vivid vision to transfigure people and transform the world.

Secretly, or subconsciously, Albert Schweitzer may conceive of his beloved Lambaréné as a cathedral of ideas with exact spiritual architecture, the first physical-moral sanctuary of reverence for all life and a working laboratory for servants to discover through meditation and service how to follow the play of the universal will-to-live and will-to-be-free.

If true, what a dream this was for a humble Alsatian, perhaps the greatest human spirit since a humble Galilean healer said, "I am the truth, the way, and the life."

An Evening With Dr. Schweitzer

On the morning of my third day at the hospital, a messenger brought a special invitation from Dr. Schweitzer to visit with him privately in his room after supper. Here was my long-awaited chance to clarify some philosophical and religious issues.

That evening, arm in arm with Madame Oberman, by now my inseparable companion at interviews, I eagerly rapped on Dr. Schweitzer's door. Dr. Schweitzer was seated at his desk, scratching with an old-fashioned dip pen. He looked up, smiled warmly, and gestured his welcome.

I observed that his room was modest and unadorned. As I had expected, Charles Darwin eyed us from the portrait on the wall. My glance passed over the plain iron bed covered with mosquito netting. Beside it was a crude night table with a small lamp. The famous old battle-scarred, zinc-lined piano with organ attachments presented to Dr. Schweitzer by the Paris Bach Society was visible in the closet-sized annex made, in part, from packing cases. In the lamplight the room appeared to have been disordered by gusts of wind. Pieces of paper and mail were scattered over the Doctor's desk. A bright pressure lamp on the desk threw beams and shadows over the room. There were many unstacked books about, extruding paper markers. True to legend, chapters of Dr. Schweitzer's unpublished manuscripts hung on nails like "a brace of geese."

Dr. Schweitzer opened the conversation by saying, "Let's not talk philosophy or religion tonight."

I had come prepared to probe Dr. Schweitzer. I did not realize that *I* was to be gently but thoroughly scrutinized like a frog in a biology class. It was not apparent to me until the evening was

over that I had been encouraged to do almost all of the talking.
They found out much about me. I found out very little that
was new to me from Dr. Schweitzer's sparse comments. It was
through indirect avenues and reflection that I learned much.

Dr. Schweitzer unveiled in his gestures and his mobile eagerness as a listener great currents of personal magnetism. I saw
new depths in his blood-warm personality. The vibrant presence
he expressed in his gestures I find too elusive to capture for
my story.

I can tell you that Dr. Schweitzer has Voltaire-like, epigram-
matic keenness and Shaw-like wit and humor. One must see
his wrinkled smiles transformed into creases of concern and
then to a classic of sculptured anguish, to know that this man
is a mirror image of a great spiritual reality.

Right from the beginning there came the inevitable question
that set diversionary machinery in motion. Dr. Schweitzer
asked, "How did you first become interested in the things we
are doing here at Lambaréné?"

I feel it relevant, though perhaps immodest, for me to introduce here the sketch of my life that I recounted, or rather
confessed, to Dr. Schweitzer. It flashed through my mind that
if I told the story of the events that really occurred from my
initial curiosity in ethics to my presence now in Lambaréné,
Dr. Schweitzer might be tempted to speak out on some vital
issue. This (more than all of his writings) might help me plumb
the depths of his personality. My plan worked, but only in
the most indirect way.

As I recounted my narrative to Dr. Schweitzer I was brooding
over the fact that he had just turned me down on the ambition
of my visit—namely, to discuss Dr. Schweitzer's philosophy
with him in the light of the current crises of the world. While
I talked about myself, I schemed how I might indirectly probe
my host and persuade him to reveal more of his deeper motives,
his secret hopes, and his practical plans.

For the most part Dr. Schweitzer listened to my self-portrait with his eyes either almost closed or fixed on the distant, unseen horizon. Though much of the time he listened in silence, the ever-changing expression of his face was proof to me that he was gathering data in his capacious mind.

I was surprised at how frequently he indicated by a gesture that translation was unnecessary. I realized again that Dr. Schweitzer understands much English but apparently does not trust himself to speak the language.

I was born in 1910 on the fringe of Chicago's famous slum area known as "Behind the Yards." My mother was a selfless semi-invalid, whose meticulously decorous mind had one unconventional recess that housed a secret love of adventure, though because of illness all her explorations had to be vicarious.

My father came from Canada in infancy and at nine was employed in the stockyards of Chicago when they were a brutal jungle. He brought his pay envelopes to his devout mother, who prayed that her eldest son would become a servant of the Lord. In his early twenties Dad did indeed become a lay minister with deep fundamental conviction and evangelistic urges.

Dad's career collided with the religion of science in his studies at Northwestern University Dental School, which he entered without formal schooling beyond the seventh grade. Science shattered his faith. The impact splintered to fragments his former Methodist religion, but diminished in no way his zeal for human betterment. His greatest distinction came when he served on a select national health commission appointed by President Hoover and later enlarged by President Roosevelt.

My childhood community, though outwardly religious, saw more than its share of poverty, delinquency, drunkenness, and gangsterism. My neighborhood was, despite crime, church conscious. The boys in the juvenile gangs, as well as their parents, seldom missed their weekly confessional and Sunday Mass.

Despite murmurings about mortgages and interest on loans, my sister and I knew a degree of abundance and privileges rare in any community. Though every trip meant a loan at the bank, we traveled extensively and comfortably. And we trekked to our country cottage on the Indiana sand dunes every week-end.

In the summer of my sixteenth year, fortified only with a junior partner, I started a taxi business on the sandy beach at the dunes. With our hopped-up Ford I cleared enough money to pay for my first independent adventure, a motorcycle tour through nine countries in Europe in the summer of 1928.

In college, I was somewhat better in sports than in scholarship, but I was undistinguished in both. Minor eye defects plagued me. At the University of Chicago I managed to acquire a bachelor's degree in the biological sciences in preparation for a career in dentistry.

Upon graduation I launched my second somewhat eccentric adventure. As a penniless bum I mooched my way in and out of hobo jungles across western United States. I rode freight cars and slept in jails. I concluded that summer by working my way through the Panama Canal on a freighter. I supplemented my meagre earnings on board by doing laundry for the sailors. I came home by plane. The experience delighted me then, and reminiscences concerning it refresh me now. My story was published in a local magazine.

My career in dental school was unspectacular. I developed warm friendships with the scientists and theoreticians but was little drawn to instructors and clinicians. By attending summer school, I completed the four-year course in three years.

My last year in dental school was spent in the delirious clouds of romance. My bride was not only uncommonly fair of countenance but gifted most generously in the mechanics of scholarship that were so irksome and at times embarrassing for me.

I conjured up for my innocent bride a most exotic honeymoon. From dental museums I corralled a foot-engine and portable head-rest. I encouraged my co-adventurer to assemble a portable manicuring kit. The last day of my state board examination, without benefit of a dental license, we started west. I had never had a private patient, and my accomplice had never given a manicure; but we were setting out almost penniless to earn our way around the world "by tooth and nail." Dr. Schweitzer's hearty laugh made me think that my pun was not lost in translation.

In the middle of December, 1934, we started across the Pacific on a small freight boat. Once at sea, the rough and ready captain granted me permission to become "ship's dentist." On Christmas Eve a sailor developed a serious toothache. After that, it became fashionable for officers and crew alike to patronize our sea-going office. Business in the dental department remained brisk throughout the trip. My bride was the sole woman aboard our slow boat to China. Nail polishing had to be filed under "failure."

In gentle Nippon, it was our extreme good fortune to meet the renowned Toyohiko Kagawa, whom we found laboring with peasants on farm problems. I made it clear to Dr. Schweitzer that it was many years later that we realized how little we had understood the forces in this Oriental nation and the powers within this saintly man.

Once we landed on the huge continent of China, we headed inland for those remote regions known to be inhabited by groups of fellow Americans isolated from modern dental conveniences. Most of these outpost island clusters of "foreigners" in China's vast sea of non-Christian humanity were Christian missionaries. We worked with, listened to, and observed missionaries of every conceivable Christian denomination. Some cooperated, others competed disgracefully with one another.

I reminded Dr. Schweitzer that this was the period in mission affairs when the Hocking report on re-thinking foreign missions was being discussed everywhere. He nodded that he was familiar with that report, but he did not make any comment.

We stopped for a short stint of dental service and financial resuscitation in the Peking Language School. For reasons unknown, we presumed that the internationally acclaimed scholar-philosopher, Dr. Hu Shih, would we willing to talk to us. We called on him, uninvited, and were courteously received. Later, Dr. Hu Shih became Chinese ambassador to the United States. As Occidental would-be scholars, we were impressed by our brief interview.

We left desperately poor, brooding, unhappy China, realizing from our experience of being shot at twice, that a bloody time was going to come. At the port of Tsingtao, we embarked on a German boat operated by a militant Nazi crew. Their national fervor had a genuinely religious flavor. They were righteous fanatics. Despite arguments, they patronized us generously as their temporary ship's dentist. After briefly glimpsing such famous port cities as Yokohama, Shanghai, Hongkong, Manila, Singapore, and Medan (Sumatra), we disembarked at Colombo on the Buddhist island of Ceylon.

We were lucky to land just before the occurrence of an odd annual religious ceremonial that was of great professional interest. The capital of Ceylon is Kandy, situated high in the verdant tropical mountains in the midst of vast tea plantations. Kandy has a Buddhist temple; the temple has a tooth. This holy tooth, as affirmed by legend, belonged to Buddha himself. The sacred cuspid is paraded through the streets of Kandy once a year with great ceremonial pageantry involving great fleets of elephants.

I told Dr. Schweitzer that I had very recently become familiar with his book, *Indian Thought and Its Development*. I explained that it had clarified many ethical issues that had bothered me for two decades. It gave me some insight into the way ethics determines human relations. I said I was gratified for his skillful presentation of Buddha's enlightenment, which had seemed extraordinarily rational in Buddha's lifetime. I said I feared that in Tibet, China, Korea, and Japan Buddhism had been betrayed.

"You were certainly right about one thing," I said to Dr. Schweitzer. "At least according to my limited experience Buddhism in its original form is so alien to modern thought processes that it takes heroic re-thinking to reconstruct the thought-world of Buddha."

I said that it was a great regret to me to have discovered Albert Schweitzer's literature late in life instead of during my school days. Dr. Schweitzer offered no comment.

Before starting our six months' visit in India, we made a side trip to Australia and New Zealand. This phase of our trip bristled with adventures that properly belong in another account, but I mention it here because we touched on two unique varieties of human relations. The aborigine of Australia is virtually unaltered by the impact of Western ways. And the dark-skinned Maoris of New Zealand are so thoroughly integrated, there is virtually no color bar. The question I asked Dr. Schweitzer was this: "Is social compatibility a matter of race or ethics?" Dr. Schweitzer's answer was, "Prejudice is a matter of culture. It is my feeling that races are for the most part equi-potential." That is all he would say.

Although we met, in the course of our travels, several maharajas, titans of industry, and colonial nobility including the Viceroy of India, by far the two most memorable experiences that we had in India were our brief but intimate meetings with Rabindranath Tagore, India's Nobel prize-winning poet, and Mahatma Gandhi.

In Dr. Schweitzer's book, *Indian Thought and Its Development,* I found a discussion of both Rabindranath Tagore and Mahatma Gandhi.

When I read Dr. Schweitzer's evaluation of the philosophy of Tagore, I discovered it was no string of platitudes that Schweitzer uses as his measure of a man. Finally I found the underlying yardstick Dr. Schweitzer uses to measure all men—even the

greatest. It is the standard he applies to himself. Being familiar
with Albert Schweitzer's evaluation of Tagore, I thought I
might get some intimate insights if Dr. Schweitzer would forget
his pledge of silence on controversial issues and speak out on
both Tagore and Gandhi.

I said in effect, "Dr. Schweitzer, I was overawed with Tagore's
magnificent personality and seeming wisdom from the time I
met him at his university, the 'Abode of Peace,' until I read
your appraisal of him. He then became a person of parts, good
and bad.

"As I recall, you felt he had made two major philosophical
blunders. First, he allowed the false Western image of the
Creator God to supplant the higher Hindu wisdom that visualized
the universe as enigmatic, inexplicable, unoriginated and timeless. Tagore left this wisdom and became lost in the dilemma
of monism versus dualism without ever realizing the paradox
and the error.

"Tagore's second error, you said, was superimposed on his
greatest achievement. In a culture that denied the value of
life and held aloft as ultimate good the escape from the law
of reincarnation and endless successions of rebirths, Tagore
voiced a joy of living and an affirmation of life and an active
ethic of service and love. His Himalayan mistake was in claiming falsely that this optimism was the correct interpretation of
the ancient Indian wisdom.

"As I understood you, Dr. Schweitzer," I continued, "in
substance truth is discovered within one's personality. It needs
no historical justification. It belittles truth to force it to speak
through the lips of ancient wisdom. It corrupts the ancient
visions to be confused with current truth. Tagore's achievements
in truth would have been more liberating for humanity if bequeathed to the world, not as old Indian thought warmed over,
but as human truth achieved by the act of self-knowledge.

"Dr. Schweitzer, you seemed to say that racial, national, and
religious loyalty betrayed Tagore, whose highest wisdom was

universal, timeless, and above the meanness of history. Human love is so liberating, it need not be assumed to be the law of the Hindu God or any other."

I spoke my piece on Tagore with an air of certainty and expectancy; but whereas I was sure I saw animation playing hide and seek on Dr. Schweitzer's face, he did not affirm or deny my presentation. He merely said noncommittally that Tagore is the Goethe of India and one of the noblest sons not only of India but of humanity, and not only of our age but all ages.

I waited in vain to hear him enlarge on the exciting subject. In a moment or two I was resigned. I would have to be content with his written statement on Tagore. Dr. Schweitzer waited patiently for me to proceed with my tale of the roundabout road I had followed for twenty years to get to Lambaréné.

I next started to tell Dr. Schweitzer of my tragic experience with Mahatma Gandhi.

I explained to Dr. Schweitzer that when I left America I carried a letter from one of Gandhi's most enthusiastic biographers, Rev. John Haynes Holmes. Because it came to me indirectly through a much revered professor, the letter of introduction was more extravagant in its appraisal of my understandings and sympathies than was warranted. Not knowing this, Mahatma Gandhi, upon receipt of the exuberant letter written in our behalf, promptly sent a wire of welcome to us, setting an early date for a visit.

We hustled across India to the village of Wardha. There we visited Gandhi on three occasions. After leaving Wardha, we organized our notes most carefully and then prepared a short article of our interpretation of Gandhi's great significance. In order to be certain that we were not misquoting the spiritual general of India, we sent our manuscript to him for appraisal prior to publication. I was sure I had captured the essence of

Gandhi's movement in my manuscript and had communicated it with some charm and competence.

You may guess how I choked when I opened the terse message from the leader of India's millions and read: "I have received your article. What you have written is true, but I am sorry to say you have entirely missed the point."

For two decades I was ignorant of the meaning of Gandhi's searing rebuke; for, as I explained to Dr. Schweitzer, it was not until I became acquainted with Arnold Toynbee's theories of history's mechanism and later with Dr. Schweitzer's own philosophy of ethics that I felt some rational power to appraise the eloquent life and spiritual achievements of India's humble and yet imperious saint. I came to realize that he was tempered on the anvil of adversity into an unyielding instrument of national freedom. He drew his ethics with consummate skill from the archives of universal wisdom, and acquired through exercises in self-mastery a spiritual freedom that moved multitudes.

Knowing that Dr. Schweitzer had appraised the ethical contributions of Mahatma Gandhi with his own ethical system of values, I suggested that Dr. Schweitzer was waging a spiritual war at the global level for all life whereas Gandhi fought at the national level for the Indians only. I submitted that Gandhi had liberated his people from the yoke of colonialism and Dr. Schweitzer was trying to liberate all peoples from the bondage of dead ideas that burden the human spirit everywhere and today threaten the race with nuclear extinction.

I felt that Dr. Schweitzer wanted to comment on my observation. But he has often been misquoted on colonialism and matters pertaining to Christianity, and frequently he is attacked even by modern Hindu and Moslem leaders for belittling Indian religions. He said with an air of restraint and modesty that he was afraid I overrated his own importance.

At this point I would have given six teeth to ask the following basically moral questions: Is the non-violent, non-cooperation force that is typified by Gandhi's selfless courageous campaign always more moral than violence, or do the principles that motivate group force, violent or non-violent, determine its morality? Was violent Jefferson less moral than non-violent Gandhi? Is all group force immoral as an infringement on the natural rights to freedom of individuals? Is the group force exerted by nations against one another moral or immoral? Is national freedom that Gandhi fought for always a sovereign good, or is nationalism an evil? How far do you go when you say that nationalism today threatens not only the freedom of individuals but the survival of humanity? Would a world federation of nations liberate individuals most, or will one central global government be the solution to man's dreams of perpetual peace?

I recall telling Dr. Schweitzer that through our veil of ignorance we were often smitten with the solid truth that religions have dominated the course of history. The cultural map of the world is undoubtedly a spiritual blueprint of the past religions of the world. Frontiers are erected by conflicting ethics. Wars are clashes of ethics. Material objectives become motivating when clothed in moral symbolism. Essentially man is a value-motivated creature.

Dr. Schweitzer looked amused and I thought pleased with my little oration, but he only waited for me to proceed with the saga of my physical travels.

I told of bouncing over pot holes through the walls of the Khyber Pass to Kabul, the capital of Afghanistan. Even in this rocky, mountainous country, where mere survival is something of a miracle, we found the people deeply religious and methodically prayerful.

These people are fanatically anti-Christian and also fanatically moral according to their own Moslem lights. Hooded women threw rocks at our car until my wife covered her "nude" face.

Public anger had recently flared up deposing a king. Pressured by priests, peoples marched against their monarch decrying his Western fashions, particularly his new fad of unveiling women's faces. He fled to permanent exile charged with breaking the sacred will of Allah. Public ethics, not kings, ruled Afghanistan.

After this, we returned to Bombay, India, and tarried there a while.

After loading our dental equipment aboard a British boat, we sailed up the romantic Persian Gulf to the city of Basra. Perilously, we made our way across this arid land which once flowed with caravan traffic bound to and from the Babylonian seat of culture that flourished between the Tigris and Euphrates. In the twentieth century Arab marauders raid travelers in Fords and Chevrolets. We arrived at Bagdad exhausted from some harrowing experiences with lawless Arab pirates terrorizing this sea of sand. These brigands are fanatical followers of Mohammed.

Next we visited the Holy Land. But we found the Middle-Eastern cradle of the three world religions rocking with hate. We speculated in our ignorance on the reasons why the Judeo-Christian inspiration had fanned out westward only, leaving the Moslem faith the eastward course.

I said to Dr. Schweitzer that I had resented the fact that my education had been so meager concerning the early thought-world of Jesus and his age. One particular remark I recall turned out to be quite inappropriate. "Dr. Schweitzer," I said, "you were most fortunate to have discovered the historians Philo, Pliny, and Josephus. You were lucky to know of the Essenes, now a famous sect of Jews, long before the discovery of the Dead Sea Scrolls and the Essene monastery."

With genuine modesty Dr. Schweitzer merely acknowledged that he had been fortunate in many ways. Luck does not describe Dr. Schweitzer's method of obtaining knowledge.

I continued my narrative by telling next of our month of dentistry in the Land of the Pharaohs. By special dispensation we were allowed to practice dentistry at Luxor, Egypt, adjacent to the wondrous Valley of the Kings.

Egypt is a most exciting laboratory for studies in ethics, because of the religious motives and illusions that drove Pharaohs to the extravagance of subterranean tombs and incredibly mountainous pyramids, now relics of a fossil faith that has no living spiritual descendants.

I think I next told Dr. Schweitzer about the Italian hospital ships that were then passing through the Suez Canal. They gave us cause to ask the searching question: "Why was it that Mahatma Gandhi, the non-Christian, was fighting with weapons of non-violence in India to end colonialism, while Italy, a world center of Christian Catholicism, was sending Fascist soldiers and weapons of violence out to Ethiopia to subdue and colonize the only independent Christian country in Africa? Why did Fascism start in the devout country of Italy? And why did Vatican City sign a Concordat with Mussolini?" I am sure I would remember if Dr. Schweitzer had answered these momentous ethical questions.

The next big hop I remember recounting to Dr. Schweitzer was a marathon of economy. We had decided we could not return to America from our experiences with Shintoists, Buddhists, Hindus, Moslems, Jews, and Christian missionaries abroad without peeping behind the curtain of atheistic Russia.

Our Russian plan presented a problem. We could not earn our way through Europe or Russia by dentistry. Therefore, we curtailed spending with utmost parsimony. We chose cheap, high calorie foods and ate sparingly. We entered Moscow third-class.

After witnessing the long lines in front of Lenin's Tomb in Moscow in sub-zero temperatures, we concluded in 1936 that Communism, though opposed to all time-honored religions, is not itself to be considered irreligious, as we had supposed. Antireligious talk against other faiths has always been the hallmark of a new faith. Marxism we found is in reality a new secular world religion.

I told Dr. Schweitzer of my diagnosis. "We had felt," I said, "that this fierce and fanatical new authoritarian world religion was making its greatest strides in areas where contemporary religions had accustomed men to authoritarian ways in politics and religion, or where cynicism and despair had created an ethical vacuum. We were not convinced that poverty and only poverty necessarily predisposed peoples to the Communist faith."

Dr. Schweitzer nodded his assent to these allusions to Communism as a new world religion, but he was careful not to make any quotable comment.

Hoping Dr. Schweitzer would forget himself and discuss my educational mission, I observed that when we returned home we were sure of one thing. American schools, following the tradition of freedom *of* religion, have long been criminally guilty of sanctioning freedom *from* religion. "In America most of us," I said, "are really religious illiterates. We know nothing of the vast heritage of man recorded in all world religions."

Dr. Schweitzer observed noncommittally that our trip must today provide us with a reservoir of wonderful memories. I momentarily abandoned the hope of talking about my educational mission to Lambaréné and proceeded to sketch in the next twenty years.

Dr. Schweitzer seemed surprised when I told him, as a sidelight, that I spent my first savings on an airplane and became one of Chicago's first air commuters. His face was wreathed in smiles when he mumbled something in French to the ladies present. The women laughed at Dr. Schweitzer's remark, but his comment was not translated.

I tried apologetically to explain the pressures acting toward social and economic success in America. My excuses for following the "bitch goddess" sounded empty when laid before the man who had turned his back on more fame and fortune that I had dreamed about. At any rate, I assured Dr. Schweitzer that as I climbed the ladder, world adventures had to be shelved. Soon we were blessed with two sons and thereafter we were embarked on the rewarding and bewildering, semi-sedentary adventure of parenthood.

Our modest professional practice blossomed. The fates decreed for us a comfortable life gradually ascending in economic security. Our spiritual tranquility did not keep pace.

I am not sure I told Dr. Schweitzer all of the following changes in fortune in my life, but I know I conveyed the substance of the narrative that follows.

After changing my practice from "Behind the Yards" to the fashionable South Shore and thence to the heights of a city skyscraper, I returned to school and spent two years on a half-time basis acquiring a master's degree in oral surgery. I stayed on at the school to instruct for two more years. I remember these days of baby-tending, bread-winning, studying, and teaching as an unmarred pleasure.

In due course we made a down payment on a home in exclusive suburbia. We were conforming nicely. I was attracted to the people connected with advertising, and I found that some of my friends were notable characters in the field of "hidden persuasion." We met many marketing executives in church. We turned in a fairly good attendance record ourselves in the village Union Church. More revealing, we contributed to its financial support although we did not become members.

One day in a moment of madness, I accepted as a duty an appointment to the board of trustees of a small college. Later I was surprised to find that my new chores became one of my keenest interests. Actually, in addition to learning something of the art of extracting gifts painlessly, I became fascinated by the core issues in American education.

I was slowly driven to conclude that no one seemed to know what an education really is.

My academic interest as a trustee carried prestige in the "crowd culture" that surrounded me. I cultivated, however,

a somewhat less widely admired academic pursuit. I was loath
to admit in some circles which scorned long-hairs my hobby of
participating in Great Books studies. I recall that I confessed
to Dr. Schweitzer without a grain of guilt this egghead enterprise.

I admitted to Dr. Schweitzer that we read superficially, often
for diversion. I said with a spark of pride that I even started
a Great Books Group myself in a plush social club. Dr. Ernest
Cadman Colwell, then past dean of the theological schools and
president of the University of Chicago, became an occasional
co-leader of my group. Soon he was one of my dearest friends
and companions of the search. Dr. Schweitzer remembered that
this was the eloquent gentleman who officiated at the presentation of his honorary degree from the University of Chicago in
1949.

I told Dr. Schweitzer a homely truth. After years of debate
on the classical issues of history, it became apparent to me that
only an ethical system of values could measure intellectual
achievements. Debates always collapsed on the core question:
what is the nature of good and evil? We had no authorities.
Without ethics all things were relative. Great books do not
map the road to ethical wisdom. Dr. Schweitzer whimsically
smiled his unspoken approval of my conclusion.

I observed to Dr. Schweitzer that we had suffered from the
epidemic disease in America called spiritual restlessness. Perhaps it was the changing horizons of nuclear science and the
growing horrors of war that kept Americans spiritually insecure.
I did not believe this epidemic disease was more severe in our
home than in most. There were many people who felt as we
did. At times it seemed that all of us were living on the ir-
idescent perimeter of a beautiful bubble.

I recall telling Dr. Schweitzer that we had continued to watch
at long range the amazing Gandhi epic. One man in our age
before our eyes was galvanizing a people into a single moral
purpose.

AN EVENING WITH DR. SCHWEITZER

When the historian Arnold Toynbee made his appearance at our hearthside in book form, many of our homespun convictions conceived on our travels became confirmed. We were convinced that Toynbee had presented indisputable insights into the mechanism of history and social change. The material was there to give modern man ethical power over his perilous destiny. His prophecies seemed uncanny in accuracy. Yet few listened to Toynbee, and life spun on to the vortex.

I contrived to meet Dr. Toynbee on several occasions and managed to discuss with him questions dealing with freedom and religion. I became convinced that his genius lies in explaining history, not in making it. I began to suspect that only prophets know the things about humanity that are hidden beneath the surface events of history. Gandhi had known secrets of social change unilluminated by external events of the past. He called his autobiography *Experiments in Truth*.

Despite his aloofness, Toynbee's scholarly insights seemed to glue our attention on the unique feature of current civilization. Striking power in warfare has achieved cosmic significance from energy stores locked in cosmic clay. Virtual annihilation of all combatants would soon be possible.

The ideological cold war between the two rival colossi, America and Russia, was staged over an abyss of thermonuclear horror and universal cremation. The urgency for waging a victorious peace produces a crisis never before faced in man's long, bloody record of periodic reversions to bestial habits of self-destruction.

As I read in Toynbee how periods of adversity and crisis challenge society to produce prophets, redeemers, revolutionaries and saviours, I dreamed a dream. I reasoned that if he were half right our age was over-ripe for a new Messianic figure. Perhaps our material supremacy clouded the moral adversity. How tragic it would be if a new spiritual leader would come forward only to be overlooked by our moral blindness. What would a creative prophet look like? What would his gospel be?

How could he and his disciples, apostles, and Gospel writers save the human family from utter destruction by blast and radiation? Would man prove himself worth saving? What could a modern saint say to the modern skeptics?

I believed the stage was set for a strong moral personage with a positive program. Free peoples and neutral nations had to be united on moral issues. They had to learn how to heal themselves and to win the confidence of all peoples who would oppose by cold war measures the forces of tyranny. But how?

Destiny, through adversity, had created a role for the new liberator. Where was that liberator?

I could see my host was getting uneasy. He probably was already sorry he had asked me to explain how I became interested in him and his hospital. He dislikes the thought of idolaters, hero worshipers, and cultists. He could not be sure where my story was going.

I told the doctor about reading his volume, *Out of My Life and Thought.* I was immediately alerted. By intuition I knew that I was discovering a Western moral leader of the stature of Gandhi. I told the embarrassed man that his dedicated deeds, his great and gentle heart, and his love of beauty constituted the moral traits that initially linked him in my mind with Gandhi. But I saw no evidence of political strategy, no moral tactics, no moral militia.

I told Dr. Schweitzer next that it was the wide range of his scholarship and the vastness of his orderly mind that came to my growing sense of ethical appreciation with his book, *The Philosophy of Civilization.* I said the real eye-opener came to me in the next book I read. I told Dr. Schweitzer that I knew even on my first skimming of *The Quest of the Historical Jesus* that this was a deeply reverent but completely revolutionary document. I did not understand what kind of reform was called for in the challenge.

Dr. Schweitzer protested, saying he must never, after the bloody French Revolution, be called a "revolutionary."

I said something to the effect that names are harmless symbols to moral men, and I quoted instances from his books where he himself recounted episodes in which he was a disturbing, provocative, exciting moralist with an unorthodox mission. I said Lambaréné to some was a Mecca of unprecedented spiritual interest, and to some it was an epicenter of a call to action.

Dr. Schweitzer seemed genuinely amused when I spoke of my feet acting like the uncontrollable needle of a compass. I said that my wandering feet, that had behaved so long, became self-willed. Indulging a metaphorical whimsy, I said that after reading his books, my feet and my heart, unbidden, turned toward Africa, toward the heart of the great Dark Continent, toward Lambaréné.

I told Dr. Schweitzer as we were about to pick up the tickets to Lambaréné, we heard via the grapevine that he was on his way to his home in Gunsbach, Alsace, in the heart of Europe. Dr. Schweitzer had at that time finally accepted an invitation to speak at Oslo, Norway, where a year earlier he had been awarded the Nobel Peace Prize. He had, incidentally, used all of his prize money to buy corrugated sheet-iron for the walls and roof of a sanitarium to house lepers in Lambaréné.

The ticket agent thought we were quixotic when we suddenly changed our destination from Africa to Europe.

I asked Dr. Schweitzer if he recalled any of the strange events that occurred on my first short visit with him in Gunsbach two years earlier. I was flattered but worried when he said "Yes." My visit had ended in an embarrassment of sorts. I decided attack was the best defense, and half in jest and half in earnest I accused him of crushing my finest dream. His reaction indicated that he did not remember much more than the physical fact of our visit. But now he was concerned, and I had to tell the indelicate story in detail.

I told him that I had not had time at our hasty first meeting to explain my self-imposed, naive, adventuresome mission. The following paragraphs review the story that led to the special purpose of my journey to Gunsbach.

Back in 1954 I had settled in my romantic mind that I was going to visit with Dr. Schweitzer in Europe. I had consulted some of his American friends and was told that exchanging mail with the harassed doctor is often slow or altogether impossible. I was advised to go unannounced and trust to luck and his famous on-the-spot hospitality.

While I was planning our family trip to Europe, I talked over my impending meeting with Dr. Schweitzer with a few intimate friends. Joseph Lohman, Chicago's scholar-sheriff, one day heard my interpretation of Dr. Schweitzer's gifts. I suggested pontifically that great historical movements radiated from moral personages, and that the anti-Communist world might have an undiscovered gospel and a prophet in Albert Schweitzer. I suggested naively that were he willing to be drafted, he could be a secret weapon for free peoples in their moral war against tyranny.

Dr. Schweitzer shook his shaggy head, apparently much disturbed, when I told him that out of the blue Mr. Lohman said the idea ought to be given to "the boys" in psychological warfare.

Mr. Lohman was a figure to be reckoned with. He had served under two Presidents, and had been commissioned by the Eisenhower administration to counsel with some of the American prisoners of war who had refused repatriation during the Korean truce.

Without further ado, he phoned the Pentagon from a public phone and arranged a meeting with the general who was head of psychological warfare.

The men carrying the burdens of planning war were working on the new concept called Militant Liberty, which has since been published. I reached into my portfolio and gave Dr. Schweitzer a description. Militant Liberty was premised on what I considered an historical truth which I had arrived at in my reading and traveling. They stated it thus: "We as free people . . . have many times been incoherent and lacked the verbal ability to explain or defend completely what liberty is and thereby have forfeited the field to the Communists. . . . Communist ideology can only be defeated by a stronger dynamic ideology."

I flew to Washington. I was met at the airport by the general and was driven to the Pentagon. The general and his associates listened to my thesis with interest and courtesy. I believe, however, that they merely filed it in their voluminous archives of ideas. They called on me thereafter on one or two occasions as a consultant to observe the development of Militant Liberty, the project on which they were working.

I found myself in agreement with the purposes of Militant Liberty but not with its scholarship or methods. The document attempted to devise ways to measure degrees of freedom and degrees of responsibility of allies and enemy nations. This idea, in my judgment, should be applied to individuals, not nations.

Just before flying to Portugal, Spain, Switzerland, and thence on to Gunsbach by car, I told Dr. Schweitzer that I decided on an exciting detour.

I had long considered Albert Einstein a world figure as much for his modesty, humility and charity of heart as for his revisions of scientific and mathematical errors in our thinking about the physical universe. Dr. Einstein had frequently expressed tributes to Mahatma Gandhi, Albert Schweitzer, Leo Tolstoy and other men of ethical stature. I told Dr. Schweitzer it seemed quite natural to me that I visit Dr. Einstein before my visit to Gunsbach.

Actually I could not resist the temptation to stop at Princeton, New Jersey, to ask the philosopher-scientist about the speculative prophetic role we had assigned to his friend, Dr. Schweitzer.

I told Dr. Schweitzer, who was listening eagerly, that five minutes after we arrived at the house on humble Mercer Street in Princeton and pushed the doorbell labeled "A. Einstein," we were bidden by the genius to sidestep his secretarial guardian and come up to his room.

I told Dr. Schweitzer we were awed but not in the least anxious in the presence of this great and gracious man. I said, "His hair-do was much like yours, Dr. Schweitzer." The old doctor laughed heartily. I said, "Also his eyes were like yours. They had an x-ray quality about them, but they were kindly. They were also bright, as if polished by stardust imported from infinity."

I told one Albert of how I presented my notions about him to the other Albert. Einstein had listened to my proposal of using the Schweitzer symbol, personage and philosophy for world unity, peace, and freedom. He was very thoughtful until I used the phrase, "unite the free peoples." Then with a loud laugh he asked derisively, "What free peoples?" I amended the phrase to, "unite the non-Communist countries," and proceeded.

Einstein deliberated and then said, "I agree that your idea is most worthwhile. Albert Schweitzer is the one and only man who might accomplish this necessary purpose. The job would have to be done sincerely and on a very large scale."

Dr. Schweitzer seemed pleased with his valued friend's good opinion.

Dr. Schweitzer spoke with undisguised personal sorrow as he told of receiving the news of the death of Albert Einstein. He stated that the agnostic pantheist follower of Spinoza was in reality a deeply religious person. We agreed that he was primarily a philosopher of matter. We concurred in judging that he was not a profound scholar of systematic ethics. However, he was not just a brilliant, socially indifferent scientist. Although he was a skeptic concerning human freedom, he was an earnest advocate of social justice.

Dr. Schweitzer said he had been profoundly moved by Dr. Einstein's agonized sentiments toward H-bomb explosions. He was shocked that some Americans feared the liberal thoughts voiced by Einstein. He seemed pleased that I had organized a public memorial service for this gallant gentle soldier of truth. I showed him a prose poem I had composed, in which I featured Einstein in the company of Moses, Jesus, and Schweitzer. This evoked no apparent surprise and no special comment.

Then Dr. Schweitzer's eyes twinkled, and he related an incident that occurred during his only visit in America, in 1949. When he was on his way to give the Goethe Bicentennial Lectures in Aspen, Colorado, a fellow passenger on the train mistook him for Dr. Einstein. He said, "I was the wrong Albert, but I signed his name anyway, writing below the signature, 'By his friend Albert Schweitzer.' "

Dr. Schweitzer did not seem overly surprised when I confessed I had written to Einstein contrasting the philosophy of Karl Marx and Albert Schweitzer and had received a reply citing points of agreement and disagreement.

He grinned and asked, "Are you leading into a discussion of philosophy by the back door?" I countered, "Is there going to be a front door?"

My question got carefully lost in translation, and the next thing I knew the subject at hand was Robert Oppenheimer. He volunteered the opinion that Oppenheimer had been cruelly misunderstood. Dr. Schweitzer remembered that several years ago this controversial American had invited him to the Institute for Advanced Studies to complete the books he had in progress. He had sent regrets because he felt he could not leave his work in Lambaréné.

After this diversion, I was asked to return to the main thread of my narrative. Without further reassurance about the proposal I chose to submit to Dr. Schweitzer in Gunsbach, and with no certainty of an interview with the overburdened man, we enplaned for Europe, joining our sons in Switzerland.

I reminded Dr. Schweitzer of the final hours preceding our arrival at his home in Gunsbach, Alsace. In the heady Alpine atmosphere we had decided on one last detour.

At a small barber shop in a suburb of Zurich, we made inquiries concerning the exact address of Dr. Schweitzer's daughter, Madame Eckert. We had phoned her, and she had invited us to visit her. Apparently to show respect to the Schweitzer legend, the barber insisted on closing his shop, escorting us to the home of Dr. Schweitzer's only child, now a mother of four children and a devoted owner of four growling chow dogs who did not for an instant take their hungry eyes off us.

This very charming, forthright young woman listened respectfully but incredulously as we told her the very special way in which we had come to regard her father. I said, "Your father is a very great man."

She said, "Who? Daddy? Actually he has always just lived and worked the way he wanted to."

Then she said unaffectedly, "You will find my father does not like to be called a great man."

Obviously Dr. Schweitzer's daughter loved and revered her father. But apparently he had not been regarded as a prophet in his own home.

After hearing of our European mission and our hope for an interview, she volunteered to make a long-distance call to Gunsbach in our behalf. To our amazement, within three minutes we had been graciously invited to dine with Albert Schweitzer in his Gunsbach home the following evening.

Mme. Eckert came away from the phone looking radiant. She said, "I want to thank you for being the cause of my having a visit with my father. I never like to call and disturb him unless I have something important to say. He asked me if my clothes were ready for the trip to Norway this fall."

We said, "Oh, are you planning to go with your father?"

"It is my father's wish, and I will of course go," she replied, with obvious delight. "But I had to tell him my clothes are not ready. And he laughed and told me not to worry, for his speech is not ready, either."

I could not tell how much of what followed Dr. Schweitzer really remembered. But he encouraged me to tell the details. Mme. Schweitzer later said she remembered our visit very distinctly.

When we had arrived at the appointed hour at the Gunsbach home, Dr. Schweitzer was not there. We discovered in talking with Mlle. Mathilde Kottman in our fractured French that he was walking with a young Negro organist to the train. To the annoyance of many eminent visitors, Dr. Schweitzer had interrupted his day to listen to the boy play. He had never before seen the young man who dropped by unannounced. The Nobel Peace Prize speech was left untended. A Bostonian, Mrs. Julian Rogers, was thwarted in plans to make recordings for her radio program. Nies-Berger, a New York conductor, had been neglected. A sculptor from Munich whose name escapes me was delayed. Viennese-born Erica Anderson, the movie photographer, waiting to work on a documentary film, had been put off. All waited in a subdued frenzy. As for us, we were more nervous than impatient.

Suddenly the enormous delicacy of my problem stunned me. If Dr. Schweitzer abhorred halos and appellations of "genius," "giant," or "saint," how could we discover his sentiments in regard to our main inquiry? Would he be wrathful if asked about so momentous an issue by a stranger? I nervously tried to re-phrase the question that had to say in effect: What would you do, Dr. Schweitzer, if the free peoples of the world adopted you as a focal and unifying symbol and your ideals as a battle cry in their fight for freedom? I wondered what he would say to a systematic effort made by friends and well-wishers to oppose the tyranny and collectivism of Communism and Fascism with his cherished principles of reverence, freedom, and individualism.

In the midst of our distressing apprehension, the seventy-nine-year-young man strode through the threshold in a wave of warmth, vigor, and magnetism. Since we were the only newcomers, he had extended to us a genuine two-handed greeting.

He pulled the circle of chairs closer and said disarmingly through the translator, "Welcome! I understand from my daughter that you want to talk philosophy."

My moment had come. Twenty carefully prepared preliminary questions burned on my trembling tongue, but opportunity might slip through my clumsy fingers. I blurted out, "Would you be willing for the free peoples of the world to adopt your principles of Reverence for Life as the gospel of freedom, and you as the central prophet of freedom?"

I had finally delivered my question. There it was in all of its brash presumptuousness, its simple candor, its blushing self-consciousness.

I asked Dr. Schweitzer if he now remembered what he had said to my question in Gunsbach two years earlier. He said no. I refreshed his memory.

His swift answer had in fact come like ice water to my impetuous flaming hope. Now I had come to judge it to be a magnificent prophetic parable.

He said in essence: "The honor is too much. I did not even dream that the ideals I had sown would bear such fruit in my lifetime. The planter of ideas does not see the harvest. Yet I knew that some day my ideas would become universally accepted because they are true. The principle of Reverence for Life I raised as a cow. I gave the cow to the world. The world may do with it what it will. And now, how would you like to hear some Bach music right after dinner?"

Now here in Lambaréné, two years afterwards, the incident looked funny to everyone present, even myself. Dr. Schweitzer had been smiling at the trials I had had with him and his eccentricities in Gunsbach. Now he could contain himself no longer.

I thought I had never heard so merry a laugh—certainly never at my expense. Smiling, I congratulated Dr. Schweitzer on the skill with which he had diverted me in my big inquiry at Gunsbach and for the way he had sidetracked me during the remainder of that memorable evening. Talk had been deftly switched to trivia. Well-planned interruptions intruded every time I tried to reopen the subject. My philosophical interview had lived only for seconds. His response, though provocative, promising, and prophetic, had been utterly inconclusive. I had to yield to the one sure judgment. He was certainly not going to be an active promoter of his own leadership. Maybe he would not even be an interested spectator if his friends elected to assign a new prophetic role to him in history.

Immediately after a delightful, non-political dinner, smiling broadly he had said to my wife and me, "Do you think organ music would hurt you now?"

For two hours he had played Bach music in the village church once served by his pastor father, on an organ that he himself designed. I sat on one side of him on the organ bench, and my wife sat on the other. The music was magnificent, but I churned with the desire for a quiet philosophical visit that never came. Actually, farewells were given in the middle of the darkened street in Gunsbach.

I told Dr. Schweitzer how unlike Gandhi he was in matters of answering socio-political questions. Gandhi had given us staccato answers to every question. Understating the facts, he said he guessed his habits in many ways were unlike Gandhi's.

I told Dr. Schweitzer that his friends often answered questions for him. I told him we had stopped at Basel to see his very good friend, Reverend Fritz Buri. Dr. Buri is a keen scholar and author of analytical books and many penetrating articles about Albert Schweitzer.

After I recovered from the shock of my failure with Dr. Schweitzer, I was infinitely grateful to talk at great length with his friend of long standing. Dr. Buri answered every one of our twenty burning questions "favorably." He also helped us understand Dr. Schweitzer's reticence.

The Early Plan of the Albert Schweitzer Education Foundation

It will serve a useful purpose to review the small part of the network of individualists that Dr. Schweitzer recalled as I related my encounters with members of an unorganized, far-flung fellowship united by his ideals.

Dr. Schweitzer showed astonishment when I brought from my portfolio a picture showing the panel of his American admirers who spoke at the observance of his eightieth birthday at Northwestern University. He was uneasy that 1500 people had troubled to attend, and more disturbed that a like number had had to be turned away. He did not seem in the least shaken when I told him that the ministers of two local churches had turned down the unusual observance. He conveyed by gestures that it seemed natural to him that the University was more spiritually understanding of the novel observance which the churches had rejected. It was the Chaplain of Northwestern who insisted enthusiastically that the affair be expanded as interest grew.

Dr. Schweitzer raised no eyebrow when he was told that all of the speakers were theological liberals. I showed him some telegrams conveying birthday greetings that were read at the occasion. One from Albert Einstein. Another from President Eisenhower, the only other non-Briton besides Dr. Schweitzer to hold the British Order of Merit.

I showed Dr. Schweitzer the clipping that appeared in the *Evanston Review* after the birthday observance had snowballed to success:

MANY TURNED AWAY FROM SCHWEITZER TRIBUTE MEETING

The public response to the Albert Schweitzer birthday observance held at Cahn Auditorium, Evanston, on January 14, was overwhelming. Many people could not be accommodated.

Even though the site of the observance had been shifted three times, Howes Chapel, capacity 60, to Lutkin Hall, capacity 400, to Cahn Auditorium, capacity, including overflow lounge, 1,500, the interest exceeded the accommodations.

The magnetism of Albert Schweitzer as the symbol of goodness and the power of his deeds and dedication surprised and bewildered the sponsors, it was explained. The committee in charge has submitted a letter of apology in which they say, "It was grotesquely contrary to the spirit of the meeting that anyone was turned away."

Apparently no presumptiveness of self-importance slumbers beneath the surface in Dr. Schweitzer's nature. He was right in believing that the people who came in droves were not honoring his ideas so much as his deeds of dedication. As we shall see in a later chapter, his prophetic certitude is in his ideas, not his deeds.

I asked Dr. Schweitzer if he realized that birthday observances had been held in several cities in the United States, including New York, and several countries in Europe. He nodded his head, but said no more. The picture of Adlai Stevenson among the panelists brought up the 1956 presidential race in America. Before I could even launch a question on politics, he raised his hand indicating "No comment." He did say with obvious disappointment that he was sorry Mr. Stevenson had bypassed him in his first African safari. He smiled with pleasure and embarrassment upon hearing that Stevenson, from whom I carried greetings, spoke of him as the foremost citizen of the world and the best emissary of the Western world because he brought Western medical skill intimately to people, no strings attached. Dr. Schweitzer mumbled, "My friends are far too kind."

I brought forth a birthday book of testimonials assembled by Dr. Homer Jack, the Unitarian minister in Evanston. It contained words of affection from admirers and friends all over the world. Dr. Schweitzer sighed, "Why do these good people

do so much for me?" With that he showed me a similar book
of testimonials in German assembled by Rev. Fritz Buri, the
courageous liberal theologian of Basel, Switzerland. There was
a third book, *Hommage à Albert Schweitzer*, containing testimonials from many authors.

Dr. Schweitzer was most eager to have a personal report
from me of the hospital founded in his name in Haiti. I told
of my meeting with Larimer and Gwen Mellon in Deschapelles,
and I assured him that in many aspects the spirit of the Schweitzer hospital was being perpetuated. He in turn was pleased
that the Mellons had made innovations and were not slavishly
obedient to his model. I showed him an article I had written
in the *Christian Century* describing the germinating power behind the Mellon Hospital. The Mellon story is so remarkable
a tribute to the vitality of Dr. Schweitzer's prophet image and
gospel that I shall include below excerpts from my own article.
Dr. Schweitzer read it with no sign of pride.

At eighty-two, Albert Schweitzer has managed to avoid
becoming the focus of a cult even though he has become a
yeasty ferment in the lives of many individuals in many lands.
Following the leading of free scholarship to true wisdom he
has found the meaning of Jesus compelling in his own life,
and through him others make the same discovery. "Reverence
for Life," his absolute ethic, has oneness, wholeness and
universality, and it awakens slumbering treasures that modern
man has buried in the abysses of his unconscious. Last Christmas I had the opportunity to observe what the catalytic action
of the Schweitzer symbol has meant in the life of a prominent, culturally intrenched American family.

My wife and I corralled our two sons for a Yuletide vaca-
tion with a purpose. We flew to Haiti to see the Albert
Schweitzer Hospital, founded by a grandnephew of the late
Andrew Mellon, one of the wealthiest men of his time. There
we saw with our own eyes how the example and spirit of
Albert Schweitzer, impecunious, socially humble and politically

inconsequential, had transformed the grandnephew of Andrew Mellon and his family.

We arrived at the Mellons' home on the day before Christmas. Our family of four was warmly invited to share potluck with Larimer and Gwen Mellon and their two younger children. (Their two older boys were in military service.) When questioned, our mild-mannered, modest host and hostess were unable to dissect out their motives and compulsions, but our inquiries brought to light an extremely interesting story of a strange contagion carrying all the cardinal symptoms of conversion.

In 1947 Larimer Mellon, along with millions of other Americans, saw in *Life* magazine a compelling picture and brief narrative of an obscure missionary doctor. *Life's* account planted the germ of an idea in the fertile soil of Mr. Mellon's mind and heart. Nothing observable in William Larimer Mellon's background would indicate that he would be susceptible to the transformation that soon took place. He grew up a dutiful son of wealthy parents. He attended Princeton, but left after his freshman year to gravitate into the Mellon National Bank and later into the family-managed Gulf Oil Corporation. Still later he became owner and operator of a huge ranch in Arizona. He was a successful businessman-rancher when the Schweitzer contagion caught him.

After reading the *Life* story, Mellon started a library adventure in Schweitzer's ethics. It was at this early stage that his ranch manager came to him complaining of exhaustion and requesting a vacation. Mr. Mellon did the unconventional thing. He urged his ranch manager to visit Dr. Schweitzer in far-away Lambaréné in French Equatorial Africa. The manager went, and he returned glowing with vitality and enthusiasm.

Seeing him and hearing him talk about his visit, Larimer and Gwen Mellon began to suspect that, while they were graciously drifting through their middle years, an old jungle doctor with far fewer material blessings was marching forward in a richer and more meaningful way. So they too went to Lambaréné, and after that "wonderful experience" resolved

to redirect their lives and follow the Schweitzer plan of creating
a modern missionary hospital.

Thus it was that at 37 years of age Mr. Mellon sold his
Arizona ranch and started back to school. In the next seven
years he completed his college education and earned a medical
degree at Tulane University in New Orleans. His wife, who
spontaneously joined in the decision, studied nursing, laboratory techniques, and hospital organization and administration.
The four Mellon children continued their schooling while
their student parents also burned the midnight oil.

In following the Schweitzer pattern the Mellons founded
their hospital in the Artibonite valley in Haiti. This small
rural area, with a population of one million, is the most
underprivileged, overpopulated and medically needy region
they could find. There, as free citizens of rich America, they
are voluntarily dedicating themselves and their substance to
the desperately poor, dark-skinned, largely illiterate descendants of the slaves of the early French colonists. The Mellons
do not intend to proselytize, but their example represents free
man at his ethical best. They are giving themselves in service
to humanity, asking for no reward except the knowledge that
they are meeting human need. They are emissaries of the
abundance of the free world, not as it is but as it could become
were free men really good neighbors.

Most of the patients cared for at the Mellons' hospital come
from huts devoid of the simplest household objects such as
are found even in the worst American slum homes. The
average Haitian family earns and perforce lives on less than
$65 a year. Thus in building courtyards with spring water
and open stone hearths Dr. Mellon has provided the accustomed comforts of life for families who have brought their
old and sick many weary miles and who will stay at the hospital until their loved ones are well again. All the attractive
landscaping around the courtyards has been done with an eye
to the practical as well as the beautiful: most of the vegeta-
tion is edible and the trees are fruit-bearing. Cattle and dairy
herds are being rounded up on a near-by farm. In this enter-

prise Dr. Mellon's ranching experience stands him in good stead.

Larimer and Gwen Mellon say they have never known such happiness as has come to them at their hospital in Haiti. Yet they do not speak of sacrifice. They consider themselves fortunate to be able to bring the Schweitzer symbol as a seedling into the western hemisphere. They have no ambitions or illusions of grandeur, but this voluntary plan has inadvertently made them effective and exemplary instruments of interracial and international good will. All who know of their experiment in ethical living hold them in reverential esteem.

Oh yes, I mustn't forget the ranch manager who, at Larimer Mellon's suggestion, visited Dr. Schweitzer at Lambaréné almost a decade ago. Like the Mellons, he also went back to school to study hospital management, and with his wife he is now living on the hospital grounds in the capacity of manager.

When their hospital was about to begin functioning the Mellons received a message from the aging, ageless jungle doctor of Lambaréné: "Let me tell you how touched I am that your hospital carries my name. I am truly moved, more than I can tell you, at this expression of understanding. I send you my best wishes for your opening. The beginnings are always difficult. But you are courageous."

Dr. Schweitzer seemed intrigued with the title, "The Spark That Leaps the Seas." Mostly he reflected surprise or perhaps incredulity that a hard-working dentist should be interested in writing about ethics. There was not the slightest trace in him of vainglory. Dr. Schweitzer said simply, "It is heartening that Dr. Mellon discovered for himself the importance of the ideas in Reverence for Life. I am glad he did not follow my model but developed his own innovations."

I told Dr. Schweitzer of my faltering efforts at persuasion when I had tried and failed to interest the Board of Trustees of a small, struggling college to attempt to create an island campus where the influence of Albert Schweitzer's ethics on the young could be evaluated. The idea was to establish his ethical approach to scholarship to give order to the core of the educational program as an experiment.

The small school in question was a satellite in the orbit of a large university which was itself in a life-and-death contest for survival in an urban community that had suffered many civic reversals. The idea of a test-tube pilot experiment in a country setting was bypassed by the worried men in general headquarters.

My first failure served only to reinforce my conviction that the basic idea of having Dr. Schweitzer's insights in ethics available to American education was overwhelmingly worthwhile. A fellow member of the Board of the little college arranged for me to confer with Percival Brundage, then director of the U. S. Budget. Mr. Brundage had been instrumental in collecting funds for the Albert Schweitzer College in Switzerland. I flew to Washington for the meeting, which was attended by Harold Stassen, former Provost of the University of Pennsylvania and previous pilgrim to Lambaréné; and Emory Ross, treasurer of the Albert Schweitzer Fellowship in the United States.

The meeting was thoroughly gratifying to me. Mr. Brundage advised me to consult and pursue the idea with his trusted friend, Dr. James Luther Adams, then at Meadville Theological Seminary of the University of Chicago.

I found Dr. Adams most eager to be helpful. By pooling our efforts, we gathered some of Dr. Schweitzer's friends at a conference to explore the wisdom and method of achieving the educational objective. Dr. Gilbert White, former president of Haverford College, Douglas Steere, professor of philosophy at Haverford, and several professors from the University of Chicago, attended the meeting.

One thing became clear: any idea that presumed to use Dr. Schweitzer's name would have to be approved by Dr.

Schweitzer himself before we could proceed. I volunteered to make the pilgrimage to Africa to get his permission and counsel. Now I could look forward to the trip with double delight. As I thought of visiting Lambaréné, it flashed through my mind that Dr. Schweitzer has often said that no one really knows him until he has seen him working at Lambaréné.

Dr. Schweitzer seemed to be listening eagerly. I told him of the next episode that led to my educational mission to Lambaréné. I had given Dr. Schweitzer all of the letters from universities from which I shall quote in this section.

About this time I was involved in arranging a Dead Sea Scrolls program at Northwestern University with the aid of Dr. Edmund Perry, chairman of the Department of History and Literature of Religion. In one of our meetings I told him of my convictions concerning Albert Schweitzer's potential significance in education. Some time later he called me and asked if I would present my ideas to a committee at Northwestern. The following excerpts from a letter, sent to me as a result of that meeting, will explain another milepost on my circuitous route to the man of mercy in his mission hospital in Lambaréné, French Equatorial Africa:

> I wish you to know how heartily the University Administration endorses your proposal . . . We are tremendously enthusiastic about the idea . . . It is my understanding that you are going to see Dr. Schweitzer this summer and that you will seek his consent to the establishment of a chair named for him . . . If such consent is forthcoming, as we fervently hope it will be, then you and I can get together in the fall . . . That you are willing to be a member of a group in raising funds for such a splendid purpose is deeply appreciated.

The conference arranged by the administrators of Northwestern had been attended by the Vice-President and Dean of Faculties, a prominent member of the Board of Trustees, deans and professors representing the College and the departments of religion, philosophy and history.

Thinking that perhaps an Albert Schweitzer Educational Fund might better be organized to start, and support in the incubation period, several distinguished professorships in several schools instead of one expensive "chair" in perpetuity in one school, I communicated my proposal to Harvard, Princeton, Roosevelt, Stanford, and Emory Universities. All responded enthusiastically.

I quote from several of these letters. The author of the Princeton letter made the following intensely perceptive observation:

> As one who is profoundly interested in the ethical example of Schweitzer, I feel that I should point out that the strong tendency here at Princeton in the last decade has been toward a greater recognition of the indivisibility of knowledge . . . and the creation of a genuine university rather than the perpetuation of a multiversity.

The President of Roosevelt University said in his letter:

> It is my personal conviction that an institution such as Roosevelt University would be greatly aided if it were privileged to use the name Albert Schweitzer for its entire College of Arts and Sciences. All students need the challenge of great lives, and Dr. Schweitzer lives to inspire them to reach the higher plateaus of service to their fellow men.

The letter from Stanford endorsed the proposal and said:

> To link the name of this great man to Stanford would be perpetuating his influence on the people of the broad community of the West and the Pacific Basin which the University hopes to serve . . . We are hopeful that the idea will become a reality.

Knowing that Adlai Stevenson had been interested in Dr. Schweitzer's example of citizenship and his manner of representing the Western World, I wrote a letter telling him of my proposed trip. His answer, written during his presidential campaign, did not catch up with me until I reached Johannesburg. I include it here in full because it represents even more forcefully the eloquently affirmative response I had received from others equally sincere.

July 12, 1956

Dear Dr. Phillips:

It pains me more than I can possibly say to come now upon this letter of yours and to discover upon calling your office that you have already left for Africa and that I cannot possibly reach you before your visit to Lambaréné. I can only hope that you will understand the confusion which seems almost inevitably to attend an operation of the sort we are trying to carry on here right now. Personal, professional and political matters seem to get all mixed up and to suffer in roughly that order.

You will know how thoroughly and enthusiastically sympathetic I am to the idea your letter suggests.

It seems to me cause for real encouragement that this society of ours is proving itself capable of recognizing, even during his lifetime, Albert Schweitzer's inestimable contributions to it. It has so often been true in the past that it has been left to history both to appreciate and to acknowledge this kind of service. I cannot for the moment think of any other man who has done this kind of building and who has at the same time been able himself to know for sure that others will carry his building above the foundation he has laid.

Yet you are very right that additional steps must be taken, and now, to carry this work forward. I approve wholeheartedly your idea of promoting the establishment of Chairs or Professorships in various colleges or universities where a particular emphasis might be placed upon extension of Dr. Schweitzer's ideas and ideals. If there is anything further I can do in this connection I hope you will tell me about it.

I had not seen the Erica Anderson volume and in leafing through it now I realize what an invaluable thing you have sent me.

Again my apologies, and thank you so very much for bringing this all to my attention.

Very sincerely,

(Signed) ADLAI E. STEVENSON

Dr. Schweitzer asked me if I had ever met Rev. Hans Casparis, founder and head of the Albert Schweitzer College in Switzerland. I hastened to say that I had just come from a conference with Dr. Casparis and his wife in London and assured him that I knew the school well. I showed him a letter in which Dr. and Mrs. Casparis heartily endorsed the integration of Dr. Schweitzer's ethics in American education and affirmed that it would be an indirect asset to the Schweitzer school in Switzerland.

I said to Dr. Schweitzer, "May I ask why you are not willing to let us use your name in connection with American universities?" He replied, "The idea is impossible, but perhaps we will talk of it later." I had heard that painful tune before. I was to wait until my last hours at Lambaréné before hearing his specific objections to the plans of the mission I was representing.

When I conveyed recent oral greetings and a little note from Emil Mettler, Dr. Schweitzer's host in London at the time he received the Order of Merit, he seemed animated by a flood of happy memories. Dr. Schweitzer said, "He has been a dear friend for many years." Emil Mettler owns a restaurant in London, the back room of which Dr. Schweitzer used to greet friends, admirers and celebrities. Even the testy Bertrand Russell had come to pay his respects, but Dr. Schweitzer did not comment on their discussion.

Dr. Schweitzer spoke of his surrender to the persistence of Erica Anderson from New York. She and artist Jerome Hill had worked for six years against Dr. Schweitzer's resistance to compile a documentary film of his life. Dr. Schweitzer, I knew, had refused offers from five Hollywood producers, but had succumbed to the persuasion and deep dedication of the stranger, Erica Anderson, who came to live in Lambaréné in order to make her dream come true. The story is as incredible as that of the Mellon Hospital.

Originally, it was agreed that this movie would not be released during Dr. Schweitzer's lifetime. But here again Miss Anderson and Mr. Hill persuaded him that obsolescence in technique was going to eat into the importance of the film and that it should be released now. He surrendered again.

The first showing of the movie occurred in New York in February, 1957. It promised, after the first days, to rival the documentary on Martin Luther, which was both popular and hotly controversial.

We discussed with special affection our mutual friend Emory Ross, treasurer of the Albert Schweitzer Fellowship in the United States and unofficial counsellor to our State Department on African affairs. Dr. Schweitzer approved heartily that my fifteen-year-old son was then traveling in Africa with the Emory Ross tour but expressed sincere regrets that the group had not detoured to Lambaréné. Dr. Schweitzer suggested with laughing eyes that I must not come back without my wife and boys who, he observed from a pocket photograph I displayed, were "the handsome members of the family."

I began to sense the long evening visit was coming to a close. I had come to listen and ask questions on politics, religion, and philosophy. Not only were my plans aborted, but also my educational mission had risen up only to be submerged again. I had been revealed on countless issues while my host betrayed, it then seemed, only too much modesty.

I whispered to myself in desperation that only controversy would bring out the outlines of this master mind. I tried with shameless premeditation to provoke the lightning that always lies buried in the mildest personality of prophetic stature. I bolted intentionally into the painful topic of John Gunther's scathing statements about Dr. Schweitzer's hospital.

Gunther had condemned the bad housekeeping, dirt, and dis-order in Schweitzer-ville, calling it "the most unkempt place of its kind." But Dr. Schweitzer emitted no sparks. He presented no apologies, no defense, no retaliation, no reprisals. With a sad, weary voice he used the very same words with which Gandhi had stabbed my pride: "I think Mr. Gunther spoke much truth, but he missed the whole point of my hospital."

Dr. Schweitzer laughed generously when I suggested that if I got the "whole point" of the hospital, I would write an article and call it *Inside Gunther*.

After a few minutes of quiet conversation, I sought again to gain deeper insights by raising another provocative issue that hovers on the borderland of modern theology.

"Do you know," I asked Dr. Schweitzer, "that some bolder students in theology are quoting you in regard to reporting the excitement caused by newly discovered Scrolls found on the edge of the Dead Sea near the river Jordan?"

I said in effect, "Your remarks written long ago about the now famous Essene brotherhood have acquired new significance. It is now known that the Essenes hid their precious unorthodox manuscripts in caves near Jerusalem twelve miles from Beth-lehem. It is known that the Essenes flourished just before the time of Christ. Many of these scribes secreted themselves in a monastery that has very recently been discovered and excavated." Dr. Schweitzer nodded perhaps a little impatiently that he knew all this.

I pressed forward, telling of a panel discussion I organized. I had secured a Catholic priest, a Protestant minister, a rabbi, and a divinity professor from four major theological groups. I told Dr. Schweitzer how each theologian in the debate read his creedal views into the meaning of the Scrolls.

I confessed that when I had finally failed to find a single *free scholar* to participate in the debate, I took the bold liberty of reviewing on the back of the program Dr. Schweitzer's own discussion of the Essenes taken from his *Quest of the Historical Jesus,* written fifty years ago.

Once more I dug into my portfolio and this time extracted the printed program which I had designed for the occasion. With anxiety I pointed to my composition on the back. Dr. Schweitzer scanned the material, boldly entitled "Religious Freedom Exemplified by Albert Schweitzer's Writings on the Essenes."

The two paragraphs that appear below were taken verbatim from my manuscript. These elucidate the claims I risked in Albert Schweitzer's name and the liberty I now wished sanctioned or censured.

Before 1947, scholarly literature dealing with the semi-secret, pre-Christian society of Essenes gathered dust in libraries. Before the Scrolls and their scribes confirmed hitherto sketchy evidence about the Essenes, few perceptive scholars foresaw and forewarned the Judeo-Christian Western world that we might one day have to face some revisions in our traditions because of the true historical significance of Essene communities and their activities. In reconsidering and re-appraising the few prophetic scholars who at least sounded the alarm, the name Albert Schweitzer appears prominently. He belongs to this rare, free fellowship that long ago considered in detail the possible impact of the Essene sect on our history and theology. We will, therefore, briefly revive here the pre-Scroll testimony of Schweitzer on the Essenes.

The most radical theological revolution suggested by modern Scroll interpreters can cause Schweitzer no anguish. His dedication is not based on eschatological precepts. Like Venturini, Schweitzer is thought by some to be too free, but others think he may be a living portrait of a free man at his ethical best. Essene ethics confirm his theory of Reverence for Life, which is "the ethics of Jesus widened into universality." Schweitzer discovered the spirit of Jesus through free scholarship, and found his symbol irresistibly compelling. He has lived for fifty years with the rare benevolence of an Essene in the ethical pattern and spirit of Jesus.

I watched Dr. Schweitzer's face carefully as he perused the lines written in English, which he read with some difficulty. His expression was noncommittal. There were words neither of praise nor blame. All he said was, "You give me too much credit."

Again I fished in my portfolio and came up with a copy of Dr. Powell Davies' book on the Dead Sea Scrolls. I opened it to the heading, *Schweitzer's Views on Jesus*. I explained that Dr. Davies was a Unitarian minister in Washington, D. C., and that a quarter of a million copies of his book are in print. I presented a copy to Dr. Schweitzer.

Then I brazenly asked Dr. Schweitzer the big question voiced everywhere: "Do you think Jesus was a member of the Essene sect?" Either Dr. Schweitzer forgot his moratorium on religious talk or he considered his comment too noncommittal to count. He said in effect: "Probably not. Jesus came from Nazareth, far north of the Dead Sea and its Essene monastery. Undoubtedly he was influenced by the pre-Christian Essene sects living throughout Palestine, particularly the branch cells in Galilee. Of course, Jesus cannot even be understood when ripped from the events and episodes of the era and thinking prevalent in this stormy period."

Dr. Schweitzer volunteered the observation: "John the Baptist might very well have been a member of the communal brotherhood. Perhaps he was even a member of the Essene monastery on the shores of the Dead Sea. He lived in the wilderness and baptized in the river Jordan nearby. He ate locusts and wild honey and talked like a true Essene, as they were described by Josephus the Jewish historian. However, in all probability John could not have been a member in good standing at the time of his highly individualistic public ministry."

I asked Dr. Schweitzer if he thought, as many did, that the Scrolls threatened to become noisy skeletons in the Christian closet. He answered by saying, "There is not much that is really new. Historical facts are now authenticated." He seemed reluctant to speculate further.

Displaying once again his skill in steering conversation, he said: "Speaking of wild honey, I have held the view that honey is less injurious to teeth than other forms of sweets. Do you agree?"

I told Dr. Schweitzer I had recently investigated the honey issue for a boy who was raising bees. He wished to enhance sales with the assurance that his product was dentally superior to all other sweets. I found that the chemical verdict did not support the claim.

Dr. Schweitzer next asked if I had found everything I needed for my work in his dental clinic. I answered with candor that much equipment would be needed to do fine dental work and to render complete dental health service. I tempered my criticism by assuring him that basic work could be done with the use of foot-engines and portable head-rests but that casting equipment, blow torches, soldering equipment, and porcelain ovens should supplement the instruments now in use. Dr. Schweitzer did not seem disturbed by my comments on the deficiencies of his dental equipment.

The tempo of our evening visit was slowing down when in a most casual way Dr. Schweitzer asked me if I knew a fellow American named Nelson Rockefeller. I said I knew him only by reputation. I laughed and said that on occasion I patronized the family oil stations. Dr. Schweitzer smiled, "Had you been here a few days earlier, you could have become better acqainted with him. He was kind enough to go out of his way to call on us here at Lambaréné. He dropped in from the sky in his own plane. He did not stay long."

When Dr. Schweitzer started to scratch inscriptions on some pictures of himself, the hospital, and the Ogowe River, I knew our long but delightful fellowship evening was drawing to an easy, natural conclusion.

As we went through the parting gesture of hand shaking, he remarked quite innocently it was odd that in my travels I had met so many of his friends and well-wishers. I assured him it was by design. I told him I had found that people who know him are already friends when they first meet. I said, "You are the center of a common spirit in many lands."

I was at this moment quite moved by my very great privilege. I know I stammered badly in trying to fit my words to my mood of deep gratitude. My halting message was something like this: "These friendships I have known in your name are quick to form. They are blessed by the absence of bondage of any kind. Your friends make up a world fraternity. They are one as lovers of liberty. Most of us quiver with the cosmic music of your religious freedom. You have been a better fisherman than most in the pools of truth. I do not yet know precisely how, but you are in my judgment in some way a symbol and a model of the fellowship of freedom that thrives even under the blackest tyrannies."

"You tell our friends, each one," he answered, "when you see them that they have found the secret of how to make us happy here. Tell them we think of each one of them and talk of them often in Lambaréné."

Portrait of a Modern Prophet

When I returned to my room, I wrote the diary-letter I was preparing to send home. Then I went to bed. But I could not sleep.

I got up and fumbled with the tricky combination of the oil lamp on my desk. Taking a pencil, I recorded in the unsteady light some of the vital statistics of the memorable evening.

Without counting the critics, we had discussed twenty-five individuals residing on three continents. Our thoughts had moved through eight countries. Many enterprises instigated in distant regions were offspring of this one prolific man.

An individualist in Switzerland founded an Albert Schweitzer college . . . An entrenched American resident in Arizona broke free to found an Albert Schweitzer hospital in Haiti . . . A Viennese-born American collaborating with an American artist residing in Europe had spent six years in Africa and Alsace making a documentary movie of Albert Schweitzer's life . . . Another American has searched European bookstores and libraries to start a special Albert Schweitzer library collection at Princeton University . . . Three men on different continents had spontaneously compiled separate books in different languages conveying global birthday tributes, which were delivered on the Doctor's eightieth birthday . . . Completely unrelated individuals in several countries in Europe and several cities in America organized eager groups to observe publicly Schweitzer's eightieth birthday . . . An ex-missionary, who had spent nineteen years as an evangelist in Africa, had served for many years as treasurer of the Albert Schweitzer Fellowship in America. Several individuals we mentioned had written books: biographies, books of philosophy, theology, pictorial histories, and a book of portraits of Lambaréné disciples.

The circle of friends discussed included the enormously rich and the poor, the acclaimed and the unheralded, the famous and the obscure, reverent scientists and scientific reverends. One fact seemed striking. The orthodox in religion and in science were conspicuous by their absence.

Though undiscussed, great honors played about the periphery of our casual talk. They included citations from a queen, a king, and a president; the Order of Merit; the Nobel Peace Prize; the Goethe prize; honorary degrees from universities; and dozens of other encomiums, accolades, and distinctions.

In the midst of this illumination, the most consistent emotions that I had observed in the course of this *discussion of people* were Dr. Schweitzer's overriding modesty, humility and unassuming simplicity.

Dr. Schweitzer's humility was one of calm resignation without artifice of self-deprecation, flavor of self-mortification, or pride muffled in self-contempt. He squandered none of his freedom to purchase fame. Rather, his humility, it was evident, came from the reverence with which he regarded the wonderment of his fellows, and the marvelous undeserved mystery of his own gratifying will-to-love. He felt his own fame was mostly "happenstance," and the widespread recognition of his services he traced to the goodness of people. In no sense did he seem to feel his renown with responsive people was due to his personal superiority. Even his critics were not, in his mind, vicious; they merely misunderstood.

In his shirt sleeves, unpressed pants, worn shoes, and in his unadorned cell, surrounded by the jungle Eden, with more animals about him than Noah had on his ark, Dr. Schweitzer seems to show that *true humility* and *universal love* are indivisibly one and inseparable.

No widely heralded prophet in history was ever as well-known and as much honored in absentia by unacquainted contemporaries in his lifetime as Dr. Schweitzer. Historians make no mention of Jesus. After making allowances for our age of swift, world-wide communications, it still must be conceded that Albert Schweitzer is more universally meaningful to more contemporaries than any sage of bygone days.

It struck me that we had been concerned *with people, not ideas.* In ideas Albert Schweitzer may have certitude. Admittedly he is controversial. Why? Was the humble man capable of becoming pontifical, oracular, and authoritative when dealing in fiery ideas?

Dr. Schweitzer's closest friends inside and outside of Lambaréné are liberals or agnostics in matters of theology. Dr. Schweitzer as a symbol is particularly compatible with many Unitarians who extol the ethics of Jesus but deny his divinity. There is a deep accord between Dr. Schweitzer and many Quakers, but this mutuality seems to be related to the person-to-person spirit of service that they have in common, not their theology.

Perhaps the most admired of all the men we discussed was gentle persecuted Einstein, a free thinker who was Jewish by race, a global humanitarian by sentiment, agnostic by conviction, and an old soldier of truth who spent his life storming the citadel of the unknown.

Albert Schweitzer, for all his humility, remains theologically controversial. If his friends are mild, gentle, freedom-loving liberals, then are his defamers the more temperate twentieth-century descendants of earlier violent, heretic-burning, orthodox conservatives and feudal dogmatic inquisitors? It was religious leaders among the Jews who arranged the crucifixion of Jesus, and it seems to be the most orthodox Christians, particularly fellow missionaries in Africa, who most criticize Dr. Schweitzer.

Once it crossed his mind in semi-jest that he might end his career in a cannibal's stew. This had struck him humorously too. He is reputed to have said his only hope in this contingency

would be that the cannibals would say, licking their lips, "Albert
Schweitzer was good to the last drop."

I reminded myself of a point easily overlooked. The measure
of a prophet in the final analysis is not what he says or does
but *what others do because of him*. What they do reflects what
he means to them. Creative individuals and peoples make their
own prophets. Mass-wisdom, right or wrong, is the arbiter of
prophetic truth, and the response of multitudes heralds the
vision of prophets and makes their new gospel alter history.

Still, people cannot proclaim or reject a prophet until they
grapple with the issues and the soundness of the new authority
of the convictions he exalts. So the question of Albert Schweitzer's prophetic stature hangs not only on his imperious convictions, but also on what multitudes would do if they were given
the opportunity to grasp clearly his vision of the better world.

Thus in friendship's mirror I have found Dr. Schweitzer not
only humble but also prophetically universal, pivotal to history,
personally magnetic, and theologically rebellious. All of these
qualities in my estimation are qualities of great prophets.

I was more convinced than ever that I would have to probe
into Albert Schweitzer's central ideas, particularly the heart
of his theology.

Is Albert Schweitzer of prophet stature? Is he a twentieth-
century spiritual liberator? Today's dogmas are yesterday's
liberating heresies. Today's heresies might become the common
denominator of tomorrow's world. At any rate, the theology
and the premises of Albert Schweitzer's religion were the place
to probe.

My thoughts had been thieves of sleep. It was very late, and
I would not have to wait long for the dawning of a new day.

On the following morning I received a surprise message.
The unpredictable Doctor informed me by messenger that he
planned to call on *me* in *my* quarters at 2 P.M.

Perhaps, I thought, he is coming to my quarters to deliver a
reprimand as a result of reconsidering the literary liberties

I had taken, particularly now that he had read all I had written about him. Perhaps he had come to feel that like so many others I too was well on my way to "missing the point" of his life, his writings, and his hospital.

I quickly conquered my negative thinking and began to plan positive strategy. I was convinced that to provoke his most sweeping judgments I would have to confine my questions to *philosophy* and the domain of *ideas*, not seething current issues involving individuals or peoples.

While waiting for the hour so fateful for me, I pondered on the importance of *direct action* in great prophets. Dr. Schweitzer did not often involve himself in direct action in the center of the theater of human strife. Was this fatal to the notion that Albert Schweitzer may be a major prophet? Does this retiring manner place Dr. Schweitzer outside the main stream of the great Teachers of Righteousness of other ages? Liberators in history have opposed surging trends. Prophets have had the courage for controversy and stamina to withstand criticism and even waves of persecution. Many opposed evil until they were violently destroyed by their contemporary opponents.

Our modern "Teacher of Righteousness" at Lambaréné struggled for freedom from society, and he has scrupulously avoided the petty squabbles of the marketplaces of the violent world. He has rejoiced and been exceeding glad to know this liberty of isolation and the joy of personal service in the wilderness. Factions do revile him at long range. And who can tell what inner bruising he has known, what mental nails have pierced him, and what anguish he has suffered when his cherished ideas have been misunderstood? Perhaps Albert Schweitzer had been a revolutionary of prophetic stature in the earlier years when he had written much, but maybe time had mellowed his zeal.

On reflection one thing was certain. If Albert Schweitzer were in the great league of history-shaping "religious" prophets, he has invented a new subtle technique of "strategy" and "authority."

As the appointed hour of the visit drew near, I concentrated not on prophetic method, tactics and strategy, but on the still unresolved question: Was Albert Schweitzer *in any way* unalterably authoritative? Did he *in any way meet* the authoritative half of the prophetic paradox? This was in my judgment the last major link in classifying Albert Schweitzer a modern prophet.

I had cancelled appointments in my tight schedule in the dental clinic. I was ready when Dr. Schweitzer, looking like a Moses or Abraham in short sleeves, strode into my tiny, cell-like room. He was accompanied by our interpreter, Mme. Oberman.

Smiling very broadly, and I thought somewhat roguishly, Dr. Schweitzer announced he had come to discuss philosophy in general and the history of ethics in particular. What luck, I thought. My big opportunity had arrived.

The report that follows is based on notes written after the Doctor left my quarters. The progression of ideas that I set down is, I believe, still complete and exact. However, in the rapid translating from German into English, the original words were certainly changed by the translator. The non-literal substitute words were not perfect servants. Idea identification was possible for me because I was already quite familiar with the ideas being communicated. Most of the statements I heard and subsequently outlined, then later recorded in detail, have appeared in Dr. Schweitzer's writings and in many biographies.

As I was interested exclusively in the idea images, I rewrote the interview several times. In each rewrite I attempted to express the old ideas with greater clarity. I tried to represent Dr. Schweitzer's forceful delivery by fitting eloquence. I converted the sermon into what I conceived to be not plain English but more particularly the American idiom familiar to the reading public in the United States.

A mere report alone would not justly reflect the honest, brilliant economy of expression that so excited my admiration. The chapter speaks the truth because I fortified the series of ideas that poured forth by checking each and every one of Dr. Schweitzer's own books that deal with this general subject.

The trials of literal translation, particularly in the field of ethical motivation, are exasperating. I cannot forbear to mention that when Dr. Schweitzer wanted to translate his own book on Bach from French to German, he found the task beyond him. He says in his book, *Out of My Life and Thought:*

> When in the summer of 1906, after the completion of the *Quest of the Historical Jesus,* I turned to work on the German edition of the *Bach,* I soon became conscious that it was impossible for me to translate myself into another language, and that if I was to produce anything satisfactory, I must plunge anew into the original materials of my book. So I shut the French *Bach* with a bang, and resolved to make a new and better German one.

If my reader then will bear in mind my objectives, my method of recording and reporting, and my determination to convey idea images, not words, we may turn to what was the climax of my stay at Lambaréné.

A Private Discourse on Ethics

After arranging my guests and myself around the tiny desk, on the two chairs and the cot in my cramped cell, and thinking whimsically I would one day call this "the sermon in the cell," I launched the first of my progression of questions that I supposed would disclose the prophet paradox (if present) in this man of mystery. I said, "Have you altered any of the convictions you expressed years ago in your books about the pivotal position of 'will-to-live' and its ultimate significance in your theory of Reverence for Life?"

"All of my studies and all of my years of experience have served only to confirm my fundamental convictions concerning the reality of *'will'* in the universe, the centrality of *'will'* in the life process, its supreme role as human self-consciousness, its rational connection with all good and evil in human relations, and its singularity as a sovereign value worthy of universal human reverence."

I hurried breathlessly to the next question which is asked everywhere in the Christian world: "What is the source and the nature of this 'will' on which you found your ethics? It seemed to me that in your books you used the word 'will' interchangeably with *infinite will, life force, essence, being, volition, creative power,* and sometimes *God.* In our English translations of your books these words are frequently but not always capitalized, giving them in English a semi-supernatural and part-time divine implication. Dr. Schweitzer, is the 'will' you place at the core of your ethics divine?"

"Before we get to that, let me systematically trace the history of ethics for you, and maybe many of your questions will be answered," he began with evasive diplomacy.

Except for two or three intermediate and terminal questions, our discussion was converted into a fast-moving monologue in which he did indeed string difficult and profound ethical ideas together in an orderly pattern.

Dr. Schweitzer spoke with authority. His bearing was commanding. His certitude and self-assurance were foremost. We were not talking of people. We were not talking of properties of matter or diseases. We were in the vast domain of values. These weightless, shapeless, invisible values are as real as steel. We had passed a barrier and were in the mysterious land peopled by ideas, where Albert Schweitzer had crowned himself king of his age.

First of all, Dr. Schweitzer defined ethics as the reasoned values that order, limit, and in general govern individual actions in all human and animate relations. Ethics arise from man's free reflection about the inscrutable aspects of the universe. They are man's efforts to evaluate himself and endow his life with meaning. Ethics are peculiar to man, the rational animal, because they are based exclusively on human reason.

The whole universe is composed of matter and will. The whole universe is therefore "alive." Will becomes more and more dominant in the life process, and matter in the life process becomes more and more subservient to the will.

In my judgment it is easier to understand Albert Schweitzer's *Weltanschauung* if we consider the two principles in the dualistic universe the forces of freedom and the energies of anti-freedom. In this report, however, I shall adhere to his use of the word will.

Individual animals in subhuman species are non-ethical beings because they inherit unlearned the common instinctual legacy of "will" and do not ponder what is good or evil. The impulse to action is common to all species. From the primordial impulse that stirs the free cell to activity, on up the evolutionary scale, each separate specimen acts freely as a self-determining individual. A mysterious "will" affirms and directs the behavior and activity of the community of chemical materials that compose the cell or "society of cells."

These impulse-driven creatures act ceaselessly and affirmatively, but their behavior is devoid of self-consciousness and lacks the guidance of reason.

Dr. Schweitzer insisted the point to remember is that the free animated "will" and the dead chemicals that compose the cell are both separate and elemental realities of a dualistic universe. The two realities interpenetrate each other in the cell.

Science can describe, measure, analyze, and manipulate the chemicals in life. But the "will," though equally natural and real, thus far is an immeasurable, invisible, weightless, shapeless essence known only by its special effects on the community of chemicals in "living" matter. The "will" in the simplest cell "sparks life" just as an unknown enzyme force induces millions of instantaneous reactions in higher specimens.

This elemental essence in the dualistic universe called "will" in the phrase "will-to-live" has been carried forward in evolution for two billion years by countless billions of individual animate specimens of life. Looked at objectively, this "will" is manifested in all subhuman specimens of life as an affirmative thrust. The behavior appears to us like an ego-centric, self-centered drive. It is raw, naked, elemental, direct self-devotion.

Even the simplest life uses its "will" to subjugate the energies locked in chemicals of the material world and to subdue when necessary the "wills" of natural rivals. Rival forms of will are destructive in nature.

The result of evolution is that man, too, inherits the ceaseless self-affirming urges to subjugate natural forces and subdue natural rivals, but this ancient impulse to self-devotion is somewhat altered by the growth of reason.

Will becomes darkly self-conscious in primitive man. Will begins to acquire personality and a new goal in a universe devoid of plan and purpose.

Human babies repeat pre-ethical evolution as well as ethical development. A fertilized ovum starts as an unreasoning single cell and passes through stages of growth in creature appetites and self-devotion. Children slowly become vaguely self-conscious and acquire personalities and personal goals. Still human lives are not supernatural but natural units of the universe. The affirmative nature of will is later seen as the optimism running through human affairs.

For only an instant in the last seconds in the immense geo-logical time scale on earth, will has acquired self-consciousness in man and the beginning of personality and spiritual goals. The earth is a fantastically tiny island in an infinitely large universe.

The new, learned impulse of self-transcendent behavior be-came dimly reasonable to primitive, savage men in the crudest ways and the smallest conceivable circles. Pooling individual efforts aided families and clans to subjugate and harness the forces of nature and to subdue common rivals. Each progressive en-largement of the primary circle of cooperative effort was the heroic achievement of labored reasoning.

The advantages of family unity in time pointed toward the wisdom of clan loyalties. Families and clans merged by pooling their freedom to form primitive tribes. Social order and laws developed *within* the tribes.

The raw and naked horrors of jungle justice, including the lawless anarchy of murder, rape, and plunder, still described relations *between* tribes.

Thus human history continued as an uninterrupted pageant of ineluctable events with little reasoned mastery of the process. The freedom to control the mechanism of history was so awe-some, it was thought to be in the domain of gods.

No great ethical growth above the tribal circle occurred in Western history until the Greeks became an episode in the procession of events several hundred years B.C. In the early period of the Golden Age of Greece, the Athenians conceived

the principle of the equal worth of all Greek citizens and discovered the principle of political democracy for Athenians.

Despite the splendors of their glorious age they failed, to their
everlasting shame, to extend the rights and privileges, magnifi-
cently conceived, beyond the tight-knit body of free Greek
male citizens. The Hellenic intellectual and artistic achievements were built by the freedom of a learned leisure class
exploiting a slave economy. Their widest vision excluded women,
most of their slaves, their neighbors, and all of their enemies.
Of course, wild beasts were dumb creatures, useful for food,
work, and hunting, but otherwise worthless and expendable.

Because Western historians have been sentenced at birth to
the prison walls of a provincial ethic, most of our scholars of
antiquity have totally missed one essential point. Much earlier
than the Westerners, the Far Eastern philosophers in China,
Hebrews in the Near East, and Greeks in the Peloponnesus
had independently developed a *very wide vision* of human
kinship.

Buddhists, Brahmins, and Hindus, centuries before the Christian era, envisioned the ethical dream of universal brotherhood
of man. It was part of the metaphysical concept of existence.

Seven hundred years before Christ, the great prophet Zoroaster
of Persia managed to stretch his mind to encompass in his
thoughts the whole human family bound in fraternal relations
by canons of mutual accord.

Two separate and distinct forms of unreasoning dogma kept
rising up in history's flow to clog the wheels of ethical progress:
narrow-circle provincialism and ethical *earthly pessimism.*

In all of these Eastern universal concepts, caste walls, social
barriers, economic classes, and political distinctions developed as
diseases in the ethical relations of peoples.

Narrowness of vision was the virus that paralyzed the scope
of reason and zestful, affirmative, ethical growth. Pessimism
poisoned the "will" and the natural, affirmative, creative impulse that is the chief quality of free will. Even in the Eastern

empires, these twin ills caused the old social sickness of provincial dogma and tribal taboos common to primitive relations. Ignorant, small-scale, selfish interest in salvation and unreasoning self-devotion deadened long periods making them ethically dark and uneventful.

(The names and ideas of this early company of sages Dr. Schweitzer talked about as if they were close relatives in his own family. The dates and literature chronicled by Dr. Schweitzer came too fast to fix them, but the ethical giants included other men besides Lao Tse, Confucius, Buddha, Isaiah, and Zoroaster. There probably were Meng Tsu, Chuang Tsu, Amos, and Hosea, who are mentioned in his writings on this period.)

The early ideals of the Western Greeks of the first period were optimistic and natural but provincial and exclusive. Their foreshortening ethics were surpassed in breadth and depth in the second period of Greek creativity. The Stoics and the Epicureans made one great stride forward. Like earlier Eastern thinkers, they leapt high to conceive the idea of *universal* human equality. The thought of universal humanism developed about 150 B.C. This intellectual accomplishment transfigured a few scholars; but perhaps because it was not rooted deep in the sub-soil of ethical wisdom, it did not reach out and inspire the masses.

The Hebrew prophets in the eighth century B.C. projected man's significance through eternity by imagining an internal Kingdom of God. This Kingdom transcending time and space was an enormous creative, imaginative achievement. This idea was adopted by Jesus, but seven hundred years earlier it had become the core of Zoroastrianism.

The introspective Jewish ethics remained highly provincial, exclusive, and historically insignificant factors in the episodes of world events until Jesus came into the Hebrew amphitheatre with his gospel of liberation through love—liberation in the last hours of this world and in the eternal world to come. Though Jesus adopted the Jewish idea of the Kingdom of God and late-Jewish eschatology, he believed in the imminent terminal expectation of the end of the world. He believed himself to be the Messiah of Scripture and the instrument of terminal events.

Freed from worldly concerns, the ethical personality of Jesus achieved unimagined universality and magnetism.

The uniqueness of the Jesus ethic is bound up in the ambiguity of his Jewish provincialism and his own global ethical spirit. The paradox of his pessimism and optimism concerning sinful man's weak and carnal nature and his capacity for goodness and free choice is part of the originality of Jesus. Jesus challenged the Law with courageous freedom. In the last hours, assured of his own salvation, he stretched out his healing hands to the wretched, weary multitudes. In his optimism he affirmed that mercy, meekness, poverty, even persecution for righteousness were elements of eternal goodness to be achieved in human affairs in the last hours of earthly existence. He exalted the common man by deflating exclusive Jewish nationalism, riches, materialism of possessions, and Roman wealth and power, and the vanity of fame, fortune, and secular profligacy and carnal pleasures. Jesus championed righteousness, peacemaking, and forgiveness as preparatory virtues soon to be preached in heaven by the elect. Jesus voiced approval for the humble, for inner spiritual freedom from creature appetites, and moral freedom from material worldly lusts. He valued man's capacity for self-perfectibility, his creative power and devotion to the kingdom of perfection.

Jesus spoke well of these human ethics but not with any notion that the world would survive him. He was sure he was the chosen vehicle of the end of the natural world. He was mistaken, but his courage, ethical convictions, and self-surrender to his reason, though faulty, makes him the immortal Lord of liberators.

Paul, too, was in his way an original, unique emancipator. Not only did he carry the liberalism of Jesus through the Hellenic world, but he perfected his own personality ethically and became transcendent and transfigured. By his power of reason he freed himself from the sensuous, sinful, transient world. Paul knowingly took rational, poetic, and spiritual liberties with the teachings of Jesus, for he believed that the spirit of Jesus was the spirit of truth and liberty in all things.

The limitations of Paul, like Jesus, were the fictions of dogma and the crushing earthly pessimism and inevitable provincialism characteristic of late primitive Judaism.

Jesus and Paul, both victims of Jewish provincialism, nevertheless employed freedom and reason to design and shape their ethical religion of action. Their actions were immediate and precipitous because time was running out. This immediately made them free. Reason did not, however, conquer their pessimism nor affirm their "will-to-live" for the on-going will in the universe.

The earthly ethics of actions Jesus commended became completely subjugated to his dogma of beliefs in the supernatural eternal Kingdom. This unfortunate deadening distortion occurred under the guidance of authoritarian priestly classes. Liberty was postponed for serfs to the life after death, now tied to the contagion of the image of Jesus.

Selected primitive Jewish myths, long insignificant, became pivotal to Western Christian historical events, producing the barren ethical bleakness in the cruel dark ages of feudalism. The ethical views fostered by Jesus the liberator—the commandments of universal love, the prohibition of killing and animal sacrifices, ideas of equality of the elect and brotherhood of the righteous, and special worth of the poorest and sinners that make up the multitudes of meek, humble, fallible people—were brutally submerged. Feudalism was dark and cruel because freedom of reason was not only fettered, it was outlawed by the church on pain of death.

Religious orders that pretended to follow the Prince of Peace and Mercy used torture, witch- and heretic-burning, methods of suppression, inquisition techniques of thought control, and in-human tyranny over free reason. Paradoxically "holy" wars, launched by Christians, flourished. The glory of life, the dignity of man, and the concept of love vanished under monastic orders which pessimistically despaired of earthly matters and sought eternal salvation only.

This long night of feudalism was a reflex of the old twin poisons, pessimism and provincialism in the realm of reason. Affirmative global humanitarianism, so ethically promising in the Greek period, was dead.

In an aside, Dr. Schweitzer said that pessimism is a toxic luxury of human society that would not have survived for an instant in the rigors of subhuman evolution that rewarded zestful affirmative living.

Pessimism and narrowness of vision are the epidemic child-hood diseases of ethics. Human pessimism is alien to all the self-affirming, forward-thrusting love of life we inherit from our kinship with the whole yeasty stream of "will-to-live."

Human religions that are based on pessimism or provincial-ism serve only to subjugate, by unreason and dogma, man who by nature is a freedom-loving creature. Will-to-live does not die in floods, droughts, disasters, catastrophes, or defeats, nor in the many forms of oppression. Life affirms itself ceaselessly because it is its evolved nature to do so.

The spirit of scholarship in the Renaissance was the greatest development in ethics in the whole pageant of history. Men turned from pessimism and provincialism involved in the dictates of divine revelation to the religion of reason. They acquired their new authority and power from reviewing nature and human nature in the state of nature, in the light of their new-found freedom from the theory of special Creation. They pursued with reason the naturalistic theories of the universe. They searched compulsively for new elemental and universal truths, and their thinking was passionately affirmative in the quest for the nature of goodness.

The net result of the Renaissance was total fragmentation of Church and State conspiracy, the splintering of feudal authoritarian divine rights and the cracking of faith in revelation and belief by reason.

Men of the Renaissance almost succeeded in establishing the religion of love as the central truth of reason. There followed a reign of unprecedented creativity fostered by a large, widely distributed community of ethically powerful thinkers bent on a common quest, the creation of a universal religion. Many were optimistic and outer circle in their ethics.

With the substitution of reason for revelation as a method of approaching reality, Christianity made a bold about-face and espoused much of the religion of reason. Humanism already shown by Greeks to be an ordinance of reason was re-discovered. Great monolithic, dogmatic denominations began to divest themselves of intolerance, injustice, cruelty, superstition. The torture of dissenters slowly disappeared. Burning of so-called witches and heretics was arrested. This transformation was sparked by self-evident, new-found and inalienable freedom discovered in nature. It was ordained by reason. Freedom's chain reaction liberated scores of men who climbed the ethical ladder and added new and higher rungs.

(At this point Dr. Schweitzer gave a summary of the ethical gains made by each of a long list of giants of wisdom from this post-feudal period. They included Hume, Kant, Nietzsche, Spinoza, Rousseau, Locke, Grotius, Helvetius, Bentham and many others. I do remember Erasmus was singled out for high praise for his original conception of universal perpetual peace based on humanitarian ethics. Schopenhauer thought deeply but pessimistically about the needed resignation to the real world, but he failed to discover the affirmative character of the "will" in life that is equally real and far more basic to ethics. Goethe was cited as the universal man who saw the weaknesses of rationalism but failed to found an exciting new, complete ethic.)

Hegel, though a profound thinker, is the real villain of the Renaissance. Millions today who never read him unwittingly obey him. He tried to find absolute purpose in the senseless, stormy history of man. He overlooked the more precious, tranquil, tiny stream of ethics in reviewing the ocean of history marked by a mixture of brutal and murderous, dull and torpid events and episodes. He ignored individualism and deified the state and collectivism. He presumed immanent progress, overlooking that all progress is ethical and results from free reason and free reflections of free individuals.

Hegel believed progress was inevitable. Hegel's ideals of progress made materialism paramount. He did violence to ethics by falsely equating past reality with spiritual promise. He derived "reality" from the external world. He thought that war and savagery as well as harmony and beauty were reasonable. He was ignorant of the truth that reality is derived from reason that is internal. He ignored the fact that reason shows the universe to be devoid of purpose other than that willed to reason. He missed the truth that life is itself a continuation of the immortal will preserved immortally by mortal, animate lives. Hegel never dreamed of a day when venerated ethics would master the course of human history.

Hegel is the spiritual father of the false, perilous and tyrannical ideas of reality of Marx and Lenin, Hitler and Mussolini and other authoritarian collectivists. These ideas of mechanism, determinism, collectivism, materialism, externalism, and immanent, inherent progress have made modern man a pathological phenomenon bereft of reason.

According to the internal, individual, creative ethics of reverence for the essence in life, doctrines derived from Hegel are elementally and universally unrealistic, unbiological, unhistorical, unreasonable, unethical, and irreverent.

(Dr. Schweitzer increased the tempo of his peroration.)

Thinking in the eighteenth century had defined self-evident, inalienable freedoms, human rights, legalized forms of equality, and affirmed the sovereignty of individuals and the legitimacy of government by consent.

Reaction set in before ethical effort devised a new theory of the universe to replace the feudal faith it destroyed. Swift changes came before a single common measure of goodness emerged. The trends since the utopia of free thinking may be characterized as a pageant of ethical reversals into barbarism unprecedented in all of history.

Now we come to modern times. It was just capricious fortune, Dr. Schweitzer said, that he was born into a period of spiritual bankruptcy. Ethics has regressed since the eighteenth century, and we are in a new period of primitive savagery. Civilization may well be in the process of suicide. Modern society, innocent of a theory of the universe, is again infantile in its narrow vision of civilization.

Civilization today is sick with the epidemic of thoughtless, inhumane, meaningless and hopeless conformity. Like jungle animals, nations are predatory, murderous, lawless, and amoral, but infinitely more cunning and cruel. Hydrogen bombs have made the so-called thinking animal not only homicidal but fratricidal to every living thing joined to us by bonds of will in life.

Education in the Western world, like the so-called Western nations, suffers from acute provincialism and a chronic pessimism that hides behind the tense, false, painted face of happy optimism. In a world capable of unimagined abundance, skepticism and cynicism, despair and mental despondency are rampant.

The universities in the Western world have not the vaguest notion of the meaning of education. They are mistaking outer knowledge for inner truth. They teach fragmentary facts and neglect the centrality of ethics. They hold vocational and professional goals aloft and forget to face the cardinal function of education, the liberation of the young for the pursuit of spiritual perfection. In their learned ignorance faculties focus attention on patterns of social success, material progress, and economic promise, betraying their obligation to present moral values and cultivate reason for moral judgments. They seek to mold puppets into patterns well adjusted and well adapted to a faulty, violent, inhumane national civilization instead of opening their hearts to universal understanding of common concerns and their ethical solutions.

Religious thinking in Western education is a tragic void. Man's heroic ethical struggle for a satisfying theory of the universe is ignored. Religion is no longer a force for good. Religions condone war as a necessary evil. Religion in the education of the Western world, if taught at all, comes to the young in dogmatic, eccentric, artificial and fragmented packages manufactured and ready to wear. Spiritual training for spiritual freedom and for a spiritual search is found nowhere.

As a consequence, Christianity in the West today is divorced completely from the essential idea of civilization. It has lost its power to command. The horrible proof: intensified nationalism and greater inhumanity in wars. And now we enjoy the peace of terror on the edge of a hydrogen abyss. In schools, as in nations, materialism has usurped the primacy of ethics and poses as the poorly disguised idol or god of multitudes. Naked expediency, opportunism, utility are masked behind an ignorant form of meaningless, superstitious piety.

The honorable and noble role that philosophers played as guardians of reason in the eighteenth and early nineteenth centuries is lost. Philosophy in schools as in society generally is petty, superficial and peripheral. Philosophy has destroyed much, but it has replaced nothing in the world of ethics. Philosophers have failed to see that ethics and religion have been parallel efforts with one motive and should at long last be merged. Philosophers who should pioneer new thought have become engulfed in the externalism of the religion of science.

Scientists in school and society in the Western world, proud and vain over their conquest of the mysteries of matter, have ignored their own tragic ethical infantilism and their utter stupidity about the mysteries of life and values.

Their successes in discoveries and inventions have caused a real blindness to the truth that they have contributed nothing to the world of insights, the pageant of virtues, and the understanding of ethics that have motivated civilization.

Most scientists are sub-citizens and do not participate in the human responsibility of determining social wisdom, moral justice, and decency in public policy. Their excuse is preoccupation with more important devices. Their knowledge and material control have submerged the compassionate and humane in man, to the peril of everything that breathes.

History and historians have served the provincialism of nations with an ugly lack of objectivity. History books everywhere are living culture beds of ethical lies. No one has analyzed the historical process from an ethical point of view, so that its intrinsic mechanism can help man in his ancient quest for freedom.

(At this point I asked Dr. Schweitzer if he had read Toynbee. He said, "Not the latest volumes." Somewhat surprised, and knowing that Arnold Toynbee agreed in the ethical approach to history, I asked Dr. Schweitzer if I might send him the set. He replied, "Yes, to my home in Gunsbach, Alsace, in Europe. Books disintegrate in this climate." He thanked me and continued.)

In schools as well as in society in the Western world, law suffers from provincialism and it has lost contact with civilization and elemental and universal justice. Law in its essence should be nothing more than the ethics that can be agreed upon and recorded. The foundation of law is humanity. And the application of law should not apply to the narrow confines of nations. Legal students should pass through the whole experience of mankind in their search for legal ethics.

Starting with a common respect for life, laws can be written concerning human rights which guarantee each person the greatest possible freedom for his personality within each nation and international laws that will protect his existence and human dignity against violence everywhere.

With Western education so chaotic and fragmented into departments and specialties, the wholeness of man and the oneness of truth and the supreme importance of the inter-connections between the specialists is sacrificed to this strange tyranny. We bow to the paternalism of fact-finders in sociology even though it is obvious that self-realization and spiritual perfection are not matters of statistics.

As would be expected, where thinking, reasoning and ethics are neglected, the power of propaganda is replacing the pursuit of truth. Civilians are still surrendering their freedom of thought to unscrupulous politicians who are in league with advertisers. The hero behind the modern scene is the manipulator of the mass mind, the shepherd of the herd impulses.

Modern individuals are losing their self-reliance and self-confidence and their very manhood. Many are becoming so domesticated they are content to be comfortable and cared for. They learn to loathe and detest thinking in others. Some even want their freedom organized by their parties, their denominations, their organizations, their associations and their collectivized factions.

It is in this sad state, deprived of a theory of the universe, that man pursues his dark journey into an ever deepening night.

The freedom that comes in self-knowledge, self-discipline, and self-realization through the insights in the mysterious microcosm within each of us, is temporarily lost. Free scholarship has sunk to depths unprecedented in all history. We are given to codes of manners rather than codes of morals; to fads and fashions instead of justice, reason, wisdom and mercy. Everywhere we see nations living under tensions and floundering on the abyss of a fratricidal catastrophe, wholly destitute of ethical leadership.

Dr. Schweitzer said in effect: Though I was born into this period of spiritual decadence, I remained a stranger to it. I became a champion of rational thinking, and I raised my voice in the wilderness. I opposed the age with words. My aim became that of making men free, thinking beings again. My mission has been to re-kindle thought and form an elementary fellowship of ethical scholars and co-explorers in ethics. I have insisted that knowledge is not truth or related to ethical reality. I have discovered man's true relations with the universe. I have discovered the essence of his nature and the unshakable foundations of goodness for our age. I have argued that we are all living in the midst of other life that wills-to-live. I have taught that will-to-live is a common drive of all life. This "will" is affirmative, and when seen through humble resignation it is an irresistible power and worthy of deep reverence. It can be deterred by provincialism and pessimism from its limitless, undreamed of destiny. Reverence for this "will," the essence of the life force, will one day be the common religious principle throughout the world. This religion is the ethics of Jesus widened to universality, the gospel of love expanded to include all life. It is love of life based on reason.

(At this point I injected a question: "Is Reverence for Life a new religion?" And he continued.)

Yes, all serious thinking is religion. All new religions are reasonable at their birth in their age. They are based on a theory of the universe, the meaning of life, and the nature of goodness. Reverence for Life is reasonable. Old dogmatic religious theories of the universe, life and goodness are now unreasonable and therefore irreligious. Religions become irreverent when they stop reflecting freely on truth and fail to try their precepts at the bar of reason. Reverence for life is religion's final court of appeals.

Each individual is, while living, the ultimate reality of the interpenetration of the two indivisible elements in the universe. Thus what is simple is profound, and all institutions, all governments, all education, all political and social relations can be measured by the degrees of reverence they have for this ultimate reality and the way they manifest this reverence by the scope of liberation they provide citizens. This theory which gives meaning to Reverence for Life is a self-transcendent vision of goodness. It describes the nature of man and his relation to the universe.

After one or two brief personal remarks, Dr. Schweitzer rose suddenly and abruptly strode from my room, pleading that he was late for other duties. I had indeed been given a magnificent lecture on the history of ethics, but I regretted that there was no question-and-answer period, no time for discussion, and no opportunity for cross-examination.

I had felt that note-taking would cast a pall of reticence over Dr. Schweitzer's freedom of speech. It is the regret of my life that this visit could not have been kinescoped for the pleasure and enlightenment of the world.

In writing up my notes of the interview from memory, I have tried to observe fidelity to Dr. Schweitzer's ideas and meaning rather than to his words and phrases. Scholars will recognize immediately that most of the ideas reported above appear in Dr. Schweitzer's books. Only the arrangement and the intimate details were new.

The private sermon on ethics left no room for doubt in my mind. The gentle, merciful servant was *humble in the field of personal human relations only.*

In the field of ethics Dr. Albert Schweitzer was *imposing, peremptory, and authoritarian.* As I later heard him label himself, he was a "benign illuminated merciful despot." Dr. Schweitzer had sententiously employed his absolute standard of Reverence for Life for measuring all good and evil.

Dr. Schweitzer's Views of Jesus

A momentous question that had tormented my curiosity was answered to my satisfaction. Albert Schweitzer had all major qualities common to the prophet pattern established by previous world prophets.

I was free now to switch my whole attention to a fresh issue. I turned with a new passion to the five volumes of Dr. Schweitzer's writings that I had toted on my long journey from Chicago —the books I had fought valiantly to prove were really allowable in the "free" category of "reasonable reading matter" at every weighing station on the air route.

My question now was: Why had I been so stupid as not to realize that this shy, shabbily dressed, humble humanitarian, so meek in personal relations, was a man of imperious certitude about his ethical convictions? Could my illuminating conclusion be verified from Dr. Schweitzer's books?

I hunted through his books, accumulating authoritative declarations, and laid them side by side for comparison and study. Finally they bristled before my eyes, indisputable and sure. This truth about Dr. Schweitzer's prophetic certitude in ethics now stood out sharp and hard as diamonds. I was reminded of the saying, "If the trumpet gives an uncertain sound, who will prepare for battle?" Dr. Schweitzer's clarion call was clear.

Albert Schweitzer shows a non-violent form of *aggressiveness* in such confident statements as: "Sooner or later the idea *I* here put forward *will conquer the world*."

Like other absolute authoritarians of history, Dr. Schweitzer makes such imperious statements as: ". . . with splendid pedantry we measure *all* principles by the *absolute ethic* of Reverence for Life."

Again he says prophetically: "The world is inexplicably mysterious and full of suffering . . . I have been born into a period of *spiritual decadence* in mankind . . . Through . . . Reverence for Life . . . I am ready to deal with each [problem] . . . In that principle my life has found a firm footing and a clear path to follow. *I therefore stand and work in the world as one who aims at making men less shallow and morally better by making them free to think."*

Dr. Schweitzer says with no shyness, "I think I am the first Western thinker who had dared to be *absolutely* skeptical of the objective world without renouncing ethics. . . ."

"For me the certainty of the existence of an ethical world-will is an *absolute and indisputable fact based on my experience of its workings in my own soul."*

While looking at the raw materialism of Western lands, Dr. Schweitzer says, "I am undertaking what has never been attempted . . . to make the Western search for a world-view come to a halt and take account of itself." He told a friend that his contribution to the world resides in the fact that he has "*forced* religion and philosophy to return to a basic ethic."

Prophets like Jesus espouse some minor aspects of their tradition and disavow most of the older conventions in accordance with their new truths. Is Albert Schweitzer's new gospel a continuation of Christianity, or is it designed to destroy Christianity? Jesus said, "Think not that I have come to destroy the law and the prophets. I am not come to destroy but to fulfill." This fulfilling, however, contrary to plan, launched a new and separate missionary religion that has struggled evangelistically to supplant every other religion on earth.

Perhaps Albert Schweitzer in fulfilling Christianity would destroy it and other religions as well, in the interests of one common, global religion—not a composite religion but one based on the religious equivalents in all.

Whether Albert Schweitzer will fulfill Christian history or suffer oblivion by history's Christian hands remains beyond our power to prophesy. A new form of an ancient struggle can be anticipated and projected.

Mentally I reviewed two books which now more clearly testified to the centrality of this momentous issue. Is Dr. Schweitzer to be or not to be considered Christian? The authors present opposing evaluations of Dr. Schweitzer's historical role in relation to the Christian tradition. John Middleton Murry published a book in England, *The Challenge of Schweitzer,* purporting to prove that the theory of Reverence for Life is an offense to the Christian faith.

An English Dean in the Church of Ireland, the Very Reverend George Seaver, Dr. Schweitzer's first English exponent and biographer, published a counter-thrust called *Albert Schweitzer, A Vindication.* I now judged that the issues were far more dynamic than implied by this theological controversy. The brilliant rebuttal insisted that Dr. Schweitzer is a Christian; Christian or not, he is the most religious man of our age. We may judge Dr. Schweitzer's place in the Christianity puzzle as we appraise *The Quest of the Historical Jesus* in this chapter.

The Western world is a Christian world. It carries the name of Christ. Jesus too spoke of the universe, life, and goodness. What relationship then does Albert Schweitzer have to the Galilean prophet? Is he a restorer, a redeemer, a savior to our age? Is he a reformer or a revolutionary? Is his special leaven planned for religions or all human relations? Will he make history or suffer eclipse by events beyond his control?

I turned to the monumental book, *The Quest of the Historical Jesus,* to see in the light of my new insights what was the true relation of Albert Schweitzer to Jesus.

In Dr. Schweitzer's study of Jesus we see more of the affirmative side of the golden coin Albert Schweitzer would circulate as moral currency in a new civilization. Actually this study re-

veals Albert Schweitzer's true self fully as much as it reveals
the original undistorted image of the Nazarene.

Dr. Schweitzer's affirmative view of the original Jesus without
his robes of splendor, denuded of centuries of bizarre accretions,
far from being a shock to me, was one of the most moving
experiences of my nomadic life of ethical adventures.

Dr. Schweitzer admits in the introduction to the *Quest of the
Historical Jesus,* written fifty years ago, that writing about Jesus
betrays volumes about the author. He says, perhaps in part
as a confession, "There is no historical task which so reveals
a man's true self as the writing of a Life of Jesus. No vital
force comes into the figure of Jesus unless a man breathes into
it all the hate or all the love of which he is capable."

Albert Schweitzer, the theological scholar, had to invent a
new historical method of research to fit the special problem. He
explains, "There is really no other means of arriving at the order
and inner connections of the facts of the life of Jesus than the
making and testing of hypotheses."

Dr. Schweitzer, the historian, says from reading the literature
about Jesus that the sketches actually enlighten us more about
the authors and their historical epochs than about Jesus himself.
He says, "Each successive epoch of theology found its *own*
thoughts in Jesus . . . each individual [author] *created* Him
in accordance with his own character."

The author who injects a reflection of his own convictions
into the portrait of Jesus in a book about ethics is caught in a
two-fold tragedy. The subconscious effort of superimposing
conviction on the image of Jesus enfeebles the vigor and the
convictions of the author. It saps the vitality of his scholarship
to project ideas backwards into history simply to make them
speak with Biblical prestige out of the past. According to Dr.
Schweitzer, it also betrays, weakens, distorts, shrivels and belittles the original image of Jesus. He accuses modern theology
of being guilty of creating "narrow and peculiarly insipid" conceptions of Jesus, with which most modern Christians are

familiar. He says, "Hence it is that the Jesus of modern theology is so extraordinarily lifeless."

Dr. Schweitzer names the central flaw in modern theological thinking when he says, "We have never really grasped the thought-world of Jesus."

To understand the original Jesus as Dr. Schweitzer found him, stripped of the false faces ascribed to him by innumerable would-be historians and interpreters, we must prepare ourselves to enter a totally alien ancient thought-world.

According to Albert Schweitzer, the New Testament scholar, there is no doubt that Jesus thought himself to be the divine instrument of the end of the world and the coming of the Kingdom of God. He considered himself a vehicle of God's will. But what of the repeated questions by his contemporaries? Why did the disciples say "Who art Thou?" Dr. Schweitzer brilliantly speculates that "this knowledge about his future dignity became his secret." This hypothesis makes many of the paradoxes of the Bible story understandable and plausible.

"For one thing is certain," says our scholar, "the whole account of the last days at Jerusalem would be unintelligible if we had to suppose that the mass of the people had a shadow of a suspicion that Jesus held Himself to be the Messiah."

Jesus thought himself to be the Messiah, but strangely enough John the Baptist—"the greatest born of woman"—was not sure what exalted role Jesus was to fulfill. He said that Jesus was the "one who is to come" (Matt. XI:14). Jesus said that John, though the greatest born of woman, was less than the least in the Kingdom of Heaven (Matt. XI:11). Dr. Schweitzer thinks John meant that Jesus was Elijah, the Forerunner of the Messiah. But Jesus betrayed that he secretly believed himself to be the Messiah when he tells his disciples that "the Baptist himself is Elijah who is to come." That Jesus did not confess to Messiahship publicly and that he evaded questions to test faith, Dr. Schweitzer says, is a weak, unscholarly rationalization, "an outcome of the embarrassment of commentators." This theory merely "opened the way for many bad sermons."

It is Dr. Schweitzer's view that Jesus retained the secret that he knew himself to be the Messiah until the last days of his public ministry.

According to Dr. Schweitzer, when Jesus decides with God-like certainty that the hour for the end is about to come, he "hastily sends His disciples, two and two, into the cities of Israel that they may spread the news (that the end is at hand)." He warns them to expect tumultuous times of persecution and perhaps death, and then the immediate dawn of the Kingdom. "He does not expect to see them (his disciples) return, but assures them that the 'coming of the Son of Man' will take place even before they have gone over the cities of Israel."

Shockingly enough, this first cosmic expectation of Jesus was not fulfilled. Dr. Schweitzer says, "His announcement was shown by subsequent events to be wrong." His disciples suffered no persecution, and not one sign of the Messianic Kingdom had appeared. This devastating development, explains Dr. Schweitzer, "Jesus can only explain to Himself by supposing that there is still some event which must take place first. . . . "

"There dawns on Him the perception that it can only come when He, as the Messiah to be, has by suffering and death made atonement for those who have been elected to the Kingdom." Jesus believes, according to Dr. Schweitzer, that this sacrifice will enable the elect to bypass the terrible, turbulent times of persecution called for by Scriptures. The resolution of Jesus to suffer an atoning death was probably justified by Scriptures, particularly the text of Isaiah.

In the neighborhood of Caesarea Philippi, Jesus makes known to his disciples for the first time his solemn secret. He tells them with certainty of his Messiahship. He reveals his new secret plan for his self-chosen death. Dr. Schweitzer says, "He discloses to them He is the same who at the dawning of the Kingdom of God will be that personality."

At Passover time Jesus goes up with the festival caravan of Galileans to Jerusalem. At that time no one except the disciples knows whom Jesus believes himself to be. Dr. Schweitzer declares that "the rejoicing at His entry into Jerusalem is not for the Messiah but for the prophet of Nazareth of the House of David."

Perhaps one of the most perceptive and persuasive points in Albert Schweitzer's hypothesis concerns the betrayal of Jesus by Judas. He says, "The treachery of Judas does not consist in betraying to the Sanhedrin where Jesus can be arrested, but in disclosing to that body the claim that He makes to the dignity of Messiah."

At his trial, Dr. Schweitzer says, "He tells His judges that they will see Him as the Son of Man seated at the right hand of God and coming on the clouds of Heaven."

The multitudes that rejoiced when they thought Jesus to be a lesser prophet cried, "Crucify Him, Crucify Him," when they realized his lofty view of himself as Messiah. Dr. Schweitzer feels it is reasonable to suppose that "His arrest and crucifixion are only possible because He Himself surrenders to the authorities who condemned Him during the night, and in the early morning almost before Jerusalem was awake had already crucified Him."

Jesus realized the second momentous error of his short life before succumbing on the Cross, when he cried out in bitter agony, "My God, my God, why has Thou forsaken Me?" This simple shattering cry of anguish in the unheeding cosmos speaks volumes of human pathos, of sincerity, reason and love. The cry utters in a paroxysm of honest doubt a courageous confession of error, a deep disillusionment about the very nature of the universe this sacrifice was designed to change. Never before nor since has human agony been so poignant or tragedy so tender and human character so victorious and liberating.

According to Dr. Schweitzer, this act of futility that has become so memorable and fruitful ended the historical career of Jesus of Nazareth. On the time scale that Dr. Schweitzer uses, the public activity of Jesus lasted perhaps five or six months—at most, nine or ten months.

With this description of the public ministry of Jesus fresh in mind, old horizons that hemmed in my vision backed away. I saw for the first time quite suddenly Dr. Schweitzer's inclusive cosmic view. I believe it is in its essence new and original.

I had puzzled over Dr. Schweitzer's description of Jesus as a perfect will. He says for example, "The true understanding of Jesus is the understanding of will acting on will." Again he says, "Jesus is an authority for us only in matters of will . . ." He even identifies gods and God in all places and among all peoples as the reflection of human, semi-reasonable will projected onto the cold features of the planless, goal-less universe. Dr. Schweitzer says emphatically, "The God of the Gospel of Jesus is living, ethical will."

The general theory of the universe in Christendom presupposed that God created the unfree matter of the universe and freedom of will in man. However, most scientists labor only with the laws of the material universe. They deny all degrees of freedom, calling liberty an illusion, a jest of the molecules jostling in our heads.

Dr. Schweitzer visualizes no evidence of a separate, creating God apart from the universe. There are, however, forces of will in the universe. In the interplay between the forces of will and matter, it is will that grows in its control over matter and the energies associated with matter. Below man, "will" in the dualistic universe is devoid of purpose. In man, "reason" is an immaterial vehicle of the forces of universal will. The nature of will is mysterious, but reason can partially direct human destiny. It is Dr. Schweitzer's reason that discovered the freedom given to man by his ethics and the liberating quality of love.

Dr. Schweitzer believes that "every life is a manifestation of the one, infinite, inscrutable, universal will."

It is, then, in this cosmic sense that Dr. Schweitzer said, "The God of the Gospel of Jesus is living ethical will." Using theological symbols, in the same sense he says, "My life is completely and unshakably determined by the mysterious experiences of God revealing Himself within me as ethical Will."

He speaks with certainty in saying, "I live my life in God [living ethical will], in the divine personality *which I do not know as such in the world* but only experience as a mysterious will within myself." The will in the universe has become self-conscious in man and in man takes on the qualities of personality. The highest trait of will is love. Universal love of all will is the most liberating ethic ever conceived. Will grows best in the atmosphere of love. In this warmth will, the seed, flowers into the perennial blooms of love. Love is most liberating when the circle of love is universal and limitless.

The "will-to-love" we may call our God within, because this is the creative force that has created all the gods of history. It has become different from the forces in nature that indifferently create and crush. To say that these are powers of one good but inscrutable God, Dr. Schweitzer says, "is to delude ourselves."

All the theories of gods and deities of the universe, and the ethics at the center of the moral achievements of human history, result from the creative act of human reason. Dr. Schweitzer laments that "the spirit of our age . . . *refuses to admit* . . . that all spiritual progress up to today has come about through the achievement of thought. . . ."

It may seem a shock to many who are disturbed over Dr. Schweitzer's concept of God being recognizable within man as living, ethical will to discover that he only uses the word God to convey the picture of the sovereign good. He once explained to his friendly adversary Oskar Kraus in an incompletely published letter in that author's book, *Albert Schweitzer: His Work and His Philosophy,* that he uses the term "God" only when he employs "the traditional language of religion." He

says in the clearest statement he ever made describing the relation between will-to-live and God: "I never speak in philosophy of 'God' but only of the 'universal will-to-live' which
I realize in my consciousness . . . It has been my principle
never to express more than I experience as a result of absolutely
logical reflection. . . . "

Dr. Schweitzer says in effect that he does not really experience God in the conventional manner accepted in Western
Christianity. He says, "I prefer to content myself with the
description of the experience of reflection (will-to-live) leaving
pantheism and theism as an unsolved conflict . . . that is the
actuality to which I am always being forced to return." He
says, "I use the word 'God' in its historical definiteness and
indefiniteness just as I speak in ethics of 'Love' in place of
'Reverence for Life.' For I am anxious to impart to others my
inward experienced thought in all its original vividness . . . "
And he continues with a most revealing phrase, " . . . and in
its relationship to traditional thought."

In short, Dr. Schweitzer tells us not only that "in spite of
external differences in form I feel that Jesus' *Weltanschauung*
[world view] is identical with mine," but he says that the
God of Jesus and the God of all peoples everywhere is not
really a mystical personality but the inner ethical will being
misinterpreted as an external God. To Dr. Schweitzer the idea
of God is a manifestation of the will in the universe being reasonably explained by itself in man's consciousness. The properties of God may be the properties of will which Dr. Schweitzer
says "stands in the center of all my arguments." It is only in
this sense that he can say, "Only through the phenomenon of
Being [will] does my being [will] communicate with Infinite
Being [will]. The only actuality is the Being in phenomena."

God is equated with will, will with freedom, and freedom
with self-realization by human reason of the *vital* aspect, not
of matter alone but of phenomena, which is the interpenetration

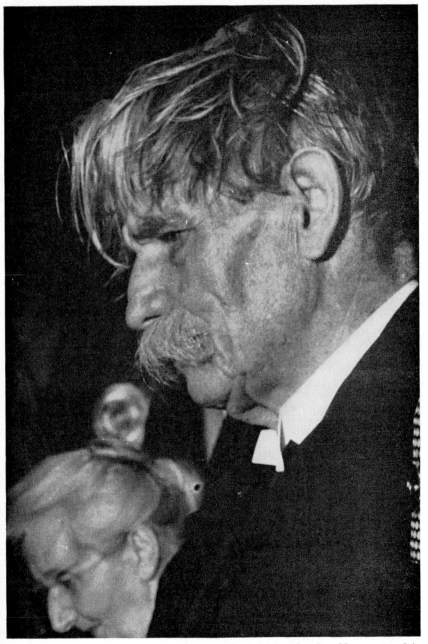

Picture by Arne Svendsen, Morgenposten, Oslo.

This was taken in Oslo when Dr. Schweitzer received his Nobel Peace Prize. Though the late Madame Schweitzer quietly accompanied her famous husband when he received honors, those who knew her felt she was more than a meek wife in the giant comet's wake. She had special illumination of her own, as rare as a Florence Nightingale or a Jane Addams.

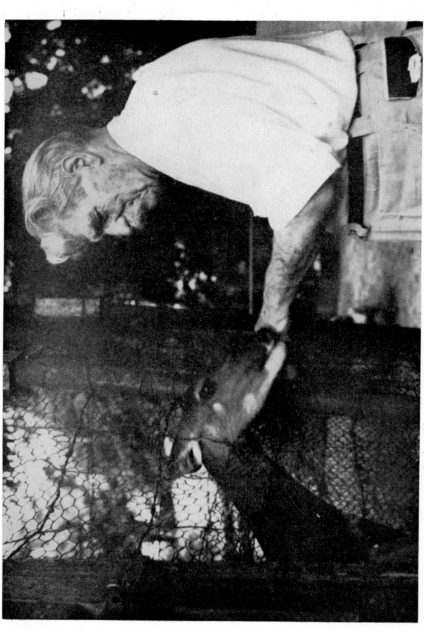

Dr. Schweitzer practices reverence for all life. The animals that come as "patients," sick or lame, receive courtesy treatment and often remain as pets and permanent guests. This picture was taken by Clara Urquhart, close friend of Dr. Schweitzer

Erica Anderson, author of the picture book, WORLD OF ALBERT SCHWEITZER, and photographer of the Oscar-winning documentary movie, "Albert Schweitzer," and one of her cameras.

Madame Oberman, volunteer servant at Lambaréné who acted as my faithful interpreter. The broad, sullen river is the swift Ogowe.

(Standing) Doctoress Van der Kreek; (lower left) Miss Trudy, Pied Piper personality with children; (right) Albertine, an angel of the hospital for the staff and foreign guests. In the background, row of "cells" used as living quarters.

Believing in the kinship of all life, Dr. Schweitzer is host and friend to a great variety of forest dwellers.

Dr. Schweitzer and Erica Anderson watch over the pouring of the homemade termite-
proof cement footings for new dwelling places in the leper village.

Photo by F. B. Knoop.

A special Studebaker truck was contributed to house and transport an unusual gift—
a herd of goats specially conditioned in the Cincinnati zoo for the tropics. The herd had
to move over to accommodate last-minute dental equipment. Twenty thousand dollars in
chemotherapeutic drugs were donated and stowed in the upper tier of the truck. A New
Orleans steamship company provided gratis transportation for Dr. Byron W. Bernard, a
veterinary, and the modern caravan to Port Gentil, Africa, where all was loaded on barges
destined for the Lambaréné hospital.

of will and matter in the universe. This, then, is Albert Schweitzer's theory of the universe.

It is in this ultimate sense that Dr. Schweitzer can say with certainty and unalterable conviction, "The last and deepest knowledge of things comes from the will." The lack of this universal insight Dr. Schweitzer feels "is the ultimate source of all of the catastrophes and miseries of our times."

Aside from denominational differences, according to Dr. Schweitzer, what are the false features in the modern portrait of Jesus created by modern Western man?

Like all Western boys, Albert Schweitzer at an earlier age than most was persuaded to believe the prevailing Western Christian dogma. As an infant he was encouraged to accept literally Old Testament stories of the flood and a Moses with horns. He was encouraged by his parents, his community, and his teachers to accept faith by faith, not reason. He did believe by faith at first, but not for long.

Thus young Albert Schweitzer was very early generally deluded by social forces, over which he exercised no control, into thinking that Jesus meant to establish the idea of earthly churches like that of his father, the church which he loved so much. As he left babyhood he believed the recent liberal variations of the Gospel stories, particularly the fantasy claiming that the story of Creation had only a symbolic meaning to the peoples of the Old Testament. The metaphors could be interpreted, as he was told, symbolically without doing violence to justice and truth.

Young Albert Schweitzer, like other Western boys, but earlier than most, was deceived by the hypothesis that infallible Jesus thought in a modern way about modern souls, baptism, and continuous salvation and resurrection. The boy Albert Schweitzer was encouraged to accept the idea that Jesus was known by the Wise Men and other contemporaries as the Messiah. Dr. Schweitzer now claims that this was a mistake, that Jesus was not known by his age as the Messiah from cradle to Cross. Jesus did not declare himself as Messiah to his disciples or the

Jewish priests or the multitudes until the last few hours of his life.

At first Albert shared with his young contemporaries the mistaken notion that Jesus, in the first century, preached of a *distant* Day of Judgment and an *ongoing* Kingdom of Heaven available to *all generations* of the righteous. Among modern errors, he believed Heaven to be an ever-ready eternal reward to which he would go as a person after his earthly death.

Albert Schweitzer, along with his young contemporaries, was urged to adopt the presumption that Jesus also originated the idea of a Kingdom of Heaven on earth, which fostered the earthly love of neighbors, love for all enemies, and peace among the ever-changing nations of the world. He believed in spreading the word and the sole truth about God through evangelists and missionaries.

Albert Schweitzer's earliest heritage of dogma imputed to Jesus the whole charter for eighteenth-century principles of equality, inalienable rights of man under God, and the brotherhood of all men in God's universe. In a vague way he accepted the gross myth that Jesus died for these eighteenth-century thoughts of freedom, liberty, and fraternity. Jesus, he was loosely taught, founded democracy. Jesus, it was widely believed, died to save the souls of generations of free men yet unborn. His divine work for this world he consecrated, so it was said, as the ascended Son of God. Also in a perplexing way Jesus was God.

Doubt came to Albert in his eighth year and then slowly, after years of emancipating scholarship, Albert Schweitzer learned that religious dogma of each age is the prank of the internal impulse of the will. Olden dogma appears as the cruel jest of surging will in the heartless universe. All dogma about the changing mysteries of the universe is the reflection of the "will" within individuals and epochs. It was a phenomenal achievement, considering Albert Schweitzer's ecclesiastical background, that he discovered the place of "will" in the cold cosmos and was able to conjecture that "the God of Jesus is living ethical will."

It is little wonder that liberated Albert Schweitzer was ignored in orthodox circles, and judged to be Europe's *enfant terrible* even in circles of the most liberal theology. More than half a century ago he had the audacity to say, "The Jesus of Nazareth who came forward publicly as the Messiah, who preached the ethic of the Kingdom of God, who founded the Kingdom of Heaven upon earth, and died to give His work its final consecration, never had any existence. He is a figure designed by rationalism, endowed with life by liberalism, and clothed by modern theology in an historical garb."

Albert Schweitzer says, "I myself have suffered in this matter of destroying the portrait of Christ . . . But I have devoted myself to it with joy because I am certain that truthfulness . . . [and] unrestricted liberty . . . in all things belongs to the spirit of Jesus . . . He [Jesus] does not think dogmatically. He formulates no doctrine . . . Nowhere does He demand of His hearers that they sacrifice *thinking* to *believing* . . . I am rewarded by the disclosure of the secret of spiritual independence. I become a partaker in *unguessed at freedom amid the determined destinies of life.*"

It appears to me that only the greatest, freest Christian scholars in the widest circles of free thought have understood and have therefore been awed by Albert Schweitzer's affirmative theological insights and deep vision expressed in his special relationship to Jesus.

How does Dr. Schweitzer manage to reconcile himself as a Christian in the light of his bombardment of most of the cherished institutions in the heritage of the Christian West? How can he call himself a Christian and say, "Christianity . . . has been so terribly unfaithful to the spirit of Jesus"? How could he say he answered the call of Jesus, "Follow thou Me," when he set off for Africa over four decades ago to establish his unique mission? Why did he call his short-lived relations with

the Evangelical Paris Missionary Society one of "symbiosis"?
Why have his deeds of dedication resembled the pattern, the
spirit, and the ethics of Jesus, when he disavows so much of the
modern Christian theology? Perhaps, prophet-like, he thinks
he is the only Christian. Much was still dark for me.

However, remembering it is the spirit, not the dogma, of
Jesus that the Doctor venerates, we may explore his thought
further. But there are still elements that belong to the age of
Jesus and not to his uniqueness.

We get a most suggestive clue to what Schweitzer venerates
in Jesus when we read, "In reality Jesus is not an authority for
us in the sphere of knowledge." Dr. Schweitzer does not even
believe the things Jesus believed about himself.

The things Jesus thought he knew—his divinity, his sonship to
a heavenly Father, his physical and medical miracles, his simple
cosmology, his Messianic destiny, his apocalyptic role—Albert
Schweitzer consigns to the wealth of material accumulating in
the archives of mythology. Myths reveal only the nature of
"will" within us all.

In order to get down to the skeletal image of Jesus that
Albert Schweitzer believes is the true portrait of the original
Jesus, I continued to drop all of the "knowledge" Jesus claimed
to have of the material world. Dr. Schweitzer points out again
and again that Jesus was a victim of late-Jewish dogma about
the nature of the material universe. This meant he was deceived
by the cosmic illusion proclaiming that the end of the natural
world was near. He succumbed to the prevalent superstition
that the kingdom of God was at hand. He accepted angelology
and demonology as causative agencies in disease and social
events. Natural law was the pervading will of God.

What then did Jesus add? What distinguished him beyond
the errors in knowledge of his time? His own fantasy of Messiahship, his own reasoning about his atoning death, and his singular
courage in presuming that his own sacrifice would end the
natural world and bring the Kingdom of God, are indeed more

mistakes. But they involve heroic self-liberation and self-fulfillment, self-mastery, and a supreme identification with the highest
goodness then visualized. He strove to be a cosmic instrument
for eternal goodness. Jesus was prodigious in seeing, with the eyes
of his intuition, moral and ethical verities that are proving to be
enduring if not immortal.

In the comparative study of religious equivalents, the certainty
of the end of the world was a reasonable cosmic hypothesis
in the Biblical age of austerity and recurring violence. The
grandeur of believing that eternity is near may have provided
a sense of epic liberation that made the ethics of the Sermon on
the Mount reasonable and believable and consistent. Plans
for eternal freedom from the tyrannies of life and the finality
of death have always stirred multitudes who are denied the
fruits of freedom in their lives of adversity. The Christian
heaven is a symbol of eternal freedom. It promises an escape
from mortal woes and assures immortal meaning to individuals
in grand heavenly style. Hell and damnation were cruel metaphors that wore the transparent mask of hated anti-freedom.
Hell was a place where self-will was mocked by hot fetters. It
was unique that Jesus had no worries about his heavenly status
or his candidacy for hell. What he did was not for his salvation
but for the eternal well-being of others. Actually Jesus was
concerned not with heaven and hell but with the Kingdom of
God, a haven of sinless morality which he thought his actions
would bring to the whole world of the elect.

What then is the uniqueness, the originality, the dignity, the
majesty, the splendor, the power, the magnetism and contagion
of this Nazarene stranger who lived about twenty centuries ago?

I tried to grasp the unalloyed spiritual qualities of Jesus,
the affirmative essence separated from all errors about material
matters, and from historical episodes and celestial events and
local dogma of contemporaries.

Albert Schweitzer sees many positive though ephemeral elements in the spirit of the original Jesus of Nazareth and Galilee.

First, while Jewish worshipers of the law worried about their own salvation, Jesus unsparingly identified himself intimately with the total salvation of the elect. He was a selfless, heroic, courageous instrument of lyric creativity and a human symbol of the universal good as he understood the universe.

In a letter to Oskar Kraus, former professor of philosophy at the University of Prague, Dr. Schweitzer wrote, "In spite of external differences in form I feel that Jesus' *Weltanschauung* [universal view] is identical to mine." He cites "the simplicity, the infinity, and the heroism of His ethics" as parallel to his own. Though the eschatological presumptions of Jesus are "fantastic," Albert Schweitzer says, "That which attracts me so tremendously in Him is the simplicity of the rationalism inherent in His fantastic *Weltanschauung* . . . Through the *Weltanschauung* and view of life which gradually developed in my mind I was able to understand the eschatological views of Jesus and was thus able to do justice to the historical Jesus."

These qualities in the personality of Jesus transcend the importance of all knowledge of the physical universe, even when the knowledge is demonstrable and scientific, which the knowledge of Jesus was not. The qualities of character suggest, if they do not define, what Albert Schweitzer means by "the ethical, living God who cannot be found through contemplation of the (physical) world but reveals Himself in man only. . . . We experience Him in our lives as Will-to-Love."

If the image of an omnipotent God is a primitive mirror image of man's instrinsic will projected on the sky, the canon, "Thy will be done," became in the hands of Jesus a vision of immediate, imminent, and perfect duty. The immediacy of the kingdom gave Jesus the keen, inner eyes that saw the beatitudes as ordinances of perfect living. If you and I were utterly convinced that heaven was at hand, externalism, materialism, commercialism, war, hate, pride, vanity and avarice would be replaced by righteousness, meekness, humility. We would say, "Blessed are the poor," and "Love thine enemies," with compelling reason. We could temporarily love those who hate us. One could love a neighbor as oneself, forgive trespasses, and give cloaks and coats away as well, and turn the other cheek if "the end of all things was at hand" and God was really known to be judging.

In his cosmology Jesus identified himself with God's unlimited freedom to determine the destiny of the universe and man. How far removed is this optimistic side of Jesus from the pessimism of the scientific view that man is a soulless machine devoid of freedom! Nothing science has done is as liberating to the spirit as the bold view Jesus had of himself and his powers.

The highest goal of modern man remains to master the physical world of matter and the obstacles to human freedom in nature and society through a spiritual perfection of individuals. Here again Jesus is a model, and Dr. Schweitzer is a modern model.

When Jesus discovered the natural world did not end as he first predicted it would, not only was his spirit undefeated but he was challenged to new, more resolute courage and fortitude by the reversal. If we grant the premise that the disciples did not know the secret of his claim to Messiahship, his sacrificial act must have been designed by a feat of brilliant, fearless reasoning and dauntless will. To decide absolutely alone and unaided to take the bitter cup of crucifixion in order to liberate the beloved elect was love in the highest. To provoke the high priests to this cruel extremity of asking Pilate for his death was daring and resourceful. To be sure, he was guided by prophecies in Scripture as to the high value of an atoning death, but he had to choose from many. What more glorious act of love is there than the sacrifice of one's own precious will for the salvation of those in the fellowship of righteousness?

The following is one of Albert Schweitzer's finest passages of imaginative writing. It presents allegorically the heroic, the tragic, and the eternally victorious in Jesus.

There is silence all around. The Baptist (John in Jordan) appears and cries: "Repent for the Kingdom of Heaven is at hand." Soon after that comes Jesus and in the knowledge that He is the coming Son of Man lays hold of the wheel of the world to set it moving on that last revolution which is to bring all ordinary history to a close. It refuses to turn and He throws himself upon it. Then it does turn; and crushes Him. Instead of bringing in the eschatological conditions (end of the world and Kingdom of God) He has destroyed them (the hope). The wheel rolls onward and the mangled body of one unmeasurable great man who was strong enough to think of Himself as the spiritual ruler of mankind and to bend history to His purpose is hanging upon it still. That is His victory and His reign.

Albert Schweitzer sees himself in a fellowship with Jesus. They share a chord of unity in a common, continuous "will" that is timeless and universal.

It finally becomes clear that within the prison walls of his dogma Jesus was a rebel spiritual commander. He is lord of liberators. His will was so sure and his beliefs then were such that he thought the authority of God's will was within his being. He was not a slave to materialism nor a puppet to the law. He came to fulfill man's dreams of the Kingdom of Goodness and to unbind with his hands all that was bound. His "last minute" or "eleventh hour" advice in the Sermon on the Mount was immortal because it was to prepare for the end—seconds, minutes, hours, days, or at most weeks away.

Jesus perfected his spiritual personality to the task in his own age. His supreme identification with the least, though restricted to human creatures, is an immortal model of love. His ethical system was not unified; it was a chaotic mixture of pessimism and optimism born of the dualism of good and evil, natural truth and spiritual truth, material earth and ethereal heaven, law and will, anti-freedom and freedom. This dualism is real to all ages, but spiritual champions like Jesus and Albert

DR. SCHWEITZER'S VIEWS OF JESUS   [137]

Schweitzer intuitively and rationally choose the commands of
the spiritual world and emerge as liberators of the spirit.

Dr. Schweitzer believes that spiritual events in civilization,
including the transcendent contributions of Jesus, are all traceable to the living, ethical will in individuals.

In this context Albert Schweitzer venerates Jesus. In the first
century there came a man of mighty will. He thought his will
would deliver a new world. He died, his dogma is dying, but
his "will" has not yet failed. His worldly beliefs have surrendered, but his liberating will has lived. The heritage of his
will and his dogma have been locked in battle in the minds
of his successors. This chaotic compound has ruled for ill as
well as good, as history testifies. His anguished death by crucifixion destroyed the Jewish hope among his followers of an
immediate Kingdom of God. A precious few have caught the
flame of his elemental freedom and borne it forward, forcing
countless changes in dogma. The free often perished at the
hands of the dogmatic, and for long intervals the mysterious,
liberating spirit was submerged by dogma.

The false dogmatic followers of Jesus may still let the world
perish without discovering his true meaning of spirit and will.
In his name they lead to battle, against his own true spirit, a
host of dead ideas. This is a ghastly, ghostly army which even
rational defeat, destruction, and needless bloody death seem to
have no power to arrest or enlighten.

His true spirit would create in us common ideals and a community of sovereign freedoms that would rule the world. But
his lingering dogma in clammy, senile hands destroys this spirit.
The spiritually infantile and morally insecure hang on to the
shriveling hand of his dogma. Despite all betrayals, he continues to reign as the alone Great and alone True in the very
world he thought his sacrifice would end.

When the umbilical cord of dogma is finally cut and his
reasonable, undogmatic, soaring, liberating spirit sows new seeds
that are of boundless potentiality, then he will lead the world

to the spiritual life of inner ecstasy and perfect earthly freedom. Then the unfree natural world will be subordinated to the primacy and supremacy of visions of illimitable freedom for all.

Albert Schweitzer discovered Jesus in the compelling light and majesty of the forward thrust of universal will. It is not necessary to consider Jesus divine or infallible or even completely original to appreciate his human, still unknown, magnitude.

It is clear at this point that Dr. Schweitzer's beloved Lambaréné is a mission that has for its target the spiritual decadence of the Western world. Albert Schweitzer is absolutely humble where people are concerned, but he is at war with all institutions of regimentation, collectivization, and anti-freedom for the precious individual, animal or man.

Using the concept of universal will composed of real forces of freedom as a frame of reference, we can more easily understand Dr. Schweitzer's justly famous but obscure last paragraph in the *Quest of the Historical Jesus:*

> He comes to us as one unknown, without a name, as of old, by the lake-side, He came to those men who knew Him not. He speaks to us the same word: "Follow thou me!" and sets us to the tasks which He has to fulfill for our time. He commands. And to those who obey Him, whether they be wise or simple, He will reveal Himself in the toils, the conflicts, the sufferings which they shall pass through in His fellowship, and, as an ineffable mystery, they shall learn in their own experience who He is.

The spirit of Jesus is not modern but universal and timeless. The special freedom of Jesus has something great to say to all ages. Freedom like his has no final hour. Its time is always. Jesus becomes a deathless, peremptory commander of freedom on earth. Dr. Schweitzer says, "Christianity, thus conceived, the most profound religion, is to me at the same time the most profound philosophy."

Believing all these things, Dr. Schweitzer walks secure and undismayed in an ethical fellowship with Jesus that may grow infinitely perfect through the labors of all who belong to the fellowship of living, ethical will.

Far more important in understanding Albert Schweitzer is the second to the last paragraph in *The Quest of the Historical Jesus:*

> It is a good thing that the true historical Jesus should over-throw the modern Jesus, should rise up against the modern spirit and send upon earth, not peace, but a sword . . . He was an imperious ruler. It was because He was so in His innermost being that He could think of Himself as the Son of Man. That was only the temporarily conditioned expression of the fact that He was an authoritative ruler . . . We can find no designation which expresses what He is for us.

This, then, is the pattern and the authoritative spirit of the Jesus Albert Schweitzer follows.

Because Jesus was a willful, imperious, uncompromising ruler of the spirit, Dr. Schweitzer tells us that we can in our external-istic age—an age which is at the same time materialistic, mechan-istic, militaristic, collectivized, yet mixed with naive superstition—find no designation which expresses what Jesus is for us. Only as we try to bend history toward peaceful reverence for all life and seek to do his will; only as we throw ourselves selflessly on the wheel and enter in an infinitesimal degree into the fellowship of his suffering; only as we probe deep into our own mysterious will can we learn in our own reason, as an unutterable secret, who he is.

I confess that for some time I harbored the strong suspicion that Dr. Schweitzer was doing precisely what he accused all others in Christian history of doing, from Paul onward: namely, projecting his own value system (*Weltanschauung*) back into the image of Jesus.

My opinion that he derives authority from reading his message into the past could be justified except for one unshakable, startling fact. Dr. Schweitzer's theory of Reverence for Life is not founded on the life of Jesus or even the Spirit of Jesus, or on any orthodox concept of God. Reverence for will-to-live is absolutely independent of Jesus and comes from the ineffable mystery Dr. Schweitzer finds within the microcosm of his own spirit.

On the above point Dr. Schweitzer says with candor: "I recognize it as the destiny of my existence to be obedient to the higher revelation of the will-to-live which I find in myself . . . All vital religious feeling flows from reverence for life . . . Reverence for life is the ethics of Love widened into universality . . . It is the ethics of Jesus now recognized as a logical consequence of thought . . . Ethics is . . . reverence for . . . will-to-live. This ethics . . . has the significance of a religion. It *is* religion."

It is my humble opinion—if you will permit a personal observation from an adventurer, not a scholar—that the details of Albert Schweitzer's speculations about the story of Jesus, brilliant as they are, do not constitute the genius of his observations.

The uniqueness of Dr. Schweitzer's achievement is his self-liberation from the tyranny and the fickle, capricious nature of recorded history. He discovered that his own reason, when informed, is capable of discerning deceptions. He shows how the compulsion for will inadvertently converts history into a pageant of lies, a fantasy of hypocrisy. History becomes a sad chronicle of inhumane struggles over competitive falsehoods. History is a whole scroll of half-truths. Albert Schweitzer discovered after looking backward with great care that it is not necessary to look behind to forge ahead. The truth of the universe is where it has always been: within ourselves.

The saddest tragedy, according to Dr. Schweitzer, is the way in which generation after generation betray themselves in the process of betraying Jesus. They exhaust their vitality in manufacturing amendment after amendment to an ancient cosmic dream, without having the wit and wisdom to follow Jesus only in those things in which he was creative.

History will teach us nothing about ourselves until we find and use the code of equivalents that portray the scope of will motivating all freedom-loving creatures.

Albert Schweitzer then is a modern prophet crying in the wilderness. His gospel is built on the certainty of will in the universe. Will-to-live is the most basic element in the consciousness of man. This will must be treated as a sacred trust. It must continue to be fulfilled. Thus it is that Albert Schweitzer speaks with a humble voice of love when he addresses individuals. He employs a tongue of unyielding steel when he addresses himself to forms of tyranny. To him men are not stupid sheep that need a shepherd. They only need the scales taken from their eyes so that they can see the truth about the universe, life, and goodness, and the relationship between individual freedom and will.

The question arises: Which institutions other than the religious institutions has Albert Schweitzer indicted?

Chapter

viii

On Paul and Goethe

As the days at Lambaréné passed, I began to feel that I was becoming a fiery convert. My surrender was not quite complete, even to Dr. Schweitzer's scheme of ethical conscience. The notion of adopting permanently his model of conduct never appeared even for an instant in my mind.

In a daydream mood, however, I found I was carried away with the vision of myself in the role of a herald, a crier, perhaps a disciple or an apostle.

A passing reflection within my reverie astounded me. These fantasies, so unthinkable in suburbia U. S. A., caused not even a fleeting twinge of embarrassment to me at Lambaréné. Whence came my sense of unrestraint?

Still imagining, I pursued the dramatization of myself in the role of traveling missionary for Dr. Schweitzer's Gospel. I concluded that my seeming lofty conceit did not, when reviewed dispassionately, actually involve my ego in prodigal self-flattery.

Instead of indulging in self-ridicule for my brash apostolic illusions, I asked a more poignant question: what has gone wrong that people must be embarrassed to share and declare their finest dreams?

Why should the only prophets we ever stop to praise today be those who lived and died so long ago?

Still following my flight of fancy, I thought without immodesty that I probably had traveled farther over the globe than all of the ancient bards of Biblical fame put together. Was I not as well the beneficiary of two thousand years of accumulated celestial and earthly knowledge denied evangelists of old? I had roamed over two whole continents that none of the wisest

142

first-century missionaries had even visualized in their most
penetrating prophecies. What uniqueness did they possess outside of the heroic courage of their convictions?

I qualified in one way to associate myself with the company
of first crusaders of Christianity. The disciples who set forth
to spread the gospel of Jesus were at first undistinguished and
simple. Some had been occupied with the menial tasks associated with boats, nets, and fish off the shores of Galilee.
All were at one time or another cursed with indecision and
self-doubt. In group confusion they jointly asked Jesus, "Who
art thou?" They were ambitious, worrying over where they
would sit in heaven when lesser men were judged. They were
at times deceitful, foolish, and avaricious. They vacillated in
their loyalties, defying at times their Jewish tradition, their
Roman rulers, and on occasion their Lord Jesus.

In my reverie I asked myself, why not be an apostle of
Albert Schweitzer as Paul was to Jesus? Saul of Tarsus started
his life meanly enough. He was a soldier, a Jew in Roman
employ, bent on persecuting the Jewish folk who followed a
trouble-maker named Jesus, whom he had never seen. After
conversion, he deified that same trouble-maker, but he took
great liberties with the holy creed.

Paul became, in the mind of Dr. Schweitzer, one of the great
liberators of all history. I discovered that I savored the lyric
image of myself that the word "liberator" aroused in my mind.

Unhappily the dangerous business of prophets and their
disciples is to smash those traditions that seem to manacle the
spirit. They act to liberate the age from fetters that limit individual freedom and keep multitudes in bondage. Paul said,
"If I yet please men I should not be the servant of Christ."
Apparently a true apostle can serve but one master.

Paul shattered many Jewish traditions. According to Dr.
Schweitzer, some of these shackles that the Apostle smashed
were the very dogmas that bound the mind of Jesus to his
primitive age. But did he serve Jesus or his own gospel?

It was while I was indulging this temporary mood of apostolic grandeur that I turned to one of Dr. Schweitzer's greatest
monuments of scholarship, *Paul and His Interpreters,* first published in 1912, and fragments of *The Mysticism of the Apostle
Paul* found in two anthologies of Dr. Schweitzer's memorable
sayings.

It will be remembered that Albert Schweitzer states one
principle firmly in many books: the only hypothesis that fills
the gaps in the Gospel story and harmonizes the inconsistencies
therein is the assumption that Jesus believed himself to be the
Messianic instrument of the end of the natural world.

Because the cosmic end of days did not happen, as predicted
by Jesus, during the tragedy of crucifixion, Paul, still believing
that "the end of all things is at hand," had to reconcile with
reason the idea of a slightly less imminent end, a somewhat less
precipitous finale, and a somewhat delayed expectation of the
Kingdom of God.

Paul taught, believed, and lived as if there would be a "short
intervening period" before the end of generations. According to
Dr. Schweitzer, the idea of baptism and sacraments "as already
established and accredited (in Judaism) Paul had only to
take over." But now the idea of the resurrection and the return
of Jesus had to be made a reasonable part of creedal doctrine.

Paul created the missionary idea of carrying the new meanings
of the message abroad. While Jesus thought only of the "elect,"
Paul was under a new, wider, inner compulsion to carry the word
to a greater circle of humanity. Dr. Schweitzer says, "He maintains the view that there is a pressing necessity to carry the
Gospel abroad. It is under the impulsion of this thought that
he becomes the Apostle of the Greeks."

It is often said that Paul's missionary zeal was sired by
practicality and politics. Dr. Schweitzer maintains that when
Paul exempts the Greeks from the Jewish law on his own authority, "he is not led to do so by the experience that this
was reasonable and practical. He declares them [the Greeks]

free because the logical implications of his doctrine [his own sense of freedom] compel him to do so. What Jesus thought about the matter is just as indifferent to him as his opinion regarding the legitimacy of preaching to the Gentiles. For this limited period the watchword is: He who is under the law shall continue to observe it; he who is free from it shall on no account place himself under it." Thus Paul smashed the rocks of dogma that had entombed Judaism within national boundaries.

Early theological historians and modern scholars of exegesis exercised "cunning and ingenuity" to harmonize Jesus and Paul, because it is embarrassing to the uniqueness of Jesus to consider Paul a co-creator of our Christianity. Our Lambaréné scholar and historian says that pseudo-scholars manufactured connecting fictions by "psychologising," "spiritualising," and "modernising" the events of those early days. They made play with distinctions between religion and theology. Their tricky discoveries cloaked "concealment of contradictions and antinomies."

Honest history shows that the theology of Ignatius and Justin is creative, new, and dissimilar from both Jesus and Paul. "There is something more in this than simple oversight . . . The conditions under which he [Paul] created his system must be for them unimaginable . . . May it be that the intensity of the eschatological expectation [imminent end of the world] has so declined that the mysticism associated therewith can no longer maintain its ground?"

In dealing with the breaks in continuity in the story of Paul as with the gaps in the life of Jesus, Dr. Schweitzer believes that free speculation alone is the method of obtaining insights. "Arguments and counterarguments must be drawn from the contents . . . The only thing we have to deal with is the self-witness of the Epistles which can neither be strengthened nor shaken by indications drawn from elsewhere." Paul's creed is more positive Christianity. His is a growing religion of reason, liberty, and widened love.

This speculative technique, Dr. Schweitzer admits, "will appear distressingly negative to those who look for results which can be immediately coined into dogmatic and homiletic currency." Although Dr. Schweitzer created this method of historical research, he shows his own independent prophetic certainty by labelling his resourcefulness the salvation of positive Christianity. Christianity will join hands with Dr. Schweitzer's own theory of the universe and his philosophy of Reverence for Life if it hopes to live.

Dr. Schweitzer ends his great study of Paul with an imperious challenge to authoritarian, anti-freedom dogmatists. His challenge is to the followers of Peter, those faithless to freedom in both Protestantism and Catholicism. He says of the dogmatists, "Their opinion is of small importance. It is the fate of the 'Little-Faiths' of truth, true followers of Peter, whether they be of the Roman or Protestant observance, that they *cry out and sink in the sea of ideas,* where the followers of Paul, believing in the Spirit, *walk secure and undismayed.*"

What, then, are the timeless teachings of prophet Paul, who lived as an apostle? Which of Paul's innovations is true for every age and every religion?

Paul did not distinguish between Christianity and Judaism. With reason he made necessary alterations in the one true religion. He penetrated to the uttermost depth of the meaning of Jesus when he said, "Where the Spirit of the Lord is, there is liberty." He was speaking for freedom when he said, "Quench not the Spirit." He carried the liberating essence of Jesus as well as his eschatology throughout the Greek world, telling all to "Stand fast, therefore, in the liberty wherewith Christ hath made us free, and be not again entangled with the yoke of bondage."

Paul was a powerful, elemental thinker within the limitations imposed on him by the thought-world of his era. He grappled successfully and reasonably with the special character of the period between what was to him the resurrection and the re-

turn of Jesus. He proved that faith has nothing to fear from
free thinking, and in fact must be based on it.

According to Dr. Schweitzer, "Paul moves within the narrow
bounds of eschatology *as a free man.*" The Doctor also dis-
covers that Paul never for a moment allows his loyalty to the
prevalent eschatological view "to rob him of his direct humanity. . . ."

> With tremendous certainty and precision he goes in all
> things straight to the spiritually essential. Amid multitudes
> consumed with the excitement of the expectation Paul almost
> alone among the disciples and early believers dwells on the
> significance of the ethical in Jesus Christ. He was not over-
> whelmed nor blinded by his beliefs in the glorious supernatural
> events to come. He persisted in teaching Gentiles that the
> faithful of the pretenders to Christianity must place themselves
> under "the absolute authority of the ethical."

According to Paul, all believers must also draw tenderness
from the warm springs of sympathy and radiate humane concern for as many days as the cold natural world lasts. All must
tend the flames of human, earthly love. Charitable actions and
deeds of devotion designed to fit the coming of the Kingdom of
God must be practiced by the elect, who become in part by
so doing super-earthly beings in this transitory and preparatory
period.

Thus in his personal freedom and in his adherence to the
essential liberating power of living, ethical love, Paul alone was
"the true disciple of Jesus."

Besides being a thinker, Paul was in part then an independent
liberator. He did not let the ways of the world interfere with
his own self-perfection as a simple, profound, humane person.
Dr. Schweitzer says of Paul, "For the external abandonment
of the things of the world he substitutes an inner freedom from
them." His freedom transforms him into a fearless, courageous,
and incorruptible instrument of the living ethical will in the
universe.

Though Paul was molded by an inescapable Jewish cosmic view (eschatological expectation) which for us is, in the opinion of Dr. Schweitzer, "completely obsolete," he transcended the bondage of his period as a champion of thinking. His ardor was contagious. He kindled many fires for earthly freedom.

Albert Schweitzer characterizes Paul as a fellow in freedom. The following is his summary:

> Paul is no *mere revolutionary*. He takes the faith of the primitive Christian community as his starting point: only he will not consent to halt where it comes to an end, but claims the right to think out his thoughts about Christ to their conclusion, without caring whether the truths which he thereby reaches have ever come within the purview of the faith held by the Christian community and been recognized by it . . . Paul vindicated for all time the rights of thought in Christianity. Above belief which drew its authority from tradition, he set the knowledge which came from the Spirit of Christ. There lives in him an unbounded and undeviating reverence for truth. He will consent only to a limitation of liberty laid on him by the law of love, not to one imposed by doctrinal authority.

Through all of Dr. Schweitzer's praise of Paul runs one deep accusation that serves also to indict most prophets, theologians, philosophers, and historians. Almost every deep thinker spoils his own creative thoughts by reading these elemental convictions into the past. Paul mixed and thereby confused his genius with that of Jesus. Dr. Schweitzer says: "The system of the Apostle of the Gentiles stands over against the teaching of Jesus as something of an entirely different character."

Later in a similar way Ignatius and Justin pretend to take over Paul's thought; but instead, without admitting it, according to Dr. Schweitzer, "they create in their turn something new."

Still later, ascribing their own ideas to Paul, men of the Reformation attacked and destroyed feudal Catholicism in northern Europe and they engineered the revolt "in the name of Paul."

Thus peoples have tagged their finest ideas onto Paul in the same way that Paul read his ideas into Jesus "in order to receive them back again clothed in Apostolic authority."

This to Dr. Schweitzer is the great crime of history and the most vicious form of self-betrayal.

With this powerful revelation about Apostle Paul's one colossal inadvertent act of self-deception fresh in mind, it dawned on me that perhaps I was tumbling into the ancient trap. If I became a Schweitzer apostle, I would create a two-headed infamy. Like others before me, but unlike Dr. Schweitzer, I would be admitting that I was a weak reed, too cowardly to set forth unattached the convictions of my own heart.

Perhaps I had been guilty already of great error, mistaking my search for truth for the search for prestige or a haven of sanction for my own ideas. Perhaps I too was reading into the object of my fascination my own inner convictions, muddling both Dr. Schweitzer's perceptions and my own. My notion of being a disciple or apostle of Prophet Schweitzer collapsed.

If I would not be a blind apostolic herald or a devoted disciple, what legitimate kinship was there between a giant of reasonable ethics like Albert Schweitzer and an ordinary man like myself discovering Dr. Schweitzer's ethic to be for the most part true? How can men hold on to their independence and ideals in such a relationship?

I was led to re-examine Dr. Schweitzer's role in relation to Johann Wolfgang von Goethe. Memories of Dr. Schweitzer as a modern herald of Goethe swam through my mind. Turning again to his books, I considered the precise way in which Dr. Schweitzer paid homage from lecture platforms in many lands to the strange complex of virtues manifested by Goethe.

Dr. Schweitzer admits that he has greater affection for the free eighteenth-century genius of Frankfort than for freedom-loving

Paul. Unlike Paul, Goethe was not trapped by late Jewish eschatology or by the poignantly dramatic modifications of the supernatural expectations associated with Jesus. Albert Schweitzer said in a private letter, later published in part, written to Charles Joy: "Goethe is the personality with which I have been most deeply concerned. St. Paul, who I think has had a decisive influence upon me, belongs to an epoch far away and too different from ours." Much of Paul, like Jesus, is embedded in the ancient, rough rocks of a stony land in an alien age.

In trying to isolate for analysis the rational ties of fellowship between Goethe and himself, Dr. Schweitzer inadvertently presents us with another wonderful key to his own hard-to-grasp simplicity. He confesses much when he says of himself and Goethe: "What binds us together in the deepest depths of our being is his philosophy of nature."

Goethe was called a "pantheist." He was labelled "pagan" by so-called Christian contemporaries because he could not find God "outside" nature. God was in nature and all through the universe, not separated from it.

Goethe steadfastly reduced the three-way Christian concept in which God the Creator made life and earth. All things were explained as the interplay between physical matter and volitional forces that characterized nature. All this included God within the process.

Dr. Schweitzer expresses the principal tenet of Goethe's philosophy in saying: "He seeks for God not outside of nature and co-existent with her but within her alone. With Spinoza . . . he believes in the identity of God and nature."

Goethe held to one concept that made his view distinctive and quite different from Spinoza's view. Knowing that Spinoza renounced the notion of freedom and accepted a universe ruled by necessity, and knowing that Goethe believed in degrees of freedom, Dr. Schweitzer takes pleasure in placing his hero squarely in the procession of freedom's fellowship. He says:

"Stark necessity cannot exist for the man who writes, 'Our life, like the great whole in which we are contained, is made up in some incomprehensible manner of both freedom and necessity.' "

Albert Schweitzer grows to love the erring, guilt-laden Olympian of Weimar, not by sentiment but by a whole-hearted, hard-headed analysis of his intellectual achievements.

Goethe, like Kant but unlike Albert Schweitzer, believes in an immanent progress, "the progression from some unknown center to some unrecognizable goal." Like Kant and unlike Albert Schweitzer, he thought he saw in nature the ferment of an impulsive "categorical imperative."

Dr. Schweitzer remains objective and withholds his affirmation when he finds that Goethe's nature-God not only "reveals itself—in the fundamental phenomena of ethics" but also "in fundamental physical phenomena." Goethe names the riddle running through all creation a yearning, surging, restless "piety." Dr. Schweitzer says, "In *Faust* he proclaims that love has its origin in the infinite and plays its part in human destiny . . . Every ephemeral being is only a manifestation of an eternal being."

Dr. Schweitzer accepts with Spinoza and Goethe the pantheistic universe. With Goethe he adopts as his own the great dualism that Goethe proclaimed about the universe. There Dr. Schweitzer stops abruptly. What Goethe pictures from faulty "observation" Albert Schweitzer cannot discover "through experience." Dr. Schweitzer suspects Goethe when he says, "Love is to be found in nature." Dr. Schweitzer says, "I cannot see it . . . I see nothing of love in nature . . . It has emerged in the spiritual evolution of mankind." Dr. Schweitzer experiences nothing that could be called God, purpose, immanent progress or categorical imperatives outside of man's ethical experience based on human reason.

Albert Schweitzer reveres Goethe for his life of action in an age when servants like Kant yielded to the pursuit of contemplation. The wise man of Weimar strove to perfect his total personality in freedom by wide, inclusive varieties of activities. The speculative thinkers of the day were busy drawing plans to perfect society and to deliver freedom by legislation or mob rule.

According to Dr. Schweitzer, Goethe stood against the tide that said the greatest good for the greatest number should be the golden rule of all politics. He maintained that goodness comes only "as each individual develops within himself in the most perfect and personal way." Goethe was one of the first to foretell man's doom by the elephantiasis of over-organization. He felt that man would sink into a sickening hyper-submissiveness to society. He would in anonymity merge with organization and yield up his spirit to brainless mob rule and crowd culture. These are vicious symptoms that Albert Schweitzer sees and seeks to cure today, and this makes Dr. Schweitzer and Goethe fellow-workers in the cause of freedom.

Goethe "wants freedom for his people." Toward the wars for freedom he is "hesitant in attitude . . . This premonition is the basis for his unconquerable aversion to all revolutionaries. The revolutionary is for him the will of the masses bent on overthrowing the will of the individual."

With mysterious foreboding Goethe stands for personal, individual perfection in freedom and unconsciously against new economic forces which in Dr. Schweitzer's words "eventuate in such a destruction of the independence of the individual."

In a moving paragraph Dr. Schweitzer illuminates Goethe's prophetic nature and in a rare insight he predicts Hitler, Mussolini, and Stalinist activities by movers of masses.

After all, what is now taking place in this terrible epoch of ours except a gigantic repetition of the drama of Faust upon the stage of the world? The cottage of Philemon and Baucis burns with a thousand tongues of flame! In deeds of violence and murders a thousandfold, a brutalized humanity plays its cruel game! Mephistopheles leers at us with a thousand grimaces! In a thousand different ways mankind has been persuaded to give up its natural relations with reality, and to seek its welfare in the magic formula of some kind of economic and social witchcraft, by which the possibility of freeing itself from economic and social misery is only still farther removed!

Once again we see that, in history, philosophy like theology is always the saga of man's struggle to explain and defend freedom in the universe or bypass the lack of it with transcendental dreams of immortal freedom.

Goethe was always a prisoner of uncertainty, but Albert Schweitzer admits with candor and a prophetic kind of modesty that he was himself cut from harder wood. Dr. Schweitzer is resigned to some immutable elements of necessity and determinism but his faith in growing degrees of freedom never flags.

Freedom in Goethe's nature philosophy is the thought that links him to the Doctor at Lambaréné. Goethe was the first to feel a premonition that institutions, states, organizations, parties were destined to rob the individual of personal freedom, and Dr. Schweitzer sees the tragedy more clearly. It is in anxiety for precious human personality and freedom that Albert Schweitzer acknowledges in his tribute to Goethe the essential fact that in different ages men can thrill to the joys of co-discovery.

My own destiny has brought it about for me that I can experience with a vividness that goes to the very marrow of my soul the destinies of our time and anxiety about our manhood. That in an age when so many whom we need as free personalities get imprisoned in the work of a profession, I as such a free personality, can feel all these things and, like Goethe, can through a happy combination of circumstances serve my age as a free man . . . [that freedom] is to me an act of grace which lightens my laborious life. Every task or piece of creative work that I am allowed to do is to me only a return of gratitude to destiny for that act of grace.

My freer self-analysis soon revealed to me that I called Albert
Schweitzer the Prophet of Freedom because I believed in a
new idea of cosmic freedom. According to Dr. Schweitzer's
reasoning, I had the right to claim a kinship to his ideas. But
I must not persist in calling my ideas the convictions belonging
to Dr. Schweitzer.

I became surer than ever that this jungle Doctor abhors
hero worshipers. He wants co-adventurers and co-discoverers
and co-creators engaged in the labor of finding and proclaiming universal truths in ethics. He believes in a renaissance of
freedom. He prefers to make men free thinkers and free
scholars. If Dr. Schweitzer is correct in his speculations and
observations, others will independently find that the basis for
Reverence for Life is true. Dr. Schweitzer says, "I would be a
humble pioneer of this Renaissance and throw the belief in a
new humanity like a torch, into our dark age."

Like Jesus and like Paul and Goethe, Albert Schweitzer had
to make his own amendments in the theory of the universe
handed to him by custom and habitual thought. But Albert
Schweitzer takes pains to prove that his ideas about the universe
are not just amendments. The synthesis is his very own. His
thought system is derived from his own knowledge of the will-
to-live within himself. He never says his view belonged to
Moses, Jesus, Paul, Kant or Goethe.

I could not be an apostle then after all. I am a co-
adventurer and co-discoverer and perhaps, I hope, even a co-
creator.

A conceit confessed is half redressed, and an adventure shared
is a freedom dared. With this lame preface, at this juncture
I will admit that I, too, have a theory of the universe. I think
it is similar to Dr. Schweitzer's in general, but I arrived at it
quite independently.

At all events, the reader has a right to know my point of
view and then judge whether the idea image of the universe,
life and goodness is, as stated, similar if not identical, to that
proclaimed by Dr. Schweitzer.

Catalysis and Free Will

In 1955 while wandering through the stacks in the Technological Library at Northwestern University and looking for books on indeterminacy and freedom in the realm of physics, I discovered a book called *Catalysis and Determinism* by Alwin Mittasch (1938).

I mention this book because I was unable to find a single person at either one of two major universities to transmit the message in the book to me or even pass judgment on the validity of its content. I invited a German teacher, two German-speaking enzymologists, a Nobel Prize-winning physiologist, and the leading philosopher in the area to attempt to interpret the book. All tried. None succeeded.

To this day I do not know what the book contains in detail, but the title was surprisingly parallel in implication to the one I had considered for a book I was planning, then called *Catalysis and Free Will.*

The title of this German book intrigued me because I was toying with the notion that catalysts are distinctive carriers of forces that reflect the invisible forces of freedom, forces that have no mass and might be thought of as anti-matter but not voids. I had considered that the unit of life was not the cell but the enzyme, which by definition is an organic catalyst. In my view the cell is a changing association of catalysts engaged in chemical chain reaction that in effect "cause" the physical-chemical aspects of the mysterious life process. They direct the destiny of certain mass actions among inert chemicals.

Biologists I consulted quoted only ancient articles of "scientific" faith and dogmatic dicta to oppose the view that each

unit of life is a vehicle of freedom, and evolution is a process
that involves the survival of the freest enzyme systems. This
inner universe, more valid than the physical cosmos, is little
known to science. In physics catalysis is not regarded as a
special dynamic phenomenon but a mechanical extension of
material energies.

I needed time to adventure with this idea about catalysis and
freedom. An interested physician-friend suggested Alaska. He
and his wife joined my family and me. With a large number
of books we started west and then embarked at Vancouver
for Alaska.

I stopped at universities coming and going, to discuss my
project with specialists and department heads. No one had any
remote clues about the origin, development and course of
human freedom. And many biologists, chemists, and physicists
insisted that freedom is an illusion.

While floating past glaciers in the inland passage adjacent to
northern Canada and Alaska, I read documents on freedom
approaching the subject from every conceivable angle in every
possible field.

I refreshed my memory on the concepts of freedom that
intellects in young America borrowed from eighteenth-century
Europe. I was disappointed to find that of all the recent books
I was lugging and reading en route, none attempted to give
freedom an elemental cosmic definition. Most were reliving
old victories. They reaffirmed freedom by faith, not original
reasoning and refined rethinking. Freedom of will, conscience,
thought, press, assembly, religion, education, and freedom in
politics, economics, and social relations were for the most part
the earlier concepts fervently confirmed. Modern authors were
not seeing new interconnections between these fragments of
freedom nor were they making additions to the family of freedoms. They failed to shore up the defense of freedom by new
reason. It seemed that these precious freedoms are now merely

fashionable habits of mind, not perennial inspirations reanimated and extended by re-discovery.

The doctrines of Leibniz, with his theory of immaterial centers of forces without parts or configurations, had much in common with my thoughts on catalytic forces that dealt with incorporeal realities, but I could not see his evidence for the extra-religious reality beyond the twin factors of matter on the one hand and eddies of force on the other. His separate category of religious forces that presumably pre-planned perfection and immanent progress in the universe was beyond my reason, my perception, and my experience. After conceiving of a divine beginning that installed inner harmony, Leibniz equated the growth of freedom with the growth in mutual help and coordination between monads and entelechy.

I became familiar with Schopenhauer's Oriental notion of world will that had to be opposed in a negative way by inner human freedom, Nietzsche's agnostic faith in a dualistic universe composed of matter and freedom (spirit) only, and Hegel's concept of institutional freedom as the manifestation of the Absolute.

I was impressed with Bergson's concept that freedom is being inserted more and more into the evolutionary process, and Hume's idea of freedom-giving consciousness flowing into the realm of matter, the eternal enemy of freedom. I laughed at and recorded Shaw's vision of residual witchcraft in modern science, which is so devoted to the dogma of anti-freedom. I found that many scientists of today still agree with Spinoza, who said in the seventeenth century, "There is no such thing as free will."

Most modern scientists are naively paradoxical on the proposition of human freedom. They scream like eagles when academic freedom is suppressed, while they deny freedom in the machine-like universe. Even the great Einstein fell into this ambiguous trap. I read in Einstein's autobiography that at twelve he was liberated by a "positively fanatic orgy of free thinking." Then the same great man, who worshiped his human freedom, paradoxically disowned freedom in his Credo. He said, "I do not believe we can have any freedom at all in the philosophical sense, for we act not only under external compulsions but also by inner necessity."

I was mid-course in writing my book, *Catalysis and Free Will,* when I came to the conclusion that Dr. Schweitzer had identified a cosmic form of freedom but called the quality Will. I reasoned that Will and Freedom are two faces of the same force. I was convinced that he was aware of a weightless, shapeless, imperceptible and invisible force or family of forces whose common characteristic was that they were not composed of the "stuff" of the physical-chemical universe. I suspected that this concept was in Albert Schweitzer's mind when he carried his theory of reverence for life not only to single cells but to crystals. He implied that "will" has degrees of freedom, and that "will" comes to realize through a gradual growth in self-consciousness that it is partly free in man's reason.

Will, Dr. Schweitzer repeatedly says, *can* order physical events even as reason *could* order the flow of history. He implies that external phenomena mirror indiscernible fields of force. Instead of machine-like matter creating the illusion of free will, will is a real force that orders or governs in part the machine-like energies of matter. Perhaps will is a property of space, the content of what we have called the voids of space.

The following medley of quotations will suggest parallels between Dr. Schweitzer's view of will and my view of freedom. Substitute the catalytic concept of freedom for will, particularly in the way he uses the terms crystal, cell, perfection, and individuals, and determine by this simple exercise whether the meaning is altered or only illuminated.

> The important thing is that we are part of life . . . We are born of other lives; we possess the capacity to bring still other lives into existence. In the same way, if we look into a microscope we see cell producing cell . . . We have discovered in the

cell an individual existence in whose faculties, active and passive, we see repeated elements of our own vitality . . . Will-to-live is everywhere present, even as in me . . . The essential nature of the will-to-live is found in this . . . Everywhere it strives to reach perfection . . . in delicate blossoms, in the manifold wondrous forms of the jelly-fish, in the blade of grass, in the *crystal.* . . .

A man is really ethical only when . . . he shatters no ice crystal that sparkles in the sun, tears no leaf from its tree, breaks off no flower, and is careful not to crush any insect when he walks. . . .

The impulse toward perfection is innate in us—*being as we are endowed with freedom* . . . For when it begins to think, the will-to-live realizes that it is free . . . and capable of reflective, purposive action . . . Life as such is sacred.

In my judgment Dr. Schweitzer believes that will is elemental in the universe—in crystals, in cells, in man's reason. Will is not the cosmic dust, the human clay, the chemical elements; it consists of the forces of freedom. It is the unseen half of the universe, the self-determining dynamism, that makes all the world go around. Freedom consists of a pluralistic universe of whirlpools of force that alter the behavior patterns of inertia-dogged matter. Reason is such a whirlpool producing irresistible currents of global motivations.

The universe I visualize is composed of two elements—matter and energy on the one hand, and on the other hand, the catalytic forces that change or govern many of the matter and energy exchanges that are connected with the life processes but are themselves exempt from external control.

I call the catalytic forces the forces of freedom because they lack mass and yet exercise control over the material world.

Organic evolutions may be described as the ascendancy of control of helpless energy and matter by ever new associations of catalytic forces. The advance is in degrees and levels of freedom exercised over matter and energy.

A protein molecule—a virus, for example—may be an auto-catalytic agent, for it carries forces within itself that can cause the production of identical molecules with unvarying fidelity when introduced into a metabolic protein environment.

The universe is not composed of living and non-living agents, but of inertial energies of matter and the forces of freedom. A cell is a vast community of autocatalytic forces. The simplest organism is an enormous society of such communities of catalytic forces managing the physical elements of the body.

Man is neither alive nor dead but a thriving microcosm of catalytic forces. Real growth furthers the control of catalytic forces over the inertial element of the universe. Man is a valid unit of the universe composed of forces of freedom and unfree energies.

Evolution has been the process in which there has been a survival of the freest, and history is a clash between the highest vehicles of freedom.

Reason is the growing consciousness of freedom, and ethics are the immaterial values that catalyze more and more freedom.

Diseases are probably disturbances in enzyme systems, and often the disturbing element is a catalyst.

"Sin" and "evil" destroy higher forms of freedom. Reason dictates that the "good" is composed of actions that further freedom. There is neither good nor evil outside of man, neither in brutal nature nor in the cold galaxies.

Thoughts are forms of catalytic forces. Wisdom is the reservoir of ideas that catalyze energy. Prudence controls and harmonizes the forces of freedom. Justice in human relations is activity that distributes human freedom and the fruits of freedom. Happiness is activity in the pursuit of higher freedoms. All gods are catalysts. They "create" without diminishing their own energy. They reflect the existence of an invisible, im-material force.

The goal of all laws is to liberate. Laws restrain us in some sectors of freedom in order to further all freedoms.

Love, according to this cosmic theory of freedom, is reason's highest view of relations that liberate. Love of self, family, tribe, clan, nation, humanity, and finally love of freedom as a principle represents growth in the realm of liberty through love. Love has evolved from egocentric circles to ethnocentric limits, and in its widest scope it is ethic-centered, thus going from the self-centered love that characterizes childhood, to the adolescent love of nation, to the mature love of total freedom. Love is the sharing of freedom. It is thought to be the highest and most indivisible cosmic good.

In history man has called truth the ideas that free him from the tyranny of physical forces. Old ideas of truth become a yoke of bondage. New visions of freedom are hampered by the very ideas and values that liberated our ancestors.

Scientists today in the name of truth and pure objectivity are describing a universe devoid of freedom because the freedom of God—freedom of perfect intelligence, unlimited powers of creativity, immortality, indestructibility—was found an extreme dogmatic deterrent to scientific research, incompatible with facts. The prevailing dogma underlying science is that the universe is mechanistic, predetermined, devoid of freedom. This scientific view liberates us from past religions' view of the universe and becomes a new religion. It has given our nation prosperity and has bestowed on its adherents a psychological conformity.

The next forward step that will liberate man from the dogmas of Science is a theory of the universe in which freedom is the principal property of the cosmic freedom that has become self-conscious in man. The point is that truth is determined by one's view of the universe. Truth is the composite of the images of life that liberate this human spirit from the hazards that imperil its freedom.

The ideas of freedom devolved by eighteenth-century thinkers arose from subjection of the spirit to the monolithic force of feudalism. It was evident that they had to find natural freedoms and rights to replace "divine" feudal privileges and rights.

They decided that man is a creature of nature and creatures of nature are free. Therefore man is born free and has inalienable freedoms over which king and church may exercise no control. These global, natural freedoms were not cosmic in origin, so it was still believed that behind the universe was a Creator who endowed nature and man with freedom. Through a slip in logic, individual sovereignty became confused with national sovereignty, and individual freedom with group freedom. This view became tied to nations and formed the new basis of democratic national sovereignty.

Hegel alone devised a new theory of the universe. Freedom was God in the process of growth. The institution of the State represented his very being. The Hegelian heresy about cosmic freedom is still having an enormous effect in history. It paved the way to deification of the modern State.

The concepts of freedom that grew out of observing nature were precipitated by revolt against the fetters of the feudal order. They smashed the one-God theory of the universe and established a freedom-centered theory, with God pushed into the background as a "first cause" only. He was not retained as the governor of free men. As long as God and Church had perfect freedom, man had no freedom. If a divine tyrant had perfect freedom, the whole universe would be his slave, striving by his sufferance. This logic was easy, but the illusions of freedom observed in nature did not and could not become a new coherent theory of the universe explaining the flames of freedom that burned in the breasts of restless multitudes.

Many men in the eighteenth century could see the ineluctable laws of the physical universe. They were immutable and interrelated endlessly. But they could create nothing, cause nothing, and initiate nothing. No one saw a basis in fact of freedom-defying motions and interactions of the physical universe. No one could without looking backward to the olden God concept see an immaterial will coexisting in a timeless eternity with the universe so apparent to the senses. Evidence for the co-determining elements in growth in complexity in chemical integration were elusive. It was not suspected that unseen units of freedom were real, that they could be and were compounded and coordinated into pairs, families, communities and interdependent societies that could master-manage the corporeal chemicals.

This catalytic view of freedom gives us an inverted look at the law of causation and the first true picture of the nature of causation. Phrases like "primary causes" and "effective causes" are misguided categories in the causeless inertial realm of matter and energy relations.

All causes are catalytic. They are undetermined, spontaneous interruptions of inertial chain reactions in matter and energy exchanges. Beginnings have no meaning in any time scale. Beginnings are relative and are explainable only by this new catalytic cause concept.

The negative notion of freedom from constraint is a proposition that is based on a misunderstanding of the nature of freedom that is self-active, positive, indestructible, and spontaneous. Limitations of freedom at the primitive, primordial level of simple catalysis are determined by the limits inherent in matter. As freedoms are compounded in complex organizations of "living matter," systems of freedom may oppose other communities of freedoms. Thus the laws of freedom are revealed to man's inquiries with reason about freedom. Purpose is unobserved in freedoms below the freedom of reason. Man cannot create matter-energy units, but he can recreate compounds and combinations and new artificial and unstable elements.

The prodigious intellectual and spiritual accomplishment achieved by Dr. Schweitzer is, in my judgment, his new cosmic explanation of freedom. His theory of the universe is dissimilar from the feudal view and opposed to the Hegelian view. Like the eighteenth-century thinkers he finds freedom not in institutions but in man as a creature. But he shows that creatures are samples of a universe that has forces built in. These forces were not installed at a supposed beginning but exist as an un-originated quality. Dr. Schweitzer's supreme achievement is allowing his view of the universe, life and goodness to create Lambaréné, the modern Mecca for free spirits, a working model, testifying to the truth of freedom and its power.

In my own catalytic view of cosmic freedom, the evolutionary process is seen repeated in every human being. A fertilized single cell in the dark womb, devoid of reason, consciousness and self-awareness, is free by virtue of its catalysts to grow and this long before it becomes rational and self-conscious. However, a rational animal emerges, capable of selfless acts of love in a score of years. Virus-like genes and chromosomes carry the power of higher freedoms, including the potentiality of reason, self-consciousness, and self-knowledge.

The catalytic forces cause, create, initiate all non-machine-like reactions in matter and energy exchange in the life process.

Collectively catalytic forces may represent all the freedom in the universe. Freedom in its elemental form is known solely by its mastery over matter.

Freedom is composed of all the forces that have not been measured. The tools that disclose the truth of matter and energy will not work on freedom. All the enigmas seem to be forms of catalysts. They are properties of space. They direct and manipulate the physical universe, as powerful shadowy ideas manipulate substance in man.

Gravity, surface tension, magnetism, light, electrostatic forces, and all the forces that hold molecules together and apart, and distinguish catalytic action from matter and energy exchanges, are primordial forms of freedom, for they act without losing power to act. They have no mass or substance. They are among the eternal, unoriginated, indestructible, creative forces of the universe. They catalyze reactions.

Can the following be disproved? The *will* Albert Schweitzer visualizes as the second element in the material universe is characterized by its freedom from the rules that govern matter.

Will-to-live, which Albert Schweitzer venerates and finds in crystals, jelly fish, and man, is better described as the forces of freedom. Will without freedom is unthinkable. The words are interdependent. The idea-image in English is usually conveyed by the term free will. However, in Dr. Schweitzer's concept freedom is relative, not necessarily self-conscious. It simply orders some events in the material universe.

Reverence for life to Albert Schweitzer includes even crystals, and really means reverence for the will in the universe and will in the life process, and the will that has become self-conscious in man. This growth of *will* is marked by the ascent of freedom. The material universe shows no such signs of growth.

The values Albert Schweitzer lives by are moral. They are the strongest forces in human history. They are liberating forms of freedom. They constitute the stream of ethics. Ethics and morals and ideas of goodness are best described as the immaterial values that liberate man's "will" (Schweitzer) or his powers of self-determination and "freedom" (Phillips).

Thus I discovered through my own theory of the universe that Dr. Schweitzer's theory of the universe is an excellent presentation of cosmic freedom. He is the model of a free man and a product of freedom's power. Whereas it is not proper that I become a parroting proselyte, I can properly say he is the wisest exponent of individual freedom and may, because of his example, fulfill the role of Prophet of Freedom for the free world if not for peoples throughout the world.

Quite aside from his cosmic view of "will" that I am persuaded is better understood as freedom, we shall see that Dr. Schweitzer employs the word freedom as the sovereign good in human relations and in many personal relations in his own life.

I should stop here to relate a strange tale of coincidence. Though I had never been able to get Alwin Mittasch's book which I found in the library at Northwestern Technological Institute, *Catalysis and Determinism,* fully interpreted or translated, I wanted to own a copy of this prophetic book. I searched through many bookstores in Europe and finally in Basel, Switzerland I found two copies.

The stunning coincidence is this: I also found one copy of a book by Alwin Mittasch called *Dobereiner, Goethe, and Catalysis.* My mind jumped. Pantheist Goethe was Dr. Schweitzer's hero because Goethe believed that freedom was a property of the universe. My question then was, did Goethe learn from Dobereiner about catalysis and apply it to his own philosophy? Did catalysis hint to his understanding two centuries ago how cosmic universal freedom might be explained? Did his theory of freedom contribute to Dr. Schweitzer's view which is built on the elemental reality of will in the natural universe? I had to wait for a solution to these important, most provocative, and pertinent questions.

Also now quite independently of my cosmic view of freedom and Albert Schweitzer's cosmic view of will, we can find in Dr. Schweitzer's story and literature abundant evidence that the various freedoms, honored in fragmentary form in human affairs, are central to Dr. Schweitzer's life.

What are the affirmative canons of Dr. Schweitzer's convictions concerning the ordinances, rules, regulations and laws of *freedom,* and how are they applicable to individuals in daily routine human affairs?

If we review Albert Schweitzer's life, we shall see the specific human freedoms that he cherishes in the wisdom of his mature years. Then in flashbacks we can see the forms of freedom that he treasured in his young manhood and finally those that were dear to him in the earliest years of his youth. The evolution of freedom in Albert Schweitzer's life is a miniature re-enactment of the growth of freedom in the history of human affairs.

While the rest of the modern world, forgetting the goal of individual freedom, flings itself frantically into the production of capital goods and consumers' goods, Albert Schweitzer at simple, primitive Lambaréné sings an unending hymn of praise to the sovereignty of spiritual freedom. Spiritual freedom in his hospital settlement is dramatized as the loftiest liberty known to man.

Spiritual freedom was the foremost concern of many liberators in the past. This was particularly true of the mental monarchs of the eighteenth century. In today's darkness of abundance in the Western world, spiritual freedom has slipped from sight. In solemn words Dr. Schweitzer warns contemporaries, saying, "Spiritual freedom we shall recover only when the majority of individuals become once more spiritually independent and self-reliant and discover their natural and proper relations to those organizations in which their souls have been entangled."

The complete unfettered freedom that Dr. Schweitzer has enjoyed in creating Lambaréné with his own will, hands, heart, and head is a joyous destiny earned and deserved by few. The Doctor counsels prudently, " . . . to obtain freedom . . . in a spiritual sense is open to everyone. To obtain freedom in the outward sense will always be the privilege of the few." In gratitude for his own good fortune he says, "I feel it deeply that I can work as a free man at a time when an oppressive lack of freedom is the lot of so many."

Long ago Albert Schweitzer realized that it is reasonable to resign ourselves thoughtfully to the limitations of liberty and degrees of freedom. There is "relativity" in free will in every age for every individual. He observes, however, "Our dependence on events is not absolute. It is qualified by our spiritual freedom."

All freedoms are mutually interdependent. Any single freedom other than spiritual freedom, if augmented to the exclusion of others, becomes a tyranny. Spiritual freedom is the only just arbiter of all freedoms.

The ecstasy of spiritual freedom seems almost limitless to Dr. Schweitzer. He says, "I am rewarded by a disclosure of the secret of spiritual independence. I become a partaker in an unguessed-at freedom amid the destinies of life. At moments when I should otherwise have thought myself overwhelmed and crushed, I feel myself uplifted in a state of inexpressible joy astounding to myself, in which I am conscious of freedom from the world and I experience therein a clarification of my life views. Resignation is the vestibule through which we pass in entering the palace of ethics. Only he who expresses inner freedom from the external events, in profound surrender to his own will-to-live, is capable of the profound and permanent surrender of himself for the sake of other life."

Dr. Schweitzer finds his liberty by losing it in the stream of liberty, and obtains thereby a blessedness the world cannot give. He works with bliss on freedom's unfinished cathedral. The freedom he knows starts where language ends. There is no fear, for the riddles of the universe cannot harm the free. The free do not know the vacuity of the machine-like mind. Spiritual freedom is the sovereign treasure among human values.

It would be a tragic mistake to think that Dr. Schweitzer discounts the value of material freedom. He only challenges its primacy. He proposes that it be subjugated to spiritual freedom. He says, "The highest possible material freedom for the greatest possible number is a requirement of civilization."

All of the fragments of freedom in human relations should be ruled by reason and never by the caprice of traditions. Dr. Schweitzer affirms, "We must search for a conception of law that is founded on an idea which grows directly and independently out of a world-view. We have to re-establish human rights which cannot be infringed, human rights which guarantee to each person the greatest possible freedom for his personality . . . human rights which protect his existence and his dignity against any alien violence to which he may be subjected."

In his most peremptory role as commander of freedom's forces against anti-freedom, Dr. Schweitzer says: "Civilization presupposes free men . . . Only by free men can civilization be thought out and brought to realization . . . A man's ability to be a pioneer of progress depends on his being a thinker and on his being free."

As we review his life, we see a younger Albert Schweitzer in Europe hunting for freedom in an unfree society. He was imprisoned by unseen bars in the form of organizations, institutions, traditions, dogmas. Good people were unwittingly his wardens. He was endowed with the impulse to be free and capable of purposive actions. He wanted an opportunity for spiritual self-perfection and free and independent activity.

When Albert Schweitzer spoke of his reasons for leaving his enormous opportunities in Europe in favor of Africa, he said, "What I wanted was an absolutely personal and independent activity . . . Although I was resolved to put my services at the disposal of some organization *if* it should be really necessary, I nevertheless never gave up the hope of finding a sphere of activity to which I could devote myself as an *individual* and as wholly *free!*"

In turning the clock back to Albert Schweitzer's youth, we see a boy trying his reason with the most mature minds in his orbit. He became an inconvenience to his own family because he would not conform to discipline concerning etiquette and codes of politeness. He learned to depend on his own reason and his own scholarship. He broke the chain that tried to bind his mind in habitual circles, and dismissed all dogma. It is significant that in paying tribute to his parents one of his dearest memories was the tolerance his mother and father displayed with their children. He says with love and veneration, "They trained us for freedom." He speaks of being as free as a wild rose.

Also in reminiscing about his youth, he recorded this observation: "The conviction that in after life we must struggle to

remain thinking as freely and feeling as deeply as we did in our
youth has accompanied me on my road through life as a faithful adviser."

Young Albert was a renegade at his confirmation, because the
pastor preparing him and the other boys "wanted to make us
understand that in submission to faith all reasoning must be
silenced . . . But I was convinced," Dr. Schweitzer says later,
"and I am so still, that the fundamental principles of Christianity
have to be proved true by reasoning and by no other method . . .
This certainly filled me with joy . . . " Speaking of the pastor,
he said, "The good man never suspected what was stirring in
my mind."

How and when conscience came to Albert we do not know;
but we do know that the little rebel, before he was of school
age, identified goodness with life itself. His freedom and that of
other lives were, in his mind, inseparable, though no one told
him to believe this. After prayers with his mother, and after
she kissed Albert goodnight, he showed a facet of precocity
when he voiced an entreaty to God that he composed himself:
"O Heavenly Father, protect and bless all things that have
breath; guard them from all evil and let them sleep in peace."

Having completed my review of Albert Schweitzer's development in freedom, his interpretation of Jesus, Paul and Goethe
as liberators, his compatibility with my independent theory of
the universe and his life-long association with many forms of
human freedom, I was in a position to reappraise the prophet, his
gospel and his sanctuary in Lambaréné.

Lambaréné in the "wilderness" could now be defined as the
Mecca of liberty for free individuals throughout the world.

Ruling at Lambaréné with the power of love derived from
reason is prophet Schweitzer, the first of the twentieth-century
liberators.

Dr. Schweitzer is a cosmic thinker. He opposes Hegel's vision
of cosmic freedom with his own theory of the universe that is
now on trial in the restless, searching mind of man.

His theory accords and concurs with my own view of cosmic freedom. I am not, however, his apostle. As a contemporary co-educator, co-discoverer, co-worker, co-creator of a universal theory of freedom, I have taken the liberty of calling Dr. Albert Schweitzer the Founder of the Gospel of Freedom and the Prophet of the Gospel of Freedom.

Man is the highest agency of freedom, and liberty is conscious of itself only in reason. Therefore the individual, not the group, individual freedom, not organization, the spirit, not the cathedral, is the highest Good. All the fragments of freedom—freedom of thought, will, conscience, action—are catalytic ideas, as are the concepts of social, political, economic, and academic freedom and freedom of the press.

But the highest freedoms come from mercy, compassion, and love for the liberty of each animate agency carrying forward the liberty of the universe.

When individual freedom is the core ideal of the society of men, the control of the forces that threaten freedom will be no more. The growth of freedom on earth will rival the finest visions of the Kingdom of God.

Albert Schweitzer's Theory of Reverence for Will is the highest, widest spiritual achievement of the human mind, for the essence of will is the essence of freedom in the universe. He discovered and described the importance of the half of the universe ignored by science which is nevertheless real but invisible, certain but immeasurable, perceivable but not palpable, spiritual and suprapersonal but not supernatural, creative but not separate in its divinity from man at his highest. Albert Schweitzer is the catalyst of great goodness in a world in search of a cosmic basis for its love of freedom.

Dr. Schweitzer Plays
Bach for Me

On my last day at Lambaréné, while working at the dental clinic, I received another invitation from the master of ethics, but this message came from Dr. Schweitzer in his role of master of music. He issued a gracious invitation to come to his room after supper when he would play the piano.

I considered my dental appointments and the professional work I had started that I had to finish before my departure the next morning. I regretfully concluded I would not be through until too late for a social call.

I sent a message declining the generous invitation and explaining my predicament. I received a prompt reply saying in effect: "Come whenever you are through. I too will be up very late."

Weary but eager, I arrived at his room after ten o'clock. Dr. Schweitzer peered at me over steel spectacles from his desk where he had been writing and gave me a hearty greeting. Then his mood grew solemn. In silence he changed his bedraggled heavy-duty shoes for lighter footwear designed to facilitate the job of manipulating the pedals for the "organ-piano." *

Dr. Schweitzer played a variety of pieces. Most, as in Gunsbach two years previously, were Bach creations. I enjoyed the experience immensely, but to me the setting was as awesome as the jewel.

---

* As explained earlier, this special zinc-lined instrument is a gift of the Paris Bach Society. It is notable for its special organ pedal attachments that control the bass notes. An oversized dugout canoe conveyed it from the coast to Lambaréné.

As I sat listening to music under circumstances in which my ears would have preferred hearing ideas, my mind wandered back to an incident that occurred in Chicago just before my departure. An effervescent, gifted concert pianist—a constantly touring friend—rushed over my threshold, arms outstretched, and trilled, "Are you really going to visit Dr. Schweitzer in Africa? Put me in your suitcase. He's my ideal. I dedicate concerts to him."

Raising a birdcage to my face, she said, "Dear Dr. Schweitzer would reverence my bird. Presto adores his organ recordings."

Presto is in fact the best traveled talking parakeet in the world. He has chaperoned trips from Carnegie Hall to the Hollywood Bowl.

When the excitement of our reunion settled, I asked with innocent curiosity, "Why should you admire a missionary jungle doctor? He is an expert on the organ, not the piano. Have you read his books on philosophy, civilization, and ethics, or his tome on Indian thought?"

"Certainly not," she pouted. "All that's over my head."

"Have you read his books on Jesus and St. Paul?"

Turning serious, she stunned me by answering, "No, but I really know his immortal writing on Johann Sebastian Bach. Dr. Schweitzer made the world aware of the universal religiousness and architectonic soundness of the master. He discovered the clear, simple musical logic in the preludes and fugues. His book is my Bible on Bach. My interpretation of Bach on the piano is better because of Dr. Schweitzer's musical genius."

Suddenly smiling, she said, "Even Presto says, 'Bach is sounding better.'"

I told Dr. Schweitzer of the incident during one of the short intervals between his pieces. Alas, I myself had only scanned Albert Schweitzer's famous book on Bach to discover his philosophy of music.

As the recital went on, I tried to remember Albert Schweitzer's way of seeing music as an inseparable part of his ethical system.

I remembered Dr. Schweitzer contends that all esthetics, art forms, and particularly music are expressions of the vitality of living ethical will within all of us. What is beautiful is ethical and liberating to the spirit. Beauty symbolizes the upward struggle of cosmic freedom.

A great musician is in one way or another a free thinker possessing a quality of mental plasticity and the power to render surpassing visions and exquisite emotions in the lyric language of rhythmic melodies. The soaring imagination of the hearer becomes a co-reactive element in the ecstatic imagery of fine music.

Later when I returned to my room, I turned to a paragraph I had underscored. It was one in which Albert Schweitzer turned poetic to pay tribute to Bach.

If the text speaks of drifting mists, of boisterous winds, of roaring rivers, of waves that ebb and flow, of leaves falling from the tree, of bells that ring for the dying, of the confident faith which walks with firm steps, of the weak faith that falters insecure, of the proud who will be abased, and the humble who will be exalted, of Satan rising in rebellion, of angels poised on the clouds of heaven, then one sees and hears all this in his music.

When I watched Dr. Schweitzer that evening, I beheld a man of eighty-two with big but still sensitive hands that sutured wounds, mixed mortar and pounded nails. He now labored with aging, work-calloused fingers, rivalled by active feet, to make use of a musical gift worthy of millions to please a single guest.

It was most memorable to feel in this lamplit, cramped cubicle the melodies of the masterworks of European cultures mingling with the elemental "silent" cadence of the jungle. The symphony produced within me a joy which I confess was overwhelming. There was little conversation beyond the amenities.

I thought when the time came to say goodnight I was really saying goodbye, as I knew I was scheduled to leave the following morning before the usual breakfast hour. I lingered awkwardly after my farewell speech of gratitude. I wrestled with temptation, wishing to open a subject with which my mind was still grappling.

Except for the fact that Dr. Schweitzer had given me a flat refusal on the request that he allow American colleges and universities to use his name, my stay had been perfect. But why not cast the dice of chance once more and go for glory?

Thus it was that I urged Dr. Schweitzer to reconsider his refusal to allow his name to be used in connection with Chairs and Distinguished Professorships in American universities. I faced Dr. Schweitzer with the question, "What reason can I give your eager friends, when I return, for your unyielding refusal to lend your name to help our young people in colleges and universities in the United States?"

In answer to my "loaded" question, Dr. Schweitzer said, "Dr. Phillips, I do not believe that Reverence for Life should be stressed more in institutions of learning than in society in general. My system of ethics must not be organized or institutionalized. It should be discovered by individuals."

I leapt at an opening for debate, and posed two more questions through my interpreter. "But, Dr. Schweitzer, is not all life a process of learning? Why not try to present vital ethical issues among young people in the formative years before other institutional provincial prejudices congeal in their minds? Students should have the chance to discover the ethical approach to education on the menu of courses offered."

Dr. Schweitzer's manner stiffened as he said, "I am not convinced that free ethical inquiry and the road to moral awareness can be presented in the busy, over-organized modern vocational institutions that call themselves universities of higher learning."

I struck at that objection with all the persuasive skill I could muster. I said, "Your friends agree. In America, schools turn out great technical experts and specialists by the thousands and condemn them to a life of ethical illiteracy by oversight and neglect of ethics. But we are not pleased with our dereliction. We would fill this dangerous spiritual void if we could. On what grounds do you refrain from at least trying to assist with the use of your name, especially where the need for ethics is so tragically overwhelming?"

He answered, "I do not relish the publicity associated with your idea nor do I feel in any way worthy of the honor your proposition implies."

I felt that his defenses were cracking.

I was exuberant for another reason. This was the first time Dr. Schweitzer had faced an issue with me man to man. I said grandiloquently, "Dr. Schweitzer, publicity about you in our country is already in the hands of fickle and capricious fortune and cannot be worsened by this scholarly association. As to the morsel of honor we would be giving you, it is not proportional to our selfish gains.

"Actually, Dr. Schweitzer, many of us feel in our hearts that we are in fact *not honoring you alone*. We revere at a distance the ideals you have been privileged to coordinate for their own merit. Many of us in truth feel quite frankly *we are honoring what is best in ourselves* by identifying ourselves with your ethical achievements."

Seeing playful smiles through his transparent frown, I followed up my seeming advantage, asserting, "You admit you have stood on the shoulders of earlier pioneers. We ask only that your ethical vision and your methods of scholarship be represented by persons with understanding on a few campuses where the ideals may equitably contend with ideas already being taught by the faithful in other modern ethical systems and believers in more ancient and historic dogmas. There is an honor implied, of course, but we may be striving to strengthen the opportunities

for spiritual growth and perfection of our beloved young
people even more than we strive to honor you as the author
of what may well be the common ethics of the world tomorrow."

Dr. Schweitzer seemed not unpleased to have been shaken
in his stand, but he countered with a new and weaker argument:
"I do not think it is fair for you to ask other ethical scholars to
live in the shadow of my ethical contributions. Surely worthy
scholars will wish to be independent emissaries of their own
thoughts."

This objection was easy to topple. "Dr. Schweitzer, many of
us feel that the stream of ethics belongs to mankind, and where
the stream can be aided on its way to the ocean by the pooling
of ethical resources of one, two or five towering co-contributors,
we feel this should be done, not as a collectivizing effort but as
a parallel labor to implement individualism, providing it is
mutually agreeable. Slavish adherence is not presumed, but
ethical scholarship must be presented."

With a growing sense of success I said, "Anyway, many men
in the field of moral inquiry are only scholars of the ethics
of others. Some are ethical historians. Few of these teachers
of ethics are models of ethics. Precious few today—in fact, almost
none—are original innovators of ethical systems. You are a
scholar, historian, model, and innovator."

I continued: "You yourself have said your ethical convictions will endure only if confirmed by free scholarship everywhere. Only when scholarship turns to ethics can reverence-
for-life stand a chance of becoming the common conclusion of
co-adventurers in free ethics in the world of scholarship in
every land."

The man of wisdom may have been planning to yield before
my exuberant polemics, but as a gracious host the kindly gentleman was charitable enough to say, "Dr. Phillips, I did not
expect these arguments. You win."

When I recovered from these words, I heard him widen his
tribute. He said, "In ethical thinking I have always trusted

people. Of course, most of all I trust my friends who, themselves, are concerned with ethics."

Then came the "green light," with words of counsel and caution. "You may tell those that are interested that whereas I can do nothing personally even to encourage an enterprise that purports to venerate my name, I honor their right to utilize my literature, my methods, my conclusions, and my name to facilitate ethical inquiry. It is my sincere wish that no scholar will stop where I have left off because of a sense of loyalty to me. I will expect students of the future to go further and to get a clearer vision of both freedom and responsibility and deeper insights into moral awareness."

Thanking my host profusely for pleasing me personally and for saving my mission from defeat, I said goodnight still thinking this goodnight would be goodbye.

In high spirits I made the rounds where lamps still burned to say farewell to many of my new-found friends. My last stop was with Dr. Van Stolk. He brewed some tea over a candle, and I lingered discussing my good news and its implications till long after midnight.

Reflections After the
Music Evening

Finally I returned to my room and settled down to savor my eleventh-hour triumph. The relaxation and freedom I had known during the period when I believed my mission had failed, gave way to a new sense of responsibility. I felt I owed an accounting to the insiders expecting a report, but perhaps the narrative should be drafted for public perusal as well.

If Dr. Schweitzer's ethics were ever seriously considered by one or more great universities, I foresaw an educational earthquake on the campus involved if not in education generally. The full scope of Dr. Schweitzer's ethics had emerged in my mind during my stay at Lambaréné. The diary form of my drama could be easily chronicled as it unfolded. But how could I project the educational storm for my readers? The organization of my report became now a real concern.

The purposes of general education, the methods of liberal education, the content and the organization of curriculums would tremble with the rumblings of Dr. Schweitzer's revolution in reverence on any campus bold enough to accept his challenge.

Absolutely honest fidelity to Albert Schweitzer's ethics in the whole field of education might prove too deeply disturbing and too emotionally explosive for the most liberal parents, yet all parents involved must be informed. Dr. Schweitzer's ethics might be too disruptive for the most adventuresome trustees, pioneering administrators, courageous professors, and bold alumni. But a less than candid presentation would be unthinkable.

As I thumbed through Dr. Schweitzer's *Philosophy of Civilization* I noticed that he treated schools as the mirror images of the societies they served. They were cursed with the same evils. The chaos in society and schools was due to the fact that neither human relations nor schooling was based on a commonly accepted theory of the universe. This confused the purposes and the methods as well as the curriculum of the colleges.

Putting aside the collisions that would occur in content of departments and courses, I began to set forth in some detail the precise educational impact Dr. Schweitzer's ethics would have on *educational purposes* and *methods of teaching*. Some of the ghostly dogmas involved in these phases of education emerged as the light of Dr. Schweitzer's ethics penetrated deeper and deeper into the forest of learning.

A professor occupying an Albert Schweitzer Chair or Distinguished Professorship would be a rebel on campus proclaiming utterly new purposes for general education. Teaching under the banner of Dr. Schweitzer's ethics, such a professor would represent a new singular goal for all general education.

Education should be the process by which individuals become civilized. Dr. Schweitzer says repeatedly throughout his writings that "the spiritual perfecting of individuals . . . is the real and final object of civilization." Reverence for Life, which is the phrase he uses to symbolize his ethical system, he says, "is in a position to complete this conception of civilization and to build its foundations on what lies at the core of our being." He insists that "seeking perfection in the spiritual atmosphere of reverence for life: this and nothing else is civilization." The goals of education and civilization should be inseparably one.

When Dr. Schweitzer speaks of life, it must be remembered he refers to an essence that organizes, motivates, and provides volition in the universe and the life process. He explains:

> The essence of civilization consists in this, that Reverence
> for Life which in my will-to-live is struggling for recognition,

does get stronger and stronger in individuals and in mankind. Civilization is then . . . an experience of the will-to-live within us.

The purpose of education should consist of developing one's powers of understanding the will in the universe and human freedom.

The central core of Albert Schweitzer's ethics is reverence for individual freedom. This veneration orders and subordinates all other educational interests. Knowledge of moral awareness grows out of self-knowledge illuminated by the ethical heritage of man. Ethics, Dr. Schweitzer says, comes from thought itself. In one of his oracular statements he says: "That is why I bade our search for a world-view come to a halt in order to fix its attention on the thought of mankind as a whole."

Still speaking of his own view of the universe that is founded on the mysteries of thought, he says, "Reverence for Life is . . . the profoundest achievement of my will-to-live." In an easier idiom, this says: The achievement of my freedom of thought is reverence for the freedom in me and in the universe.

Educators have contrived many high-sounding goals for general education, but the spiritual perfection of the individual by developing keen moral awareness would be the solitary central goal around which all others would revolve.

This single authoritarian definition of the purpose of education is reminiscent of the dark age when the universities trained only spiritual leaders. Paradoxically, Dr. Schweitzer's theory of the universe makes him authoritarian only about the reality, the centrality, and the illimitable growth possibilities for will or freedom.

Ethics, once important in university life and in public affairs, is today neglected, belittled, and ignored. Ethics today is a casualty of realism in history. It is a cruelly slighted foster child in Western education, particularly in America. Knowledge of spiritual values, spiritual self-fulfillment, spiritual self-conscious-

ness, and spiritual freedom and religious responsibility are left
to the wild winds of chance. We have no vision of a civilization
with a common ideal.

Perhaps the most revolutionary idea that would slip into a
school with an Albert Schweitzer Chair is that all serious thought
tends to become religious, and philosophy and religion are now
and always have been inseparable equivalents in human thought,
though unrecognized as such.

Dr. Schweitzer states his master thesis equating philosophy
and religion thus: "Raising a dividing wall between philosophical ethics and religious ethics is based on the mistaken
idea that the former are scientific and the latter non-scientific.
But neither of them is either; they are both alike simply thought."

Dr. Schweitzer places his faith in free thought in saying,
"It is rational thinking alone which is able to pursue the
search for the basic principle with perseverance and hope of
success."

Dr. Schweitzer sees in his mirror of ethics the truth that
the university, aside from vocational training, is still in a real
sense a religious institution. Orthodox religious indoctrination
has been recently dropped from the formal curriculum. The
campus divisional dogmas represent the religious fragments into
which the feudal religion of the Dark Ages was split. The
division of humanities, division of science, and division of
social science are divided because they have come to represent
separate disciplines, separate histories, separate literature, separate
precepts, and separate methods of attaining truth. These divisions contribute to the confusion of the young.

The renaissance in Western ethics started in the fourteenth
century when free men in society and renegades in schools
began to take refuge from ancient schools, teachers, priests,
and holy books in their own free reason. Dr. Schweitzer says,
"Then thought surged like a rough sea against the world-denying
philosophy of the church." Free thinking began to by-pass
the dogma-dominated institutions of learning. Men became

intent on re-examining the affirmative nature of life in the natural world. They replaced articles of faith with canons of reason.

By the eighteenth century rebel thinkers were rounding out the infinitely promising young and vigorous *religion of reason* derived from elemental thinking about human experiences. None of the enlightened free thinkers, however, had yet found a new theory of the universe to undergird the new, growing global gospel of goodness.

For a time the brash, young religion of science, with its strong creed, and men deriving their religion of reason from human thought, worked as companionable rivals, outdoing one another in abolishing the darkness that bathed the feudal mind. Later science broke with reason and strode off in seven-league boots to start the most disastrous schism in the annals of moral warfare.

The religion of science had an unwanted child that it soon disowned. This maverick young science of sociology and social studies became a new religion. A body of truths grew up, derived from studying not man the rational-animal individual but man the social animal. Man's institutions, organizations, and herd behavior patterns came under quasi-scientific scrutiny. Statistical studies brought to social scientists the power of prophecy. This new religion offered salvation through socialization. Social studies presented analytical material that called for social changes. The field became a worthy contender to compete with men of reason dedicated to salvation through the humanities and those dedicated to pure science, who altered society by a flood of inventions.

To free education from lingering ecclesiastical dogma and control, our prudent forefathers instigated a bold but negative law. The first amendment to the Constitution states that "Congress shall make no law respecting an establishment of religion or prohibiting the free exercise thereof."

For a time private schools sprang up to re-wed denominational dogma to the educational processes, making the union almost as firm as feudalism. Concurrently tax-supported state schools timidly divorced religion and ethics from education in order to break quietly free from all specific lingering denominational control. To win out, free forces had to settle for a narrow, negative escape. The motive of the timid was merely to escape from dogmatic denominational fetters, not to affirm positive freedom of inquiry in religious and ethical matters.

Thus freedom *of* religious scholarship in American schools became merely freedom *from* deep and wide religious scholarship. Broad, world-wide inquiry in ethics, morals, and great religions has yet to take its proper place in college curriculums in private or public universities. Dr. Schweitzer insists that in ethical scholarship "we must pass through the whole experience of mankind in its search for the ethical." In Dr. Schweitzer's terms, America's narrow ignorance coupled with her scientific power imperils the world.

In America as elsewhere scholarship ignores the implications of the kinship that man must admit to in relation to subhuman creatures. This kinship becomes the cosmic basis for Dr. Schweitzer's ethical system. Dr. Schweitzer rebukes with hard words those who still cling to institutions built on a denial of evolutionary associations. He says, "The stupidities they are guilty of in trying to maintain the traditional narrow-mindedness . . . border on the incredible."

Spiritual development and ethical learning in the young in America is left to the caprice of casual and arbitrary contingencies. Today a pleasant, intoxicating frenzy of over-specialization and super-vocationalism in universities masks the ethical vacuum at the center of our modern concept of education. In the fair name of democracy, of diversity or tolerance or freedom we paradoxically promote duplicity, moral ignorance and ethical illiteracy.

Dr. Schweitzer raises his voice in protest against the modern mockery of moral wisdom in the whole Western world. In addition to the academic neglect of ethics he tries to focus our shame on the tragic fact that even our private shallow ethical thoughts "are not only kept sacred from criticism but are not a legitimate subject of conversation."

So unreasonable and unsupportable is our triviality in ethics, he says, that "everyone is haunted by a sort of terror lest anything original should be demanded from him . . . Talk does not go beyond generalities or develop into a real exchange of (ethical) ideas." Ethical growth has been arrested and scholarship has atrophied.

The purpose of a course in ethics would be the exchange of ethical ideas. Students should wrestle constantly and openly with these crucial, silent issues. Reason must reign in deep, broad matters. There is a desperate need for a world-view. Dr. Schweitzer is advising young people when he says, "The restoration of our world-view can come only as a result of inexorably truthloving and recklessly courageous thought." Ability to think in breadth and depth is a cardinal prerequisite for ethical inquiry.

In a course given in Dr. Schweitzer's name, the professor would surely attempt to prove that good manners, tolerance, and freedom do not today mean timid silence. The false fear and pretense that juvenile delinquency is a symptom of too much ethical freedom must be shelved in the catalog of mistakes in favor of Dr. Schweitzer's current view that ignorance of good causes is the ruin of confused young rebels. Freedom of religion and academic freedom should mean, as their more daring eighteenth-century authors intended, freedom *for* ethical inquiry without external intimidating pressures.

Dr. Schweitzer affirms: "To be truly rational is to become ethical . . . If free thought is to set out on its journey unhampered, it must be prepared for anything, even for arrival at intellectual agnosticism."

Dr. Schweitzer is opposed to the foolish folly that condemns doubters to a negative life of sleepwalking. Doubting is the beginning of wisdom, not the end. Freedom of inquiry, including agnosticism, should be the free man's approach to all the religious convictions of secular religions in the university, as well as the ecclesiastical prescription of virtue offered by various off-campus denominations.

In the light of our background of neglect of ethics in America and in the light of the way we imperil the world by our power guided only by our ethically immature leaders, it should be our ultimate purpose to train ethically mature citizens. In an enlightened course in ethics seedling ideas should have rich, warm, friendly soil in which to flourish, wide opportunities for cross-fertilization, and ample room to flower.

In the five centuries since feudal universities taught only ethics, scholars in the humanities, science, and social sciences have been busy dividing and subdividing external knowledge of the universe, life, and history. The revolt in Albert Schweitzer's ideas would carry the reform full cycle back to unity.

Today the foremost master of ethical enlightenment has trained his big guns of reason on Western society and Western education. The artillery is poised to cannonade the deadly dogmas in society that separate denominations and the mutually repellent fictions that keep campus religions apart. Ingrown religious rituals and divisive practices of secular religions are the same in all of the ivy-covered halls of higher learning.

Dr. Schweitzer's battle cry carries his higher concept of freedom of thought and inquiry to the ranks who form public opinion. He is pained and challenged by the false purposes of modern education. He is relentlessly challenged by the tragic soul sickness he seeks to cure. He is making a diagnosis when he says, "Our age is poorer in deep thinkers than perhaps any preceding one." His objective is to make Westerners think fundamentally about universal issues.

In my opinion, Dr. Schweitzer's single educational purpose and sole moral mission is aimed at transforming society. In schools his dicta would be designed to trigger a new movement of free thought leading toward a common concept of civilization and a single ethical ideal of a civilized man. His ethical symbol poses the question: can the gospel of cosmic freedom become the theory of the universe that will unite all men into a spirit of peace and reverence for all life?

The teaching methods employed in an ethics course under the Schweitzer spirit should be those demanded by the unified objective of spiritual self-perfection, self-realization, and self-devotion in the service of others.

At first glance it becomes clear that the course should never be listed among any of the three formal divisions of the university— humanities, science, or social science—nor in any of the thirty-two fields of concentration into which the college curriculum dealing with general education in our best colleges is hopelessly subdivided.

According to Dr. Schweitzer's view, all ethical knowledge is indivisibly one. Ethics crosses the frontiers of all fields of knowledge and forms the encircling cord that unites them and simplifies them.

The class might be listed among the "honors" courses, not because it should be exclusive but because it fits no other category in the curriculum. This course should never be degraded into a unit of credit that is in a sequence leading to a ritualistic academic degree.

In Dr. Schweitzer's value system, degrees today record time and servitude and divert curiosity and initiative. They reward docile attendance, conformity and over-concentration in fenced-in areas of specialization, limited by textbooks and syllabuses. Perhaps degrees are vocational milestones in a society that puts a supreme premium on economic success, but they are absolutely empty of ethical content.

Ethics is nothing if it is not of supreme importance in all
other fields of knowledge and central to all forms of learning.
If Dr. Schweitzer is right in maintaining that civilization is
ultimately ethical, then only that minute fraction of schooling
that is stripped of all special skills and vocationalism is really
educational because it alone is ethical. Only ethical reflection
is a self-liberating experience for students.

In a sentence loaded with meaning Dr. Schweitzer says, "The
only teacher is the man who thinks ethically and struggles for
ethics."

At any rate, the students in the course in ethics should know
at the beginning that attendance is voluntary. They should not
be tormented by examinations or grades. There must be no
counterfeit awards dangling before each student to stir him
into flurries of competitive, insincere initiative. "Spiritual happiness," Dr. Schweitzer says, "is sufficient unto itself."

Believing that learning in ethics will be the result of reasoning
and self-teaching, the professor should conduct every class
session as a cooperative round-table conference. Free and independent preparation and open discussion must be the teaching
method. The class should be a miniature democracy in action,
purged of all pedantic paternalism. Students will learn free
citizenship by *living it* in Albert Schweitzer's classes in ethics.

In ethics, students should not accept or regurgitate for approval a single idea that does not commend itself to their reason.
By foregoing examinations, grading, and credit, professors re-
linquish every vestige of academic authority over the minds of
the young. Students must cultivate their own spiritual nature
through the use of their own freedom and reason.

In stirring words Dr. Schweitzer asserts, "Every being who
calls himself a man is meant to develop into a real personality
within a reflective theory of the universe which he has created
for himself."

Besides the external revolution that Dr. Schweitzer's ethics
would tend to incite in the formal realm of academic purposes

and methods, I pondered even more earnestly about the internal tempests that would occur in the minds of senior students. The course would perforce be a comprehensive review of the curricular content they had consumed.

I was convinced that for young people spiritual freedom offers its own ecstatic reward. Real freedom starts from sublime inwardness, and its ultimate resources appear limitless. Mature freedom seeks as self-fulfillment avenues of service and does so with prudence, patience, and joyous independence.

In this new view juvenile crime is not caused by too much freedom. Delinquency is rather the result of an anarchy of a bewildered spirit loosed into an ethical vacuum. Tragic delinquents are indeed rebels but invariably without a cause. In any event some human wreckage and wastage of youth could be avoided.

I decided as an exercise in thinking to create for myself a hypothetical classroom scene in a wholly invented university setting. This class in ethics I would conjure up would be presided over by a fictional professor occupying a phantom Albert Schweitzer Chair. Well-dreamed dreams are the building blocks of ethical truths.

By employing the conjectural class, supported and kept earthbound by my library of Albert Schweitzer books, I could engineer on paper in the form of a "dialogue" or "symposium" the sample collisions between campus religions that would come to light more methodically and less painfully in such a course in real life. In a dramatic test-tube chapter we could project in fancied violent form the slower impact Dr. Schweitzer's views would have on college students.

I am confident that young people today are the one group potentially capable of coping with Dr. Schweitzer's challenge. Whether adults would be jolted from their routine is problematic. In any event, once the report was in writing, the dramatic challenge to students could be assessed and evaluated by all interested individuals.

Parents, faculty, trustees, and alumni could visualize the proposal from the "dialogue." If my one-act drama were a reasonable, fair presentation, key people could endorse or reject the whole idea of Albert Schweitzer Chairs or Distinguished Professorships easily.

To complete the imaginary and dramatic backdrop for my academic exercise in thinking and reporting, I supposed myself to be an unseen witness and recorder of the Albert Schweitzer college class in action. I supposed that the incumbent for the Schweitzer Chair would be very familiar with Dr. Schweitzer's philosophy of education and civilization. I assumed that under the blessings of academic freedom this professor would be free to speak and quote from Dr. Schweitzer's literature, whether or not specific precepts pleased parents, teachers, administrators, or trustees. Young people, admonished to reason for themselves, could be the fairest judges of the ultimate values. A few apt students might be lucky enough to receive a vision of the unlimited promise of spiritual fulfillment and self-mastery from the "symposium."

Having two boys in high school, soon to enter college, I decided to gear my thinking to their spiritual welfare. Some day they might be candidates for such a course in ethics, even readers of "Dad's" original report. One day my own boys might be victims or beneficiaries of a class such as I was now imagining. By identifying the spiritual well-being of my own boys with the welfare of all students in my imaginary class, I might prepare the script for the little drama with meticulous concern completely in keeping with my grave responsibility. The spiritual well-being of all young people would necessarily be the primary concern of any professor occupying a Schweitzer Chair.

As my plan matured, I groped for the method and content of a classroom discussion that would suggest with fidelity what a Distinguished Professor occupying a Schweitzer Chair might in justice say to students about their own traditional ethics and

Albert Schweitzer's ethics. I decided the method should be an open class discussion. But what of the content?

As I pursued the question of content, it became increasingly clear that the primary purpose of this one-act "dialogue" would be to portray in an admittedly unreal and over-concentrated form the very real cleavages between contending value-systems in the modern American college. All conventional campus clashes in values must be considered in a class in ethics.

I decided that in fairness to Dr. Schweitzer's thinking a bold but truthful policy must be followed. The various equations of values to which students cling must be depicted as "campus religions," even if some turned out to be "secular" campus religions. This liberty could be taken with a firm feeling of realism because in Dr. Schweitzer's ethical-idea structure he says with intended comfort even to the agnostics and supposedly irreligious that "all serious thought necessarily becomes religious."

My plan for the "playlet" slowly crystallized into a concentrated progression of ideas. Matters of ethical content I found could remain in sharp focus from the beginning to the end of the "playlet."

The unresolved self-perpetuating, mutually challenging, conventional campus religions could move across the stage in a procession as a pageant of colorful living fossils. All modern campus religions in fact are fragments of eighteenth-century history, when the monolithic feudal view of the universe was finally splintered into slivers that still survive with tenacious vitality. Candor would compel a professor to show that modern campus religions rest on fragmentary and diverse views of the universe. Currently campus ethics have no visible means of support from the cosmos. Not one of these campus religions harmonizes the elements of modern self-knowledge with external knowledge of human nature, science, or social studies.

The schisms and the subdivisions of the competing campus religions appear to be irrational when analyzed by the unifying and barrier-breaking religion of reason expounded by Dr. Schweitzer.

Learning the massive details of dogma in one of the special fields comprises the greatest wastage and the cruellest form of monotonous irrelevancy facing modern students fettered to campus conformity. Schools demand that students spend their time devouring and digesting mountains of rubbish, which displaces their opportunities in formative years to learn to understand themselves and the core of ethics. Enormous ergs of student energy are used up in the meaningless exercises crammed by compulsion into the programs of indoctrination in valueless disciplines that effectively displace ethical education and the wisdom of self-perfection.

In identifying the various campus "disciplines" as campus religions, it becomes possible and most realistic to compare the departmental disciplines with Dr. Schweitzer's whole ethics, which he classifies as his own serious thought system that long ago became religious.

Dr. Schweitzer thinks of his ethical system of Reverence for Life as a master religion to integrate all religions. In prophetic terms Dr. Schweitzer tells us, "This ethic, profound, universal, has the significance of a religion. It *is* religion."

I decided it would be an act of fidelity to let the thread of anti-Communism run through all of the campus religions found in American colleges. Thus in my imaginary class all students who would speak out in the first session would be hostile but helpless in answering the challenge of modern Communism. A cacophony of contradiction and confusion involving our own brand of collectivism would beat against the coordinated global religion of collectivism à la Marx in a vain, fearful, and futile way. The supreme illusion that victory by force would be condoned by most was presumed. These attitudes prevail. They are condemned as foolish by Dr. Schweitzer. The cure for the religion of Red collectivism is a more rational new religion of freedom and individualism.

The culmination of the "symposium" attempts to show the collision of the monolithic world religion of Communism with the coordinated global religion of Reverence for Life. Thus Reverence for Life emerges as it is conceived by its author as a unifying principle for integrating all Western religions into a perfectly forged *moral weapon* to fight *non-violently* the false collectivism of Red tyranny.

In his fight with institutions, Dr. Schweitzer never forgets the precious qualities of youth. I decided it would be most fitting to let the "dialogue" end with a tribute to the eternal relations of truthfulness and youthfulness and freedom, which is so characteristic of Dr. Schweitzer's religion of Reverence for Life.

Of one thing I am certain. Every reader must be encouraged to feel that all conflicts in the mythical class are occurring in an atmosphere of love. The wise professor tries to listen patiently to the chaotic diversity of ethical ideas in students' minds. He strives to sift the extraneous from the elemental. As an ethical leader he aids the youngsters in their personal search for a single moral principle and a community of ethical ideals firmly planted on resolute reason. All classmates, it is hoped, would become kindred spirits of the search. They would be encouraged to express their ethics individually while reappraising Dr. Schweitzer's ethics. The assumption is that during the course each student would search for ethics of his very own. The class in ethics would be a place where the youthful will and freedom of each student could grow.

I then wrote the following chapter called "Campus Religions."

Campus Religions

A Dialogue

Cast: Professor Revere and six bright students representing different views in the divisions of the humanities, science, and social science.

Scene: Imaginary first session in senior class in ethics presided over by a professor occupying an Albert Schweitzer chair.

PROF. REVERE: Good morning. We might do well to open the first hour in this course by getting acquainted with one another. Perhaps we can accomplish this by shedding our mantles of shyness.

We must discard all truth-concealing manners and drop the masks with which we deceive one another. Stripped of disguises, with our shirt-sleeves rolled up to work on moral issues, we shall see that much which purports to be etiquette is a hindrance to the pursuit of ethics.

While we are striving to throw off our shells, let us try to resurrect the abandoned, starved, and bloodless body of *ethics* from the graveyard of disuse.

My real purpose in this course could be likened to the function of a midwife. I shall try first to induce your ethical labor pains and then aid you as you yourself give birth to your own ethical ideas.

Our common purpose will be to reexamine the past significance of ethics in relation to our modern difficulties in identifying goodness and evil. At the outset this prospect will sound forbidding and dull to you. Admittedly ethical knowledge will

never be a big money-maker for you. Nor will this education
be a key to social success or political power. Ethical values are,
however, unfluctuating sound coin in the circulation of spiritual
currency. Our vigorous approach to ethics may revive local
interest in the ABC's of the language of ethics.

Ethics, taught with genuine candor in the atmosphere of
absolute freedom, stripped bare of all taboos, can be the most
explosive and exciting subject on campus. I believe you will
discover that our somewhat painful strife in class today will
soon make outside reading and future discussions more meaningful and far more interesting.

In this introductory session I would like two students from
each major division—humanities, science, and social science—
to give us as a starting point, their own definition of ethics.
I would like each speaker to tell us whether ethics is related to a
specific reasonable theory of the universe. Is the concept of
free will a myth or a reality? Is freedom related or unrelated
to a theory of the universe?

I have one more special request because this is our first
meeting together. When you speak out for the first time, please
identify yourself. Give the division in which you are majoring,
the department in which you are specializing, the advanced
scholarship you may contemplate, the career plans you have
selected, and your church preference.

After identifying yourself, tell in a word why you have
elected to sit in on this course in ethics.

Let us hear from a lady first.

MARY CHRISTENSEN: My name is Mary Christensen. I am
a student in the department of Humanities. I have concentrated
for my major sequence on courses in Western culture. I am
preparing to enter the divinity school to equip myself for missionary work in Africa. My deepest motivation is evangelical
work, but I will do everything possible to raise the living
standards of the natives and improve their understanding of
national independence and the democratic obligations of self-

government. It is my firm conviction that godless Communism is offering a unique threat to the spread of the Christian gospel and democracy.

I hope to serve in an American mission school supported by my Lutheran Church.

From the very little I know of Dr. Schweitzer's scholarship in New Testament theology, I fear I will disagree with his ecclesiastical ideas and evangelistic goals. I do know, however, that I admire him as a model of morality and Christian charity. I am taking this course to further my understanding of his motivations and missionary service.

I think ethics are neglected today because they have become so controversial. In my judgment, it is clear that ethics are earthly codes of action condoned by an established religion. Ethics are that part of religious study that focuses attention on the spiritual basis of moral behavior. Christian ethics are clear and absolute.

Christianity is not a theory of the universe. It is the truth about the universe. To believers, true ethics are Christian ethics derived by faith. Truth about the universe is revealed and recorded as the Word of God in the Holy Bible. Christian ethics, unlike Jewish ethics, are mainly derived from the sayings and example of Jesus, who was the Son of God.

PROF. REVERE: Miss Christensen, would you tell your own theory of the universe and its relation to your freedom?

MISS CHRISTENSEN: It is my honest belief—really my unshakable faith—that God, an all-wise and benevolent Creator, has produced the universe and our earth. I am convinced there is no other reasonable explanation for the marvels of the heavens, the beauties of nature, the miracles of living, and the mysteries of human love. Man is the special creation of Almighty God. Unlike beasts, man is given an indestructible soul.

In His infinite wisdom God gave man the right to use his free will to choose good or evil. In his heart and soul man knows God's commandments in the form of moral law. Ethics were revealed to man as the gospel of love by Jesus Christ, the Son of God. Using free will to obey God's moral laws and laws of love is man's highest purpose. Since his fall and original sin, however, man has been a spiritually blind, morally weak creature cursed with carnal appetites. Jesus taught ethics and died to atone for sins, to prepare mankind for brotherhood on earth and eternal salvation after death.

PROF. REVERE: Miss Christensen, your eloquent statement was most concise and coherent.

Now may I with candor but without offense mark for you the areas in which you would find criticisms of your views of ethics in Dr. Schweitzer's literature, and then I will note three specific criticisms.

In the first place, he would tell you that these ideas you express, though once deduced from reason, are not your own by your reason. Nor do they belong to Jesus or his reason. These values you voice so earnestly began to evolve after the fourteenth century and became stabilized as a reasonable creed during the eighteenth century. Only the notions of God, virtue, sin and immortality date back to the first century.

In the age of enlightenment, the eighteenth century, men sanctified their non-Christian beliefs deduced by reason by reading them into our Christian history. You are a victim of the religion of reason which these eighteenth-century thinkers concocted from observing human experience. You will find this view you call your view best expressed by the country minister in Rousseau's *Emile*. Unfortunately you will find none of these ideas in the Gospel stories of Jesus.

Your external view of the universe, your optimistic vision of progress, your group view of goodness, your notions of material standards, your ideas of free nations and good governments, your view of rights and freedom are of recent history, not ancient and Biblical.

Your conflict with Marxian irreligion is a nineteenth-century contention. You may recall that a measure of Communism was condoned by the Bible.

Let us look for the moment at the notions involved in your presumptions of denominational truth—your story of truth about the universe and the principle of establishing truth by faith.

Denominationalism was not called for by Jesus. Actually Christianity, as denominationalism testifies, has changed character and emphasis many times. Fractionalized and warped, but unconcerned with modern reasoning, Christianity has lost its centrality in community life and all moral authority so completely that it is today only a peripheral Sunday affair wholly divorced from national and global moral decisions. Denominationalism was forced out of public universities and now yields to secular campus religions in schools once dominated by denominations.

That the universe is an optimistic, on-going place of marvels, miracles, mysteries, and love, is not Biblical and is not scientific. It is a reasoned interim view founded in a period of transition. It is clear to free reason that the universe, outside of man's ethical mercies, is infinitely cruel, sordid, amoral, unethical, and murderously devoid of love.

Christianity as it was conceived in the eighteenth century by the earliest rationalists no longer explains the nature of the universe in learned circles. Dr. Schweitzer tells us:

> Christianity has had to give up one piece after another of what it still imagined it possessed in the way of explanations of the universe.

Your theological school will continue the deception about the universe, life, and goodness started by parents, preachers, and teachers and professors who betrayed you by failing to show you how to think for yourself. Dr. Schweitzer says:

> Obstructive erudition is the special prerogative of theology. Truly marvelous scholarship often serves only to blind the eyes

to elemental truths and to cause the artificial to be preferred to the natural.

For example, Miss Christensen, if you would use your reason freely, you could look at the universe and see for yourself that it was not made for man, no matter who has said so in the past. Dr. Schweitzer says:

> We are entirely ignorant of what significance we have for the earth. How much less then may we presume to try to attribute to the infinite universe a meaning which has us for its object or which can be explained in terms of our existence.

When Albert Schweitzer was about to be confirmed in the Lutheran Church, the pastor preparing him tried to regiment his thought by pleading the cause of pure faith. Dr. Schweitzer recounts the episode, saying:

> He wanted to make us understand that in submission to faith all reasoning must be silenced. But I was convinced—and am so still—that the fundamental principles of Christianity have to be proved true by reasoning and by no other method . . . Dogmatic religion . . . has no relation with thinking but emphasizes the differences between thinking and believing.

A moral question raises its head. You and Dr. Schweitzer differ. If he is right, is it moral for you to propagate the ideas born in the eighteenth century and label them as your ideas, Lutheran doctrine, or the gospel of Jesus?

Would you not then be following Jesus and the other authors of your views more perfectly if you thought out your own ethics freely and reasonably instead of accepting by faith traditional and denominational views, particularly if they are contrary to the stated views ascribed to the founder of your faith? Dr. Schweitzer says, "Personal reflection about final and elemental things is the one and only reliable way of measuring values."

MISS CHRISTENSEN: From what you say, Dr. Schweitzer's views sound atheistic, Marxian, and un-American to me.

PROF. REVERE: We will not dodge this issue, but let's table the inquiry for a few moments until we have heard from some others. May we next hear from a gentleman in the field of humanities?

BOB BLACK: My name is Bob Black, a Negro as you see. For three years I have also concentrated in the humanities. My major field of study is Western history in general, and I am specializing in early American history in particular. Eventually after my hitch with the armed forces I intend to obtain a master's degree in the school of education in order to teach American history or civics in some high school or Negro college near my home in Alabama. I elected to take this course because Dr. Schweitzer is for me a model of human justice in race relations.

As an historian, I have to disagree with Miss Christensen about the nature of ethics. I favor Dr. Schweitzer's view on the folly of denominational differences. I agree that the universe does not reflect the love, goodness, and intelligence of a personal God. Nor can I accept the supremacy of faith over reason. I think of myself as a liberal modern Christian and a humanitarian. At the moment I am unchurched. I do believe in God, but not as a father image. God may be a Cosmic Parent of the universe or some Intelligence that acted only as a First Cause. The laws of this Creative Cosmic Force may determine the laws of existence. I believe in the democratic teachings of Jesus but not in his divinity.

I believe that when the First Cause, Moving Force, or Omnipotent Power made the physical laws and the universe, freedom was beamed to man through nature. Man is a free agent. Man's liberty results from his nature, and the right to liberty is inseparable from man and equal among all men. Human laws and governments are derived from consent of the governed, which preserves the only innate right, the birthright of freedom.

At any rate, rights are natural and freedom is, as Jefferson observed, a self-evident truth. I believe that nations of men are in part free to work out their own destinies. Theoretically cultural and social forces weld us, a free people, into a one-class free society.

Our national ethic is unrelated to a theory of the universe. It is relative and changes constantly. National ethics grow out of the history of moral events, spiritual episodes, reasonable ideas, rational usages, and common customs concerned with good and evil found in all the nations and all the religions of the world. Though I am a member of a minority race often abused, I feel deep loyalty to the country that on paper at least guarantees my rights, my freedom, and my equality. I accept many grievances with forgiveness.

It will be a pleasure for me to teach American history. I will consider it a privilege to serve my country in the armed forces, and if need be lay down my life for our sacred heritage. I will have no hesitation in taking the teacher's loyalty oath and teaching young girls and boys to pledge their allegiance to the Stars and Stripes. This is my faith.

PROF. REVERE: Mr. Black, like Miss Christensen, you state your beliefs with convincing passion. According to Dr. Schweitzer's ethical measure, your views originate from the same period, the same world view, and the same methods of thought as hers. The views you call your own are splinters of feudalism formed by the same religion of reason that Miss Christensen draws upon. You follow the cautiously reasoned "academic-philosophic" fragment, while hers involves a reasoned "fantastic system of metaphysics." Both of you follow a well-organized group pattern of thinking that represented new creative thought in the eighteenth century. Her theory of the universe is shaky, but yours too is an unsupportable compromise.

Dr. Schweitzer says that "true ethics are world-wide," and the eighteenth-century founders of your faith made a clean sweep of nationalism. Dr. Schweitzer says, "Above and beyond

individual nations the men [of that period] pointed to mankind
as the goal toward which all ideals must be directed." Actually
patriotism is the last refuge of the ethically lost, the symptom
of social sickness and ethical retrogression. Modern nationalism
is treason to the truth revealed by the real chain of ethical
events that gave rise to the very values you have espoused. Dr.
Schweitzer laments:

> The cult of patriotism is to be considered as barbarism . . .
> The majority have offered up their personal morality on the
> altar of their country.

Nationalism multilates the fair face of freedom and shows
the ethical poverty of those who must without credit or fidelity
borrow the creative ethical achievements of others. Dr. Schweitzer says,

> The proclamation of the Rights of Man by the States of
> North America and the French Revolution do no more than
> give recognition and sanction to what in the convictions of
> the time had already been won.

The original scattered thinkers who founded the religion of
human reason thought they deduced their nature-philosophy
from human nature and human experience. They presumed an
inviolable measure of freedom from the external history of all
humanity and all human reason. Nature and nature's God and
self-evident truth are sources you give, as they did. The ante-
cedent creators of your dogma—Locke, Rousseau, Kant, and
others—did not manage to reach a new theory of the universe.
For this reason your views are grounded on shifting sands.

You, Mr. Black, have followed others who have twisted the
religion of Jesus and the religion of reason into a religion of
nationalism under a God grown very vague. Dr. Schweitzer
pulls off the veil of propaganda and says,

> Under the very eyes of our historical learning there springs
> up a manufactured history for popular use in which ideas are

unreservedly approved and upheld and our school history books become regular culture beds of historical lies . . . The fascination exercised upon us by earlier events is elevated to a religion . . . We must study the history of civilization otherwise than as our predecessors did or we shall be finally lost.

Mr. Black, liberty has no land. But more than this, its illumination must be discovered again and again everywhere. Dr. Schweitzer says, "Permanently valuable ideas are born again and again in thought . . . what is truly ethical is rational."

Do you not think you owe it to yourself, and to others you might otherwise betray by ethical ignorance, to test your canons of faith by your reason? Don't stop with national heroes. Follow the free creative forebears including Jesus and the eighteenth-century men who were the creative heroes of reasoned ethics.

BOB BLACK: I am afraid that I too, like Miss Christensen, suspect that Dr. Schweitzer is a deviationist, too odd for me. He is probably an agnostic one-worlder. Globalists are pink in my book. He is a really weird radical idealist.

PROF. REVERE: I would still like to postpone this Red issue until we have heard two students from the division of natural and biological sciences and two from the division of social sciences.

Now may we hear from someone in either of these divisions?

NAT STEELE: I am Nat Steele. Early in high school I was persuaded to limit my interests to science. When I entered college I chose the science division in my freshman year. I concentrated in the natural sciences, which includes electives in physical chemistry, electronics, and mathematics. I am majoring exclusively in the field of physics. Nuclear physics is my special goal. I have never regretted pursuing science. Actually it would help today if one could start a career of science in the cradle. After my stint with the military service I hope to find a niche in nuclear research in a university or in industry.

As to the discussion at hand, quite naturally I think Miss Christensen and Mr. Black are reading religious dogma into

the universe and history. With their answers they would flunk
out of physics or astronomy fast. Studies of time, space, and
motion would not support the view of the humanities. There
is not a shred of evidence that the Bible fantasy of Creation
is scientifically true. Likewise I know of no evidence corrobo-
rating the notion of a cosmic beginning, a First Cause, or a
Parent of us all. The cosmic history I know does not show
that freedom or human rights are floating about the firmament
or in geological jungles, for that matter.

Creative forces do not exist. The universe is slowly running
down, according to demonstrable thermodynamic laws. A sense
of freedom must be a bizarre chemical effect, a mischievous
trick of the molecules of the mind. We see some evidence for
indeterminacy and randomness, but they have no connection
with human freedom in a philosophical sense. It is primitive
and infantile to say that freedom comes from God or a Cosmic
Parent. It is not even a good allegory or a sound metaphor.
The cosmic cinder on which we live, by laws written on the
tablets of cause and effect, is doomed.

I am a confessed agnostic. I agree with whoever said, "There
is more faith in honest doubt, believe me, than in half the
creeds." Like many consecrated scholars before me in science,
I am dedicated to Truth. If there is any ultimate Truth, it is
not that which is found in the Holy Bible but rather in the
growing scientific Bible of universal facts. Truths are objectively and dispassionately discovered by observation and experimentation, not by faith or revelation, reason, or pure
speculation.

I admit and freely confess openly that I am guilty of one
paradox. Though I know that the freedom I feel is an illusion,
I detest restraints on me and on research, and all factors that
limit my liberty in free inquiry. Because I detest external
despotic discipline and regimentation, I will gladly serve our
country in making nuclear weapons to deter, or if necessary
destroy, the epidemic slavery of Communism that is sweeping

around the world. Long ago I decided you cannot tolerate people who resolve not to tolerate you. Right favors the forces with the best weapons.

I am in this course for three reasons. I heard that Dr. Schweitzer contests the importance of science. It is said that he thinks he has a theory of the universe of his own. Finally, to be utterly frank, I am suspicious of Dr. Schweitzer. I want to know why he was unjust and scientifically dishonest in his report to the world on fallout radiation. After reading Dr. Schweitzer's intrusion into the realm of physics in his statement on banning hydrogen bombs, I decided that he is either a Communist, a Communist sympathizer, or a soft liberal duped by Red propaganda.

PROF. REVERE: Mr. Steele, you are mixing moral language with scientific terminology. How do you derive your moral judgments? What is a just or an unjust act? What is wise and prudent, or unwise and foolish? Because bombs do not explode spontaneously, bomb banning must be a moral issue only. Fallout is a moral and scientific question. What limits Dr. Schweitzer's right to speak on any subject?

You find the universe absolutely amoral. Yet you are a unit of the universe. As such, are you absolutely amoral? Do you suppose the authoritarian dogma of the religion of science has blinded you, just as orthodox religious dogma produced faulty vision in Miss Christensen and Mr. Black? You deny that freedom exists because you find no evidence in matter. Could your certainty be a faulty article of scientific faith resulting from observing part truths? What relative value should world-wide public opinion place on your ethical judgments in comparison with Dr. Schweitzer's views on freedom, goodness, rights, justice, wisdom, prudence, and bomb banning? Speaking historically, do you know how closely your ethical system approaches the doctrine of Karl Marx?

NAT STEELE: I don't know about Marxian dialectics or the history of ideas. But in my field there are attitudes which clearly make individuals poor security risks. I will not even discuss Marx or his Red descendants, particularly since the rape of Hungary and the murder of the enslaved freedom fighters.

For the most part it seems good enough as virtue and most rewarding to me personally to follow my natural curiosity in the laboratory and to labor to push back the darkness of the unknown by understanding the physical universe.

PROF. REVERE: Mr. Steele, you too state your case forcefully and with the fervor of an evangelist. But should you believe your reason about external physical matters and doubt the insights of your reason concerning your own freedom? The core of your consciousness, your awareness of reason, which permits you to understand and worship factual truth, must logically be acknowledged as prior and higher truth. Dr. Schweitzer says:

> If there is a double truth, there is no truth. Let us rejoice in the truth wherever we find its lamp burning . . . It suffices to know that the whole world of the senses is a manifestation of forces, that is to say of mysteriously manifold will-to-live . . .

If freedom is a universal hallucination, then all consciousness of external facts is likewise illusion. What you called a paradox may be the dualistic nature of reality.

The sect of physical scientists more than any other religious group on campus ignores the universe within themselves. You are composed of inert chemicals, but you really act by "internal causation." You are not built like a watch or a cosmotron. Your will, your volition, your motivation, your creativity, your reason and freedom are finer, firmer realities than cosmic rays or positive electrons. Dr. Schweitzer says,

> In science man observes and describes the course of nature . . . In practical matters he uses what he has grasped of it [nature] outside his own person. But in his moral and artistic activities he uses knowledge and obeys impulses, perceptions, and laws which originate in himself.

At the hands of physical scientists and their brother engineers we have known a life more abundant than was ever prophesied, but we also know a more homicidal peril because the scientific tyranny of specialization tends to dehumanize men and makes experts neglect ethical realities. Dr. Schweitzer puts it this way:

> In all professions, most clearly perhaps in the pursuit of science, we can recognize the spiritual danger with which specialization threatens not only individuals, but the spiritual life of the community. It is already noticeable, too, that education is carried on now by teachers who have not a wide enough outlook to make their scholars understand the interconnection of the individual sciences, and to be able to give them a mental horizon as wide as it should be.

On the hydrogen bomb experimentation Dr. Schweitzer's moral message is simple:

> We are forced to regard every increase in the existing danger through further atom bomb explosions as a catastrophe for the human race, a catastrophe that must be prevented.

Is there someone else who would speak for science?

NATHAN GOLDE: I am Nathan Golde. I too am in the department of science. However, I am majoring in a biological sequence as a pre-medical student. I am Jewish by birth but unorthodox in my faith.

I admire Dr. Schweitzer as a humanitarian, and I agree with his humane view against bombs. I suppose that fact combined with his de-emphasis of race prejudice is why I am here. Of course, I am interested in him as a doctor of medicine.

I had never thought of science as a religion, but like Mr. Steele I will confess to a fervent sense of service and devotion that is a parallel psychic phenomenon if not an exact equivalent to spiritual experiences known in orthodox religious circles. In a usual sense I am an agnostic, but I believe that research in biology and medical sciences is a supra-personal calling as high as the saving of souls. Healing for me is a sacred mission.

Perhaps because millions of my ancestors have perished violently by Christian hands, and because free thinkers and early scientists were burned at the stake by Christian Inquisitors, I doubt that there is a relation between religion and ethical behavior or even history and ethical conduct. Ethics are probably a result, not a cause. Ethics may reflect basic biological drives.

I disagree with my colleague Nat Steele about ethics being an illusion, about the universe running down, and about physical determinism. Human drives, appetites, and motivations are in a sense devoid of freedom, but they are traceable to animal instincts or built-in reflexes.

Sex drives, parental instincts, aggressiveness, herd impulses, and inherited urges have had survival values to species in evolution. Our unlearned drives must be coordinated by learned reflexes if we as social anthropoids expect to act for the common good of our species.

The extreme social behavior that we witness in the anthill or beehive shows that cooperation and group behavior for the good of the species tends to be rooted in all species. The good of my kind is the basis of my personal ethics.

As for freedom, I cannot see that the infinitely complex universe within me, ruthlessly ruled by biological satisfaction and patterns of pains and pleasures, is really endowed with free will in a philosophical sense. We get our physical anatomies, physiologies, and our behavior from the evolutionary and historical past that stretches backwards in time timelessly.

I do not yet know a biological explanation for the learning process or reason or freedom. I live as if limited ranges of personal freedom were my lot; but I don't know how to decide whether freedom exists, how much we have, or how it came into the universe and into our custody.

PROF. REVERE: Mr. Golde, Darwin and Spencer would be proud of your presentation of their master conclusions. They originated the fiction of the importance of the communal life of cells, family instincts, social impulses, pack patterns, and herd mentality. They were the first to presume a biological background for altruistic human drives for social welfare. Co-operation for group survival and group good emerged as a concept. Presumably group discipline humanizes naked egotism. Eighteenth-century thinkers believed group good could result from coordinated individual altruism. The socio-biological ethics of socialism resulted from this thinking in the nineteenth century.

The biological sect of the religion of science shifted the emphasis from individual ethics to social ethics, from individual dreams of self-perfection of individuals to the community compulsiveness to perfect the social order. Individual creativity gave way to community adaptation, social adjustment, security, and survival.

Significant as was his message of evolution, Darwin is remembered by Dr. Schweitzer primarily because of the gentle, humble, sensitive manner in which he explained the kinship of all life coupled with his creative, fearless rebel reason. Darwin thought freely. His zeal surmounted poor health. He defied traditional dogma. He did not adapt his individuality to society to make a satisfactory adjustment in order to feel secure with his species. He broke from the herd. He perfected himself as a rational individual, and became one of the most creative, daring observers in history. His one fault was that he mistook organic complexity for evolutionary progress. His major failure was that he did not replace the theory of the universe he helped destroy with a new theory of the universe.

Of course, the science of biology has helped destroy orthodox religion and the pitiful and cruel superstitions that accompanied it. But also it has paved the way for a more sinister, more shallow, less intuitive, less inward, less inclusive, less vital religion—the religion of science. The scientific biological point of view has done most to disgrace, destroy, and exile the search for ethics in campus circles and the formal fields of learning. Idealism retreated before the half-real but utterly utilitarian facts of biology and social biology.

The scientist has won, by virtue of his unbroken series of technical triumphs and discoveries, a disproportionate prominence in the world of modern ethical thought that he does not deserve and an influence on human relations that his ethical knowledge does not merit. The age of reason was overwhelmed by science, but mechanical inventions and longer life have not added an inch to the spiritual status of men. Dr. Schweitzer mourns in anguish that—

> Our age has discovered how to divorce knowledge [of the world] from [rational] thought . . . Once every man of science was a thinker who counted for something in the general spiritual life of his generation . . . Today thought gets no help from science . . . The disastrous feature of our civilization is that it is far more developed materially than spiritually.

Dr. Schweitzer discovered early that truth has two indivisible faces, the factual and the rational. He says,

> Through the study of chemistry, physics, zoology, biology, and physiology I became more than ever conscious to what extent truth in thought is justified and necessary side by side with the truth which is merely established by fact.

Dr. Schweitzer uses medicine to advance the cause of individualism and ethics. He does not derive his ethics from biological knowledge. When he speaks of life, he thinks of the essence of life, the will within that animates the otherwise dead corporeal elements. He says, "There is no such thing as a scientific system of ethics . . . What life is no science can tell us."

The biologist is, according to Dr. Schweitzer, "puffed up with vanity at being able to describe exactly a fragment of the course of life." Dr. Schweitzer insists that "behind all phenomena there is will-to-live," which is still an enigma to science.

While we are on the subject of science, let us hear from someone majoring in the offshoot of natural science, namely, social science.

MARIO MARCONI: I am taking my major in the field of social science. I intend to get a master's degree in the school of commerce. I hope some day to work into my father's advertising agency. Advertising may not sound spiritual in this class, but it is really the backbone of the whole economy of our country and American values.

I consider myself a good Catholic. I have found nothing in the social sciences that is incompatible with my faith and nothing in my other studies until now that challenged my beliefs. Frankly I have enjoyed the verbal fireworks here in class.

I am taking this course because I am deeply curious about the publicity that has come to Dr. Schweitzer. I reasoned that his script must be good. I know his religion and politics are not my brand. I hope to get a good briefing in his philosophy.

As to the class debate, no one will ever persuade me that faith is not an avenue to truth about spiritual matters. Faith has nothing to do with business, politics, and social relations. Happiness and prosperity go hand in hand. In fields of human relations the common good of society is most important, and social utility determines social and political ethics. Love of fame and power act as a constant ferment to stabilize society. Prestige identification is a powerful motive that appears moral. Even in church attendance, fear of ridicule is a factor of great strength. Public opinion determines good behavior. Thus God and society work together, each with a whip and a promise, and jointly they mold the raw, wild, too-free ego. Man needs authority of firm laws and mass opinion in every sphere except economics.

It is a mandate of human reason and an ordinance of God that regimentation must be exempted in economics. I believe that the best government governs least in economics. The greatest good for the greatest number is served when the internal laws of economics are left free. Laws of supply and demand, coupled with the sympathy and compassion implanted in our hearts by nature or God, act as controls of our ego. Free enterprise driven by free egos is the most productive and humane economic system on earth. Free economic struggle is best for individuals and society. I think the free enterprise system has brought prosperity to the common people as no other form of economics could do.

In spite of what Dr. Schweitzer thinks about the state and patriotism, I am a loyal American. I am admittedly and passionately anti-Communist. I hate the atheists slinking behind the Iron Curtain. I believe that only a constant vigil in this country can prevent creeping socialism or galloping Communism from spreading here. We must export our ideas to the marketplaces of belief. Christianity and capitalism are the only weapons of persuasion we have outside of missiles and bombs.

Communism has some superficial features of a religion, but it is a perversion of the sacred meaning of religion to regard the Reds as religious. Communism, more simply, is a form of crime and violence. It is an international conspiracy to destroy democracy, individual freedom, belief in God, the sanctity of the family, and all forms of decency and real religion. The fact that godless dupes who deal in duplicity, who travel with fake names on phony passports, who pursue the lusts of murder at midnight and intrigue in the cause of sabotage and subversion—in short, the simple fact that they are willing to die for their unholy cause does not make their false system a religion, not even a secular religion. Left-wing globalists, Socialists, and Commies are all one breed of black cat.

From my minor courses in philosophy I have been inclined to accept the William James philosophy of pragmatism. I do not feel that his realism is a challenge to my religion, which I believe is the only true faith. Social utility has always been a test of human goodness outside religion. What promotes progress, provides decent pleasure, serves happiness, and does not conflict with the laws of God.

PROF. REVERE: Mr. Marconi, you can't imagine how well you have expressed the earliest form of eighteenth-century utilitarianism expounded by Jeremy Bentham, David Hume, and Adam Smith.

The great problem then was to determine what ethic would serve as a universal mechanism to perfect human society. Before Darwin and Spencer came on the stage of events, historical scientists, romanticists, nature philosophers, and natural scientists were trying to establish footings for their new modes of thought. In this ethical chaos Bentham supplied the world with a system of ethics. He opposed the notion that an individual's conscience is a reliable guide to goodness. He claimed man is ethical only when he is commanded by society to be moral. The general good is determined by exact utility values. The group theory of the greatest good of the greatest number was adopted, because it was alleged to produce arithmetically the greatest happiness. Dr. Schweitzer admits, "Bentham is one of the most powerful moralists who have ever lived, but his mistakes are as great as his insights." His tragic error is that he elevated the value judgment of society over the conscience of the individual. These men created the illusion that society is an end, not a means, to perfect individuals.

Hume and other utilitarians sought to promote the common good as the dominant principle of morality. Methods of self-perfecting of individuals sank lower and lower in this period.

Adam Smith proposed an entirely free and rational activity of egotism in economics. He believed God has implanted a feeling of altruism and sympathy as a benign regulator in all men, so that they can be trusted to promote freely the common good. Dr. Schweitzer says of Adam Smith:

> He led industry and commerce in their struggle for liberation from the petty and injurious tutelage of authority . . . Today when economic life among all peoples is again delivered

over to the most short-sighted authorities . . . we can measure the greatness of his achievement.

Mr. Marconi, Dr. Schweitzer's criticisms of the early utilitarians would apply to you. He says, "Action for the common advantage does not by any means constitute ethics." In addition, he would be critical of your sense of nationalism that was not present among the scattered rational utilitarians from whom you have inherited your views.

Your interest in pragmatism and William James would be sharply criticized by Dr. Schweitzer, who says that distinctions between philosophy and religion are arbitrary and meaningless, for both originate in human thought.

The philosophy of William James is a half-naive, half-cynical outgrowth of utilitarian thought that arbitrarily divides truth into utility value judgments and scientific facts. Dr. Schweitzer, an advocate of the oneness of all knowledge, calls this doctrine of double truth an "insidiously employed interpretation of the world." He says this "miserable" system is "dirty business." Pragmatism "plays a fatal part in the mentality of our time."

Dr. Schweitzer goes further. He summarily damns all philosophers that have emerged since the giant-sized heroic free thinkers of the eighteenth century, when thinkers molded international history. Modern philosophy, which at best has an inconsequential role in modern universities and no opinion-forming status in current society, Dr. Schweitzer incriminates as a "pedantic philosophy of degenerates."

Modern philosophy has no convictions about civilization, freedom, or the means by which individuals may make progress toward moral perfection.

And now may we hear from one more student in the field of social science? Perhaps we may have a word from the young lady from India with the dark flashing eyes framed in a truly lovely sari.

NADRA SARISAN: Professor Revere, I would like to present a rebuttal to Mr. Marconi. It would seem that two students can major in the field of social science and end up at the very gates of graduation without a single idea or ideal in common. There is no point on which I can agree with my colleague. That we belong to the same campus religion or value system is absurd.

PROF. REVERE: By all means explain your position, but please introduce yourself first.

NADRA SARISAN: I am Nadra Sarisan. I too am majoring in the division of the social sciences. I am specializing in the department of sociology in preparation for entering the graduate school of social service. I intend to do social work in India. I elected this course because I admire the pioneering group medical work and the social thinking Dr. Schweitzer is modelling at his hospital in Africa. He is not cursed with silly notions of evangelism that were the scourge of India under British rule. He is bringing the magic of modern medicine to groups of people in the extremity of desperate need. He does not restrict his services to evangelical prospects, as do some missionary doctors, or to the over-indulged, badly pampered rich, so often sick with imaginary ills, as do the urban physicians.

I deeply admire Dr. Schweitzer's courage in following his interracial policies against the swift stream of supposed white supremacy.

I am a Hindu by birth, but I am an ardent Socialist by my own free choice. As to ethics, I think you are all hopelessly mistaken about the elemental basis of good and evil. This blow of mine is aimed at the class, but it strikes at the individualism preached by Dr. Schweitzer as well. The ethics in humanities are pure romantic sentimentality. The physical scientists are morally unaware of social tragedies. They are disdainful and utterly unconcerned with positive programs to achieve real social welfare. Only the biological scientists are aware of man as a social animal, but they are lost in their laboratories.

Mr. Golde, who sounds highly rational to me, proved—and Professor Revere failed to disprove—that man is heir to social instincts. In the same manner as subhuman forbears of man, we all have inherited impulses to cooperate in families, clans, tribes, and societies. My point is that you are all overlooking the statistical, sociological, and institutional aspects of group behavior and community loyalties. There are social codes even in gang warfare. Individual morality is a product of social institutions. Crime and delinquency are products of sick societies, not bad or fallen individuals. Group therapy is needed for human ills. Someone once said that what is good for the swarm is good for the bee. Social order must be built rationally on social instincts.

PROF. REVERE: You say you disagree with Mr. Marconi on every issue, and yet you and he both speak of ethics as measures of controlling the individual ego by social institutions. You would explicitly institutionalize and nationalize all human activity, including economics. Mr. Marconi exempts economics. You are both at odds with Dr. Schweitzer, who says:

Social ethics without individual ethics is like a limb with a tourniquet around it into which life no longer flows. They become so impoverished that they really cease to be ethics at all.

Coerced ethics destroys reason and freedom and the meaning of ethics. Completely unwilled ethics defines tyranny. Society must not be trusted with human ethics. Dr. Schweitzer says to all who will listen:

Never for a moment do we lay aside our mistrust of the ideals established by society and of the convictions which are kept by it in circulation. We always know that society is full of folly and will deceive us in the matter of humanity. It is an unreliable horse and blind into the bargain. Woe to the driver if he falls asleep.

NADRA SARISAN: But I thought Dr. Schweitzer was wise enough to be a good Socialist.

PROF. REVERE: Dr. Schweitzer says on the issue of public ownership:

> In the question of possessions the ethics of reverence for life are outstandingly individualistic . . . Wealth acquired or inherited should be placed at the service of the community . . . through the absolutely free decision of the individual.

Dr. Schweitzer defines wealth as the property of society left in the sovereign control of the individual.

NADRA SARISAN: This settles one point. I disagree with Dr. Schweitzer on the subject of Socialism as deeply as I disagree with Mr. Marconi.

If we look at ourselves and society biologically and study history realistically, the blueprint of the future becomes clear. All the arrows of all of the social trends point to one conclusion: Capitalism is dead, Mr. Marconi's dream world of free enterprise notwithstanding. Socialism is the way of the world for tomorrow. We are endowed with a wonderful natural benevolence in our nature, and if we cooperate for the common good instead of competing like individual vampires, vipers, or vultures, a new age of undreamed-of abundance for all will appear.

PROF. REVERE: You used an unfortunate analogy. You illustrated evil individualism by referring to the same field of biology that you say proves we are social animals. You were using the Darwin-Spencer line. Dr. Schweitzer says:

> The ethics of Darwin and Spencer are a failure from the start because they are too narrow. The social impulse which they put in place of the [instinctual] sympathy which is assumed by Hume and Adam Smith is set at a lower pitch . . . less calculated to explain real ethics.

Dr. Schweitzer fails to see how institutions can perfect individuals. The spiritual perfection of individuals is the final

end of civilization and the only excuse for society. The point
is not only that you and Mr. Marconi would spoil humanity
by saving the world by institutional means. You yourselves
have lost touch with the reasoning powers that created the
dogma you accept. You know nothing of the freedom used
by the eighteenth-century free thinkers who wanted to save the
world by perfecting individuals by reason. Dr. Schweitzer states:

> The activities and the aims of our times are penetrated by
> a kind of obsession that if we could only succeed in perfect-
> ing . . . the institutions of our public and social life the progress
> demanded by civilization would begin of itself . . . one section
> sketches out an anti-democratic plan; others believe that our
> mistake lies in the fact that democratic principles have not yet
> been applied consistently; others again see salvation only in a
> Socialist or Communist organization of society. . . .

NADRA SARISAN: But, Professor Revere, the Socialist ethic
is scientific. It grows out of statistical knowledge of mass
behavior. If individuals merge with the inevitable stream of
progress, the individual is perfected. In swimming with that
tide one feels a sense of freedom. One becomes an important
instrument of the glories of the future. If you oppose the
forward moving glacier of historical progress, you are destined
to be pulverized to dust, remembered only as an obstructionist.

PROF. REVERE: Your fault here is that you measure material
and external items statistically and arithmetically. On this
point one thing should be clear. The free thinkers who originated
the view you now parrot as your own dealt with immaterial
images and values. Now you all deal with the material world
as if it possessed the spiritual values. The Gospel writers and
eighteenth-century thinkers talked of the folly of material possessions and wealth of men and nations but spoke of the immaterial values of brotherhood, charity, righteousness, love,
freedom, justice, and equality. These virtues seem now in-
discreet. They are championed by inaudible whispers. They

sound communistic because Marxian Socialism and Communism are Western Christian heresies. Today Communists use immaterial values to propagate materialism.

Actually all values are immaterial. Values may be assigned by creeds to goods and products, but values in man are products of reason. Man is evolving as an ethical animal. Man is not an animal become rational by viewing reason, anthropoid become realist through studies of the physical realities, or ape become utilitarian through the pseudo-wisdom of social science. Man is a part of the universe naturally growing conscious of the immaterial and the liberating values hidden in his misunderstood but ecstatic ethical immaterial experiences. This is the current counsel and recent insight of really free reason.

You are all using reason to defend ideas, not to establish them. Human institutions are real only in the minds of believing individuals, and human failures are traceable not to institutions but to individuals.

We must pause in our consideration of the ethical role of Marx to discuss one powerful influence that shaped many of Marx's ideas but no less the ideas expressed here today. Hegel not only discovered a deep and profound way to sanction non-Biblical values, materialism, externalism, and utility, but he tied the ideas of freedom and liberty to the apron strings of the state. He deified nationalism.

Every student who spoke up today deviated from the founders of the religions they represented by nationalizing their convictions. They are all obeying Hegel's commandments, as did Karl Marx. Feudalism was, like Jesus, pessimistic and lacked an earthly view of progress. Dr. Schweitzer says,

> This new orientation of the Christian world view . . . is the decisive spiritual event of the modern age.

The Western world changed the character of Jesus to fit their belief in material progress. The Hegelian view of progress and optimism was masked. It adopted what had become good

Christianity under new labels. Marx finally made a new inclusive religion out of Hegelian ideas, and did so by violently
discarding Christian associations. Dr. Schweitzer says,

> Through Marx, Hegel's belief in inherent progress becomes
> . . . the conviction of the masses. His optimistic feeling for
> reality takes the helm . . . The hopes of the masses begin to
> center no longer on what can be accomplished in the world
> by an [individual] ethical temper . . . but on what is reached
> when free course is secured [not for individuals but] for the
> *laws of progress* which are assumed to be inherent in things . . .
> The great influence it exerts rests on the fact that it preaches
> belief in a progress which is inherent in events and works itself
> out in them automatically.

NADRA SARISAN: Before I yield the floor, may I make three
observations. Americans haven't the vaguest notion of the real
social distress, grief, and wretchedness that the people face in
India. You all hate so hard you fail to see the good side of
Karl Marx that appeals to desperate Indians. Finally, you
don't realize that democratic Socialism is your stoutest ally in
opposing militant, tyrannical Communism.

PROF. REVERE: You may not realize it yet, but our discussion has arrived at a point where it is appropriate to speak of
Hegel and Marx. Because our school divisions roughly reflect
society, and because society reflects the living fossil fragments
of monolithic feudalism, we have inadvertly recapitulated history
in our discussion. All discussions in this university would fall
into this general pattern. Miss Christensen represents the
Erasmus-Luther line; Mr. Black, the Locke-Rousseau-Kant view;
Mr. Steele, the Copernicus-Galileo-Newton view; Mr. Marconi, the Bentham-Hume-Smith position; Mr. Golde is a living
emissary for the Darwin-Spencer ethic; and Miss Sarisan
evangelizes for the Lassalle variety of Socialism.

In this trend, the sanctity and freedom and ideas of the
perfectibility of the individual are notable for their absence.

Civilization defined in terms of ethical perfectibility has been retreating since the eighteenth-century flash-flood of worldwide ideas of individualism and freedom as the basis of ethics.

It is time to discuss Marx, because with him the compulsion to conform to the common good is finally enthroned with spiritual sanction. Dr. Schweitzer explains the advent of Marx and Communism thus:

> If it be granted that progress in the welfare of society depends on the application of the conclusions of biology and scientific sociology, it is not necessary to leave to the good pleasure of the individual the corresponding conduct which is to be ethical. It can be imposed on him . . . in such a way that it automatically functions as is most expedient. Thus by the side of social ethics socialism makes its appearance . . . Karl Marx (1825-1864) and Friedrich Engels (1820-1895) put forward its consistent programme. . . .

The entire Western world and everyone here has fallen under the spell of Hegel, who was the spiritual father of realism. His profound religion murdered the last remnants of idealism. He saw a new universal world spirit divorced from the Christian universe. His view of realism, Dr. Schweitzer says, "perhaps some day will end civilization." As passionate nationalists you all are obeying the laws of Hegel, and this is one way in which you all are similar to Karl Marx, who made a world religion out of Hegel's thinking.

Dr. Schweitzer points the same finger of guilt at Marx that he shook at us, except that Marx has made Communism into a global monolithic religion that evolves from forceful overthrow of the old social order and the establishment of a dictatorship of the proletariat with international promises of eventual freedom, peace, and amity. Dr. Schweitzer says,

> In the victory so fateful . . . won by Marxian State Socialism . . . we see . . . in the mentality of the masses that belief in progress has been separated from [individual] ethics and has

become mechanistic. Confusion in the conception of civilization and ruin of the [eighteenth century] civilized way of
thinking are the consequences of this disastrous separation.

What may give you an eerie feeling is that Marx welded
together the religious fragments of history which are the same
fragments this university is busy preserving and perpetuating.
Marx brashly adopts the goals of Christian brotherhood and
freedom. He uses the tinsel imitation of idealism in his realism.
But Marx proclaims that ideals must be achieved by scientific
methods applied to the control of social institutions. Dr.
Schweitzer says:

> Personality and ideas are subordinated to institutions . . .
> The man of today is a being without freedom.

This is true of all collectivized citizens, living in the East or
West.

Marx maintains, nevertheless, that the ends are so worthy
that force may be used where necessary. He scoffs at ethical
ideals of individualism and measures all progress by material,
mechanistic, and economic standards.

That Communism has every classical hallmark of a world
religion, and is equivalent in its growth patterns to other world
religions, can no longer be denied. It represents serious thought;
and all serious thought becomes religious, according to Dr.
Schweitzer. In addition, Communism has a view of the universe,
a Moses in Hegel, a Messiah in Marx, an apostle in Lenin, and
disciples by the score. Marx was an authoritarian and published
his global gospel in his "bible," *Das Kapital*. He inflamed the
faithful and missionaries with his Sermon-on-the-Mount-like
Communist Manifesto.

Hegel's theory of the universe is shaky, but the Western nations since feudalism crashed have had no undergirding theory
of the universe at all. Hence the chaotic fragmentation in the
lack of common ideals.

Dr. Schweitzer's religion is based on a new theory of the universe, in which cosmic freedom is identified as individual freedom. The will which is the common feature of all life becomes the basis of his ethics and system of reverence. His religion collides head-on with the modern religious views enslaving your minds on this campus. We too, like the hated Reds, are according to Dr. Schweitzer, collectivized, externalized, and materialistic. We do not know the cosmic meaning of democracy, freedom, and civilization. Our religious subdivisions on campus and our denominational multiplicity are a disgrace to thinking men.

As we show the specific points on which the two prophetic figures—Marx and Albert Schweitzer—clash, try to determine if you can which critical factors would *not* apply to us. What part of Marx is non-Western?

Dr. Schweitzer and Marx have opposing articles of faith, but of one thing we may be sure. Both are really motivated by ethics. While Marx claimed the truths of dialectical materialism, he himself was never motivated by materialism but by what he deemed an inevitable vision of goodness revealed by his theory of history.

Karl Marx, the founder of a new economic law in history, gave little thought to his personal economics. He and his family almost starved, and might have if Friedrich Engels had not come to the rescue. Marx the dispassionate observer failed to see that religious cultures form the units of history and map the modern world. His insights into his own nature were negligible.

In Albert Schweitzer's terms Marx was totally ignorant about the nature, source, extent, power, and history of human freedom. Marx paradoxically recommended anti-freedom to achieve freedom. He suggested the dictatorship of the proletariat to achieve the democracy of the classless society. He called for violent and forceful overthrow of all existing social order to achieve free men of good character and peace.

Unlike materialistic Marx, Dr. Schweitzer the confirmed idealist says, "I still remain convinced that truth, love, peaceableness, meekness, and kindness are the violence which can master all other violence."

The case history of Marx proves the ethical viewpoint held by Dr. Schweitzer. In his views, materialists give material labels to human ideals and then pretend that the object and the camouflage veneer are inseparable.

Violence-sanctioning Marx advised physical destruction, but he was himself non-violent. He commanded no armies. He conducted his campaigns in the libraries of London in the battle of books. His dynamite was in his pen and in his false ethics. No blood flowed in the streets of Europe when he dropped his biggest bomb, the Communist Manifesto.

Marx spoke of real warfare, bloody violence, and forceful overthrow; but his mightiest soldiers were immaterial, shapeless, weightless ideas that cannot be killed by lead or fear of blast or radiation. Only a counter-militia of moral ideas better and truer can win the field and destroy the pestilence.

Collectivism was the battle cry of Marx, and yet he was himself a free, uncollectivized renegade. But he asked for obedience, regimentation, indoctrination, and individual submission. To Albert Schweitzer the herd idea of collectivized servitude is a retrogression more primitive than the condition of subhuman existence of the free creatures in the state of nature.

Now let us turn Dr. Schweitzer's biggest ethical guns onto the tyrannical citadel of Communistic collectivism. If opposed by free peoples, joined in holy reverencing of individual freedom and ideals of moral perfection, collectivism could be crushed.

Tyranny is an evil older than the pharaohs, as cruel as the Spartans, and as spiritually barren as the Dark Ages. Its idol, the State, carries the infamy of Macchiavelli and the perfidy of Hegel. Tyranny and collectivism are impotent, atavistic, and repressive to individualism and freedom. Tyranny is not even scientific or ethically efficient. It is an offense against truth, a crime against nature, poisonous to reason, treasonous to democracy, faithless to Jesus, seriously inhumane to man, and a monstrous irreverence to sacred life itself. This is my interpretation of Schweitzer's Manifesto of Freedom against the tyranny of Communism.

The battle of the prophets is not a popularity contest. But in my judgment the deeds and dedication of Albert Schweitzer would make bitter, hard, cold, dictatorial, violent, arrogant Marx pale to anemic pallor by any comparison, especially in the realm of personal, neighbor-to-neighbor service. Albert Schweitzer is not the model of lucidity and conciseness that Marx was at times. But the Doctor's scholarship is deeper, more penetrating, more inward, more just, more wise, more reasonable, more elemental, more universal, more truthful, and more liberating.

I hope by this orientation that you in the class who have accused Albert Schweitzer of Communist leanings will now be alerted to the sinister injustices that you could commit in voicing this mistake. Too lightly we call what we disagree with Communism. To call Dr. Schweitzer Red or Pink is a scandalous slander.

Before we close this first session, let me tell you what a pleasure it is for me to be confronted with your fresh young minds. In Dr. Schweitzer's name I have accused you all of accepting thoughtlessly the precepts of the past. But it did not escape me that through your ardor for your respective and dissimilar campus religions you betray an underlying, eager idealism that shines through your chaotic convictions.

Zeal in ideals is the great gift of youth. Dr. Schweitzer says,

> It is through the idealism of youth that man catches sight of truth, and in that idealism he possesses a wealth which he must never exchange for anything else.

My young friends, though you are ethically uneducated, you are the world's most precious resource.

I want to stress that youth is not a matter of chronology as much as a state of mind. Many epitaphs could read, "Died at twenty-five; buried at ninety." With you, youth is the springtime of life and the season of hope. But I think you will discover that all great things are done by the young in years or the young in heart. Youth is an ephemeral quality. You may sense that it is slipping when you feel you are forsaking your ideals or when you feel that the temper of your opinions has hardened and the suppleness of your imagination is suffering rigidity. Your minds at any age can scale barriers, leap chasms, and roam tirelessly over the diverse lands in search of wisdom.

Dr. Schweitzer, now an octogenarian, frequently tears off his mask so that we may see his youthful soul and discover what he meant when he said,

> As one who tries to remain youthful in his thinking and feeling, I have struggled against fact and experience on behalf of belief in the good and the true. At the present time . . . violence, clothed in life, dominates the world more cruelly than it ever has before . . . The world will be theirs [the young in heart] as soon as ever a sufficient number of men with purity of heart, with strength, and with perseverance think and live out the thoughts of love and truth, of meekness and peaceableness.

Dr. Schweitzer would tell you that the key to the secret of spiritual success is to learn how to search for the ultimate cause of the things in yourself. Suddenly you will find that what you thought was immovable reality will give way to your ideals. Dr. Schweitzer says, "The power of ideals is incalculable."

Let me end with the warning that if you hope to learn about ethics you must come to honor the most precious possession that you have: namely, your free reason. Dr. Schweitzer was speaking to youth generally when he said,

> The conviction that in after life we must struggle to remain thinking as freely and feeling as deeply as we did in our youth,

has accompanied me on my road throughout life as a faithful adviser.

Dr. Schweitzer will also warn you against all adults including himself. He says,

> Grown-up people reconcile themselves too willingly to a supposed duty of preparing young ones for the time when they will regard as illusion what is an inspiration to the heart and mind.

I hope by now that we feel acquainted enough to pursue the search for ethics and a testing of our ethical convictions with our reason.

Au Revoir to Lambarene

When Dr. Schweitzer played for me and gave me the "green light" for my mission, my all too short visit had come to its last hours. When I left his small room that night I thought I was saying goodbye as well as goodnight.

My timetable was set by a departure schedule that was synchronized to the movements of the local forest-hopping, village-visiting plane. The plane flew in and out of the Lambaréné airport so early that I expected to breakfast alone long before the usual hour for the morning meal in the settlement.

When I arrived for my very early breakfast, I was startled to find that the usual places in the dining hall were all occupied. I checked my watch. I could scarcely believe that the busy routine had been shifted in the interest of one minor guest. But it happened that Dr. and Mrs. Schweitzer and the staff had turned out early to break bread with me at my last meal at Lambaréné.

After the repast, Dr. Schweitzer walked with me to my room and paced up and down on the veranda as I packed my books and tried in haste to close my bulging bags.

Apparently Dr. Schweitzer worried lest I be tardy for the plane at the airport, a long canoe ride and short, rough bus trip away. Finally he unceremoniously opened the door of my room, intruded his head, and spoke the only words in English I ever heard him utter. Smiling broadly, he said, "Herbert, hurry."

I must say at this point that Dr. Schweitzer has a way of making guests feel on arrival that they are coming to their own home away from home, and on departure that they are leaving

their own family. The whole staff of hospital workers gathered
on the river bank to see the Chicago dentist off.

The members of the fellowship waved white sun helmets and
handkerchiefs from the river bank until an island in the stream
obscured our craft. Then to my surprise many, if not all, climbed
the hill and continued waving until a bend in the river shut
off all visual communication.

The warmth of the welcome Dr. Schweitzer and his fellowship
bestow on guests on arrival and the kind gestures of regard they
send forth over the water after a departing friend, I am sure
remain as utterly enchanting memories in the mind of many a
humble pilgrim. My pleasure-pain parting is a sweet sorrow
that is with me still.

As I sat in the canoe paddled by three chanting lepers, I
remembered again, but with more insight, the malicious charges
slung at Lambaréné and its founder.

The charge that Dr. Schweitzer saves bodies, not souls, is true.
But that his life, patterned truly in the liberating spirit of Jesus,
is *un-Christian* became, in my mind, a poignant injustice both
to Christianity and to the modern liberator. Dr. Schweitzer's elemental religiousness is beyond dispute.

The charge of untidiness and de-emphasis on hygiene is
technically valid. But it seemed to me that the charge missed
the larger truth that Lambaréné exalts personal relations between people and subhuman creatures to embody in action the
kinship of life and the universal circle of love.

The charge of authoritarianism involved a striking paradox.
Dr. Schweitzer is an "older brother" in ethics, a senior in a
world of ethical sophomores and moral freshmen. But his dicta
extol individual freedom and exalt liberty and "will" without
equivocation as an ethical ultimatum to be observed everywhere.

I personally found his non-violent ethical despotism not only
unassailable but on reflection infinitely charming. If all dictators rose to eminence through moral persuasion and made the

fight for equal freedom for all as their sole goal and sovereign good, the wounds of the world would soon be healed.

Dr. Schweitzer conceives of colonialism as an evil, but it is not always the worst affliction that a people may suffer. When a people go from colonialism to intensified nationalism, in which ruthless dictatorship rules, individual freedom may be worsened. Why celebrate if the whip changes hands? Reverence for life and liberty is the measure of any governing body; and the wider the scope of common idealism, the greater is the degree of civilization. Only a universal ethic of brotherly love is rational, wise, just, and truly consistent with man's role in the cosmos.

That Dr. Schweitzer is a segregationist at heart is absurd. He has pleaded the cause for universal kinship for more than a half century. He has served Africans for all these decades man to man.

The most infamous indictment is made by the most pitiable people who by misunderstanding or disagreeing with Dr. Schweitzer on one or more points cry "Red" or "Communist" or "dupe." This infantile pretense to superior wisdom involves the vicious assassination of truth. For Dr. Schweitzer has been in word and deed a life-long articulate and consistent foe of collectivism.

It is my opinion that all the charges of radicalism, inconsistencies, paradoxes, and ambiguities come from people who have not grasped Dr. Schweitzer's theory of the universe and the fundamentals of his ethical system. The actions that grow out of ethical theory are a result of reason and value judgments.

As my canoe slipped farther downstream, in a very deep and personal way I felt as though I were leaving the mountain-top of freedom. Lambaréné *is* an oasis of liberty where man the inheritor of the earth is honored, where will *is* sacred, where spiritual freedom is understood and worshiped, and where kinship knows no limitations.

After an extension of my African safari, I would head back to the white, Western, rich, healthy, hygienic, Christian, cultured, civilized nations. But these large geo-political areas ahead appeared to have smaller and more savage ethical circles than the tiny primitive community I was leaving.

It is difficult to convey how great the folly of human strife appears from this sanctuary of brotherhood. That two great leaders among nations of the world—Russia and America—were converting their knowledge, skills, and substance, natural resources, and human wealth and labor into horrible, fantastic weapons of incineration, radiation, and blast is from Albert Schweitzer's mountain-top incredibly stupid, a carnal jest profaning the concept of reason.

Bloody, violent war is a witness to the ethical infancy of the "civilized" world. But the Lambaréné brand of moral warfare demonstrates what the nature of man may become.

The Schweitzer way to peace, prosperity, undreamed-of freedom, and human dignity worthy of gods seemed so simple, so real, so practical, and so cosmically sound that I still felt as I left Lambaréné that it should serve as the elected gospel to guide the destiny of man.

I personally would like to think that our political leaders in America would claim Dr. Schweitzer as an honorary citizen, even if it took an Act of Congress to accomplish the feat. I am sure that such a gesture of affection from our government would have a catalytic effect on the citizenship of America in their days of drifting from crisis to crisis. Furthermore, the wisdom of the act would echo around the world. It would hearten those who feel that in pursuing our own luxuriant materialism and in preoccupying ourselves with our ruthless race for power to kill men we are losing touch with our own humanity. It would allay their concern that we no longer feel the real worth of vast neutral multitudes who live out their lives at the hunger-pain level of existence.

If we honor ourselves by honoring Dr. Schweitzer, our enemies would at least have to confront the merciful image of Albert Schweitzer in their own blind march toward dialectical materialism and fratricidal power.

At any rate as far as my educational mission is concerned, Dr. Schweitzer's friends have neither a command to proceed nor a dictum to desist. We have a permissive trust to use our judgment. If Albert Schweitzer's symbol is to be planted here in academic soil to enrich American education, it will be nurtured and it will bear fruit by virtue of spontaneous activity of faculties, administrators, boards of trustees, alumni, and lay sponsors. We have a "green light," and the rest is up to the wisdom of people.

In conclusion what may be said of Dr. Schweitzer as a man among men?

In my opinion above all else this unusual human being is a creation of freedom's moral power. We might well pause to listen to his lusty voice booming through the conscience of mankind, extolling freedom. Freedom is the source of his distinction, and he warns us against the stultifying effect of social, political, economic, and religious tyranny and collectivism.

It should be heartening for all to know that this man is of the people and for the people. His mind is unshackled. But like the common man of all ages he has mud on his shoes. The sun and rain beat in vain on his sturdy vitality. The tornadoes come to the hospital, but they only rumple his hair. He is a match for nature. He may be a match for the cruel capriciousness of history. He is a model of morality, education, universality, liberty, and love. He is at once a Western citizen and a world citizen. He works with his calloused, sensitive hands prodigiously on things elemental in the life cycle. He loves and honors his neighbors and dreams of sacred things. The neighbors he venerates are you and me and the peoples of the world. His sacred dreams of spiritual treasures encompass all life.

Epilogue

1. The Real Crisis and the Educational Dream

Twenty-one months had passed between my first days at Lambaréné and the hour when I finished correcting the last galley of the proofs of this report. So much had happened that I felt obliged to append this Epilogue.

The caprice of fate sometimes gives the poorest observer the best seat at history's unpredictable turning points. Thus puckish destiny, aided, I admit, by a series of well-timed accidents, put me, so to speak, in the orchestra pit in the theater of contemporary history at a moment of great climax.

At any rate, while my good luck is a lesson in humility, I feel I must bring to my readers a rising series of surprises which now becomes a fitting finale to my safari of discovery.

*   *   *

At breakfast on the first morning of my second visit in the Lambaréné settlement, Ali Silver, my translator, said, "Dr. Schweitzer will see you now in his room. Please bring all of your material on the Education Foundation with you." Within a few minutes I was at Dr. Schweitzer's side.

I looked down at ants swarming on his desktop. The ants were busy devouring or storing the breakfast Dr. Schweitzer had just provided for them.

Most of the matters that we discussed confidentially that morning are now on the public record. Shortly after my departure from Lambaréné, Dr. Schweitzer released his views concerning the world crisis through the Nobel Peace Prize Committee in Oslo. His statements were widely quoted by mass communication agencies. The Albert Schweitzer Education

Foundation, which I helped create and over which I preside, published the English translation in full and distributed it to schools and civic leaders.

*   *   *

In connection with my personal discussion with Dr. Schweitzer about nuclear weapons, I would like to report only one intimate incident which I believe reveals Dr. Schweitzer's almost unique theory of the universe in an unforgettable way.

During our hour-long discussion of the problems of fall-out from bomb testing and the horror of nuclear war, my eighty-three-year-old host's appearance of glowing health deteriorated before my eyes. His ruddy face underwent changes in color. His wrinkled countenance paled to an alarming gray. His lips turned blue.

At first I mistook these vascular changes for extreme exhaustion until the big man suddenly announced, "This subject makes me too sick. I cannot talk about it longer."

I knew that personal fear is alien to Dr. Schweitzer's nature. I had just been made aware again in our conversation that Dr. Schweitzer feels a very special kind of oneness between his will and the infinite manifestations of will in the universe. I concluded that Dr. Schweitzer was vicariously living through a unique sensation of cosmic horror that perhaps no one has ever endured before in history.

Dr. Schweitzer cannot believe in the Christian cosmology that absolves man from ultimate responsibility. In accordance with his theory of the universe, Dr. Schweitzer feels that omissions, negligence, or imprudence on his part are acts of unforgivable faithlessness to the vision of will he discovered in himself.

Besides the infamy of nuclear war in the human family, such a foolish conflict would be also a betrayal of a wider trusteeship, for it would jeopardize the lower forms of life that would bleed and die en masse because of human stupidity.

The cosmic horror story that thus involved him personally disturbed Dr. Schweitzer's worn physiology, requiring a change of subject.

I asked if we should not adjourn until Dr. Schweitzer was composed. He insisted on proceeding despite the protests and entreaties of the translator, who doubles as a watchdog for the Doctor's well-being.

Dr. Schweitzer said, with the air of finality with which I had become familiar on my first visit, "Tell me about your plans and purposes for the Albert Schweitzer Education Foundation, in order of their importance."

Shortly after we thus changed the subject, the Doctor's complexion regained its healthy glow.

*   *   *

With a clumsy flourish, I presented Dr. Schweitzer with a photostatic copy of the Certificate of Incorporation of the Albert Schweitzer Education Foundation. I said that it had been granted in record time by the Secretary of State in Springfield, Illinois, on February 17, 1958.

Dr. Schweitzer put on his battered spectacles to acquaint himself with the following statement of purpose set forth in our Articles of Incorporation. As he read, scowling and shaking his shaggy head, he did not conceal his good will and satisfaction.

> The sole and exclusive purpose for which this corporation is organized and shall be operated is to support, assist, aid, sustain, foster, and encourage the study, teaching and knowledge of the ethics, aesthetics, philosophy, humanitarianism and reverence for life of Albert Schweitzer, in universities, colleges, other educational organizations, and community groups.

Dr. Schweitzer smiled and said, "What do you intend to do first?"

The group of incorporators and those closely associated with the infant enterprise, I explained, were most enthusiastic about developing modern audiovisual aids to facilitate the presentation of the meaning of will-to-live symbolized by Reverence for Life.

He asked, "Can you name the subjects you and your colleagues consider most important?"

I suggested the following titles for audiovisual movie shorts: Theory of the Universe, History of Ethics, Meaning of Civilization, Portrait of Jesus, Evaluation of Paul, Centrality of Inward Freedom in Scholarship, World Religions Compared, and Current Dangers of Hegelian Thought.

I said that after this much is accomplished, then his summary comments on Aesthetics and Bach, his generalizations on Goethe, Kant, and other philosophers could be integrated into the series to make the synthesis more complete.

I never dreamed I would hear the next comment from the lips of the Albert Schweitzer I had badgered for discussions on my previous trip to Lambaréné. Without a shred of his old depotism he said, "You and your friends in America would know better than I about the value of these plans."

I continued, saying that we would like to arrange and facilitate the activities of lecturers who would present talks or seminars at various colleges—such men as Adlai Stevenson, Percival Brundage, Norman Cousins, J. S. Bixler, Edwin Booth, Walter Kring.

Dr. Schweitzer was surprised to hear that these men had already declared their willingness to carry the ethical contributions to schools as their own schedules would permit.

"I think," Dr. Schweitzer said, remonstrating, "these men you mention are far too busy to help in this work, but they do understand my message and could do the educational tasks very well."

I continued my exposition, saying that as time went on, in addition to the traveling lecturers, we would like to bring to an American university a distinguished professor who would be knowledgeable in the areas Dr. Schweitzer's scholarship has illuminated—for example, Fritz Buri or George Seaver. Many universities would be interested, I assured Dr. Schweitzer.

"My friend Dr. Buri," Dr. Schweitzer said, "could not leave

his new post as director of the great Cathedral of Basel. Other than this, he would be a fine choice."

Dr. Schweitzer was incredulous when I said Dr. Buri had already announced his burning ambition to represent Dr. Schweitzer's ethics at the University of Chicago, Yale, or Harvard, where a new orthodoxy represents a trend toward a renewed dark medievalism.

I was happy to explain that I had discussed our educational plans with Reverend George Seaver when he was in New York. He was even then in America lecturing in part on the Schweitzer philosophy.

Dr. Schweitzer said of George Seaver, "No one has written longer and more authentically in the English language of my ethical system than my friend, George Seaver."

Knowing that our meeting could end at any time, I hurried to summarize the remaining objectives that the Foundation would pursue if thousands of individuals in America expressed their interest in our projects in financial form.

I made the following points:

We hope to be in a position to provide university libraries with Albert Schweitzer books.

We would like to make lectures available to the community at large when we are called upon to do so.

We hope in good time to give scholarships to advanced students interested in writing doctoral theses on Schweitzer literature and to start nuclei of advanced teacher training opportunities.

We would like to help deserving students interested in obtaining a personal service experience in underdeveloped areas and provide this character-molding opportunity in the Schweitzer tradition as an integral part of their education.

I said that eventually, to emphasize the wholeness he represents, we would sponsor some outstanding "whole" scholars who have succeeded to high academic pinnacles through general learning. As an example of this category, I suggested the historian, Arnold Toynbee.

Finally I outlined the upper limits of our most daring dream, which encompasses a conscientious search for a new religion and a new theory of the universe. I suggested that some day a summit conference could be arranged so that creative scholars in the Schweitzer pattern could organize an international Manhattan Project on Freedom. I mentioned that a philosopher-scientist like Werner Heisenberg might be the nucleus of this fellowship of freedom searchers.

Fortunately my modest report of an immodest program was at an end, for the name Werner Heisenberg diverted our conversation to the frontiers of science.

*   *   *   *   *

People had gathered outside the door for instructions from Dr. Schweitzer and Ali Silver. I asked a final question but regretted it before it was half uttered.

I said, "Would you want to write an open note of confidence to your friends who are interested in the Albert Schweitzer Education Foundation, expressing your good will and confirming the fact that we are acting with your knowledge and approval?"

Dr. Schweitzer said, "I cannot officially endorse projects undertaken in my honor. My real friends will understand my silence and need not be told of my confidence in them. Critics would not be impressed with a letter from me and might with some justification misunderstand my motives in writing such a letter. Besides, I would find it difficult to acknowledge in advance something that proposes to perpetuate my work."

I was sorry I had asked the very practical but irrational question. Actually our affirmative meeting had passed my fondest expectations. I had been given a whole loaf, and I had asked for two to make my work easier.

Cursing my gluttony, I took my leave and went back to the dental clinic to carry on with problems that had accumulated in my absence. In the torrid busy-ness of the clinic I forgave myself.

2. *Christianity, Communism, and the Religion of Reason*

During the long hours I spent in the dental clinic and in the evenings when groups chose to listen to me by lamplight, I played the role of a travelling raconteur.

The tale I had to repeat most often and in greatest detail featured Dr. Theodor Binder's Hospital Amazónico "Albert Schweitzer" in the jungles of Peru near the village of Pucallpa. I had visited this new moral outpost only a few days earlier on my way to Lambaréné.

The drama of my high Andean flight from Lima to Pucallpa brought some gasps from my sea-level listeners at Lambaréné.

The silver bird cleared the 22,000-foot peaks and then scattered numerous families of pigs on the primitive, little-used Pucallpa airstrip.

Dr. Binder met me at the airport. He has a finely chiseled, classically featured face. His steady, penetrating eyes are surrounded by Mephistophelian eyebrows.

I was distressed to discover that the very lovely Mrs. Binder has been handicapped by illness. For over a year now she has managed hospital affairs from between the rough sheets of a sick bed in temporary quarters in Pucallpa.

I was most fortunate to be invited by Dr. Binder to go on a minor medical mission to an authentic Indian village. His thirteen-year-old son accompanied us.

Though our trip in the jungle was easily made by dugout canoe, I must confess that afterwards I was indisposed for several days, recovering from the itch left by numerous blood-sampling larvae, from the toxins absorbed from bouts with miniature unmentionable wildlife, with the cumulative poisons from the ever-present militia of mosquitoes, combined with distresses caused by inescapable changes in intestinal flora.

Actually when we set out, I was in one of the most exuberant moods I have ever known.

As we paddled forward on open water alive with crocodiles, electric fish, and aquatic specimens with tails like scorpions, I probed deep into the motivation of my host. With persistence I extracted the following narrative.

*   *   *   *   *

Dr. Binder's religion of reason parallels Dr. Schweitzer's, but he acquired it independently.

At thirteen Theodor fell out of the arms of orthodox Christianity. Valiantly and at first alone, he hurled his own challenge to ecclesiastical authority. This caused a break in the family, for his zealous father was a dedicated, doctrinal, and dogmatic Christian.

Albert Schweitzer was Theodor's hero. The youthful Theodor willfully rejected prayer. He bolted confirmation. Later he refused to marry in the church and withheld baptism from his baby boy. In his impious aggression, Theodor exceeded the rebel character of his inspiration at Lambaréné. Like Dr. Schweitzer, he too played the organ in the local church for several years.

Two decades later Theodor's father recanted enough to admit that his disobedient son had uncommon, even rare, zeal for ethical goodness.

Mrs. Binder never had a soul-wrenching transition, for she was born into a wealthy, religiously liberal family. The fortunes of war dispossessed her family of their treasures. Rich or poor, she was ideologically suited from the beginning as a perfect mate for her freedom-loving, adventuresome husband. She trained as a medical technician and nurse to do mission work for reason's creed.

Like so many who dared to dissent from Hitler's tyranny, Dr. and Mrs. Binder had a harrowing escape from the Reich. The Binders suddenly had to head for the Swiss frontier. They all but failed to get across the border. So desperate was their plight at one moment on the Swiss border that the young pair, in utter despair of having to return to mad Germany, plotted a joint suicide. It came as an enormous relief that they were allowed to work in refugee camps in the republic of Switzerland.

After the war, a chain of fortuitous events drew the courageous Binders to Peru. For two years they helped build a forest hospital for Catholic nuns. They drifted to Lima, where they found it so comfortable that they postponed their own dreams of a mission of reason.

Six years of unexpected financial success made their renunciation of pure materialism more difficult. However, after a visit with their lifelong hero, Dr. Schweitzer, in his home in Gunsbach in 1955, they became re-dedicated. They vowed never to turn back. When they returned to Lima, they sold all, crossed the Andes, and poured their accumulated substance into the new plans to establish a Schweitzer-like hospital in the heart of unbelievable adversity in the upper Amazon basin.

My listeners at Dr. Schweitzer's settlement often interrupted my story with questions. They wanted to compare the details of the hospital building and the jungle setting on Lake Yarinacocha in South America with Lambaréné on the Ogowe River in French Equatorial Africa.

I got out pictures which convinced my hearers that the equatorial settings are virtually interchangeable. The statistics on diseases, poverty, superstitions, infant mortality, and the expectancy of premature death are likewise comparable in the two places. The physical features and pigmentation of the Africans and the South American Indians are of course very different.

Unlike the frame construction at the Schweitzer jungle village, Dr. Binder's hospital is built of home-made, hollow bricks covered with a smooth cement veneer. The job proceeds slowly with unskilled and voluntary Indian labor, much of it offered in return for medical services. The floors are made of local tile, but as in Lambaréné the roofing is corrugated iron sheeting.

Dr. Binder practiced reverence for all life on the edge of the primeval forest while he personally staggered through the rigors of most of the tropical diseases. Then he contracted and almost died of Weil's disease, disseminated by rat urine. This is a horrible variety of yellow fever characterized by jaundice, muscle pains, high fever, and enlargement of the liver and spleen. After this ghastly episode, he sadly instituted humane extermination procedures. His reverence changed to mere compassion. Believing that each baby rat is part of the miracle of all life, he still has pangs of guilt and remorse, especially when he sees a rat family at play.

Once when Dr. Schweitzer was one of my listeners at Lambaréné, he interjected the observation that the play habits of rats are among the most interesting and moving of any animal he has studied.

The bout with Weil's disease and the war years, and observations of the carnage and killing among the animals in the forest, have solidified Dr. Binder's first commandment of reason. He insists that reason requires behavior in the ethical man that is "other than the world." He has a reasoned concept of spiritual living that is not "biocentric" but is derived from the freedom that is uniquely human. Reason is not the end of human existence to Dr. Binder; but it leads to the supernal good, the "silent, confident reverence for reality of spirit," and it commands us to be *other than* the unethical world about us.

As at Lambaréné, the eventual accomplishments of Dr. Binder's hospital will depend on the financial response elicited throughout the world for his religious, spiritual, and moral principles.

3. Re-living Theories of the Universe in the University of the Universe

My attention had been so absorbed in Dr. Binder's tale of victory told to me en route, I had failed to observe the externals of our progress. We had been paddling steadily away from the last outpost on the frontier of civilization toward, I supposed, an isolated community of Stone Age natives.

As a respite from my incisive probing, we proceeded in a delightful, meditative, almost prayerful silence—if prayer be reverent, quiet conversation with one's own reason. We turned away from the repetitive tropical scenes of the open waterway into the intimate, confined, incessantly changing, verdant, swampy everglades.

The magnitude of the jungle made me feel that if I would know truth, I must love truth. I decided in this new reverent spirit to re-think and re-live in empathy first the ancient Christian gospel, next the nineteenth-century Communist gospel, and then the current untried gospel of reason—just as free, unshackled students everywhere must do more or less for themselves while they progress through modern universities that give comprehensive courses in natural science in addition to the prevailing local and national propaganda.

A canopy of greenery above our moving canoe shut out the retiring equatorial sun, producing a spacious, winding corridor of sacerdotal gloom. In some wider places the reverent effect resembled the atmosphere of great galleries in a giant-sized cathedral, or chambers in a rambling tabernacle big enough for Titans.

These scenes fired my mind with the graphic images of Genesis. I borrowed the eyes of the Old Testament ancients to see with fear and awe a God so great that He was able in the beginning to create the heavens and the earth from a formless void when darkness was on the face of the deep.

The special kind of solitude through which we passed was enriched with the melodious dialogues of muted forest voices. The discordant intrusions of chattering birds did not seem an irreverence amid the humming harmony of insects, the whispering breath of the breezes in the reedy grasses, and the sussurus of the big-leaf palms. If there is a God, He must be a musician to compose such divine organ music.

As we glided deeper in this paradise—or was it Eden?—we could see in the high boughs of the biggest trees lacy, hanging birds' nests. The bosoms of the oldest monarchs of the forest were often decorated by incredibly brilliant corsages of wild orchids.

On reflection one could see how some thoughtful eighteenth-century Christians were satisfied to release the paternalistic Creator portraiture of God and say that mysterious Nature was the image of God, though this view meant a fragmentation of a lovely, complete theory of the universe expressed by the vivid artists who recorded their real beliefs in the cosmology of Genesis.

Yet besides the beauty, even a child could see blood on beaks and claws in this graveyard garden. Nature's second face was ugly. The special kind of routine murder on display showed water dwellers gobbling one another. Each one among the assorted, painted birds aloft zigzagged through shadows with grace, but the mission of every abrupt turn or dive was sinister.

Why did God create the horror of life feeding on life? Why death? Was this the Devil's work? Who created the Devil? Was death really a property of life? Are not birth and death alike the price paid for infinite variation and specialization? Except for death, life would be only an endless chain of yesterdays becoming tomorrows.

Then was this immaterial spectacle of spacious serenity, of music, of harmonious beauty, of lawful order and goodness plus devilish horror and death the complete truth about Nature and God and the real universe? Perhaps the vivid poetic picture of Genesis represents the inventive capacity of man. God may represent the creativity of man. Genesis and the God of the Bible are not taught by the University of Nature today.

*   *   *   *   *

To approach the so-called scientific Marxian view with empathy was far more alien to my traditions, but in the name of more empirical whole truth I made the effort. How would the godless scientific socialist regard these natural scenes we were witnessing from our canoe in the university of the universe?

First, Newton's scientific law of inertia dictates that nothing moves or stops moving unless acted on by external forces. Each action has an equal and opposite reaction. Engels and Marx spoke of immutable material laws and motion from molecules to solar systems.

The code of conservation had been canonized by all experiments in physics laboratories. Matter was atomized into discontinuous orbiting units; but energy, particularly the heat, of all bodies flowed from high to low ceaselessly, continuously, without interruptions, according to the immutable laws of radiation.

So far this deterministic description was in agreement with my experience of the warm sun, the cooling earth, the orbiting moon, and my knowledge of molecules in motion.

These classical theories of physics carried over into biology. Here too a high school student would know that cells function as pure mechanisms under the code of deterministic laws.

As I peered back into stagnant coves, I saw blue-green algae encrusting the surface of the murky water. For a moment I wore imaginary microscopes for glasses. Sure enough, my mind's eye saw each tiny cell working with smooth stability and precision like a physico-chemical laboratory. The tiny, vaporous, colloidal robots were selecting from the varied menu only energy-rich molecules from the decaying culture broth and returning energy-degraded matter in an endless, balanced chain of continuous deterministic causation.

Every arrow of evidence was flying through the armor of ancient Christian faith. It seemed this jungle university taught nothing of immortality, special Creation, and immaterial or spiritual reality. Matter, laws of motion, the determined behavior of molecules, the machine-like precision of these marvelous cell mechanisms had obviously been invariant for billions of years. Evidence indicated that these things existed in time and space continuously, eternally, without beginnings or end.

Science did not stop with the apparent mechanical finality of Newton. Almost every new nugget of evidence, from Darwin to Einstein, verified and extended determinism.

Einstein's relativity had sounded at first like a source of freedom, but actually this great philosopher-physicist served to complete the foundations for the framework of classical physics.

Einstein said, "I do not believe we have any freedom at all in the philosophical sense, for we act not only under external compulsion but also by inner necessity."

Nuclear power brought, in addition to terror, confirmation of materialism and its predictable, predetermined laws.

My objective nineteenth century scientific view of this jungle laboratory seemed at first to confirm the assertions made by the godless Communists who had rejected Genesis in favor of classical Newtonian science. Physicists compiled mountains of evidence to support dialectical materialism. Biologists favored the mechanistic interpretation of cell behavior and animal reflexes.

*   *   *   *   *

As we continued to glide through the mysterious water trails under ethereal shadows, I turned my full attention to the problem of evaluating the religion of reason as it was long ago outlined by Dr. Schweitzer.

I felt that in this jungle setting I could also fit the truths of reason with the deepest, newest scientific truths that were represented here in the University of Nature.

To my knowledge no philosophers or scientists had attempted to reconcile the new non-Newtonian, non-classical developments in science with the religion of reason. I made it my task, therefore, to see how well the religion of reason could fit the propositions of the new science. I was determined to test the spiritual synthesis as I had tested Genesis and the scientific approach to Communism.

What I could not see in this material world of mechanistic

movements and machine-like animation I would have to imagine with reason.

Long ago Dr. Schweitzer chided classical scientists with Newtonian loyalties for being "puffed up with vanity at being able to describe exactly a fragment of the course of life." Dr. Schweitzer maintained from observing the nature of the will-to-live within himself that "behind all phenomena there is will-to-live." He insists that "all that is, is will-to-live." And he says again elsewhere, "Everything that exists is will-to-live."

Dr. Schweitzer's most profound confession is that he has reverence for "the will-to-live which is in all things." With a resounding slap at classical, materialistic, deterministic science he says, "What life is, no science can tell us." Science has not illuminated the degrees of freedom represented in the universe by will-to-live.

Thus consciousness and its implied freedom has been the area of observation for Dr. Schweitzer, who recognizes that man is a unit of the universe "endowed with freedom and capable of reflective, purposive action."

The new science, represented by such men as Niels Bohr, Max Born, and Werner Heisenberg, presumes that mechanical models and finite pictures are inappropriate to describe the immateriality which is the real truth of nature.

My problem now was to consider the new accumulated scientific facts and scientific theories of reality and attempt to bridge the gap between these truths and the truths presumed by the religion of reason.

As I listened to the deep-throated and high-pitched forest music, I felt a deep sense of responsibility to think out this synthesis and this new world view in the American idiom for purposes of communication in my homeland.

If freedom or will is not the gift of God's grace, and if freedom and will exist despite the deterministic challenge of Newton and Marx, and more recently Max Planck, Albert Einstein, Erwin Schrodinger, and Louis de Broglie, where can it be found in a jungle university and how then can the freedom of reason be derived?

After Max Planck shook the world of science with his quantum discovery, a Dane entered the arena of contending cosmologies. Niels Bohr of Copenhagen observed that both wave and particle theories of light and matter were complementary half-truths of a deeper, wider whole truth. Apparent disharmonies disappeared when the rigid, classical, deterministic, materialistic, mechanistic, conceptual framework of reality was widened.

Dr. Bohr's new inclusive view was called "complementarity." It accepted the truth of both contradictory theories as complementary propositions in agreement with underlying immaterial reality. This enlargement of the traditional view proved extremely fertile and produced many new laboratory successes.

Werner Heisenberg, a German disciple in the Danish scientific revolution, opened more doors in the haunted house of classical science. Dr. Heisenberg's mind leapt forward. He showed that single atomic events, which were now established as "immaterial" realities, had an individuality, a singularity, and wholeness about them. Reality units were probabilities.

Dr. Heisenberg showed that attempts to study simple subatomic events were blocked, perhaps forever. The single microcosmic events were altered by the act of observation, even when the finest, most delicate tools of experimentation and sensitive recording methods were employed. Distortions occurred under the most exacting conditions.

Actually a single specimen of reality had never been seen. Reality had never been measured or recorded by itself. Isolation of units of reality was by the nature of reality impossible. Only the fleeting inconstant interactions with the tools of observation were knowable as shadows masquerading as bits of recorded truth, and classical physicists had mistaken these appearances for the truth of ultimate reality.

Werner Heisenberg proved with others that specimens of reality could be symbolically represented by mathematical formalisms. Immaterial relationships *were* the ultimate realities. So true was this to him that he had faith that all immaterial relations might be expressed in one set of mathematical equations, and this could include all field forces as parts of one continuous field.

Heisenberg was aware of the force of his first scientific breakthrough, and he sensed the enormous confusion his theory would bring to philosophical speculation. He said in his writings with the certainty of a prophet, "The rigorous validity of quantum mechanics compels us to depart from the reality concept of classical physics."

Werner Heisenberg was paid high tribute by his rival, Albert Einstein, who said, "This is the only theory at present which permits a unitary grasp of experience concerning the quantum characteristic of micro-mechanistic events."

Dr. Heisenberg called his vault over barriers "a real break in the structure of modern science." As we shall see, it was a prophetic advantage to the philosophical stream of thought in relation to the conflicts between East and West that he called his theory "indeterminacy."

*   *   *   *   *

Though Dr. Schweitzer used the core of consciousness as his non-scientific but unassailable source of cosmic freedom in his theory of the universe, he sought the underpinning for his new religion in nature. He said once from his microscopic knowledge of how cell produces cell:

> We have discovered in the cell . . . and crystal . . . an individual existence in whose faculties, active and passive, we see repeated elements of our own vitality.

This, he said, is the "being manifested in phenomena."

Here is the kinship Dr. Schweitzer has lived by and taught by example. To Dr. Schweitzer, partial freedom is much more than an illusion of human pride or a trick of predetermined vanity. Semi-freedom is the essence and core of individuality, rational uniqueness in man, singularity of the world of will, and the wholeness of every specimen of the universe that is half deterministic and half free.

Today, besides the uncertainty principles and probabilities in physics, we do know in the new biology that cells are really communities of protein molecules that can exist as crystals. The uniqueness of life has been vaporized as a concept. There is no basic difference between the animate and inanimate in the universe.

Proteins are high-energy units of the universe capable of self-renewal. Metabolism appears statistically to be like herd behavior in sub-microscopic atomic events. The interplay between statistical determinacy of metabolic proteins and the individual self-determining disorder of the infinitesimal protein singularities is a primitive manifestation of a few degrees of primordial freedom.

The virus is a protein molecule crystal capable of self-replication with the perfect precision of an indestructible die. But these "living" molecules are not necessarily material. In a cell they are rather a branching, moving cobweb of continuously changing spatial relations and reactions controlled by internal field forces.

Primordial freedom is an immaterial reality that changes external reactions or relationships without changing itself.

Each protein molecule has a dual nature. Each has an incredible mutability locked inside incredibly stable energy levels that other protein molecules (enzymes) alone have the key to unlock for swift, almost instantaneous physico-chemical interactions.

All protein molecules can manifest the capacity to change otherwise stable energy levels without altering their own stability or capacity to continue changing energy levels in reactions. Enzymes act with unbelievable specificity. Enzymes can speed up some reactions 100 million times.

My reason told me that my jungle university would be inert without its billions of enzymes.

The molecular crystals involved in enzyme action are the essence of sub-living organic evolution and the evolution of life as well. In a defensible theory of the universe one might say that what we have called life may be more reasonably interpreted as nothing more than the universe itself unfolding in a fluctuating random process, in which order is manipulated by regular units of partial disorder identified with a ramifying labyrinth of field forces.

Genes, the genetic carriers of the chromosomes, are like the virus and other enzymes. They are incredibly stable, self-duplicating protein molecules which, like microfilm, carry the infinitesimal codescript for all species.

These stable but mutable micro-masters are the executive directors of the tapestry of tissues and the spatial configurations of each individual from algae to Schweitzer.

The open-faced essence of reality of outdoor life in the upper Amazon region conforms to no substance. It is an irrepressible ferment of an indeterminate surge.

The carnival of cannibalism in my University of Nature is a tempestuous hunt for a shadowy form of immaterial self-realization called freedom or will-to-live. Each sudden, quanta-like movement is part of the relentless forward thrust of freedom. Though the compulsive will-to-live is divided against itself in a million ways, billions of whole singular wills coalesce as freedom's power and are triumphant and victorious.

This mysterious ferment is what Dr. Schweitzer calls "the secret spring of life as life is in itself . . . the sparks of the will-to-live; the impulse to self-realization . . . the eternal spirit . . . an enigmatic creative force."

It took no special genius to reflect that the species around me were not the result of a continuous stream of upgraded changes. Evolution obviously took place by the characteristic wholeness of quanta-like jumps. Every mutation, good or bad, involved individuality, singularity, and unique probability expectancies. The leaps occur in evolution in the spatial arrangements in genes.

There is a power of freedom. It is seen where a tiny force master-manages statistical masses of elements or microscopic machines without changing itself. Freedoms are partially predictable. There are laws of freedom. Freedom fragments can occur in super-units of indeterminate complexes of singularities and independent packets of probabilities.

Thus ranges of freedom expand from whole quanta to electrons, to atoms, molecules, enzymes, cells and cell societies, the highest of which is man, who is dimly aware of freedom's processes. Ethical jumps sponsored by reason go from self to family to tribe to state to nation to humanity to the oneness of, and preciousness of, singular wills in the universe.

One thing was apparent to me as I gazed through the gloom and listened to the singing circus of life about me. Darwin's deterministic description, survival of the fittest, did not suit the scene. Fitness is the mark of all specimens, despite injuries or disease. As I linked the activities of the algae with those of the birds to the mystery of my own reflections, I was convinced anew that evolution is a survival of the freest. Fittest can only mean freest.

As I glided along in our dugout canoe reflecting on this newest, most elemental, naked, immaterial reality behind the new rational theory of the immaterial universe and my own dim but marvelous heritage of perception, I could feel no separateness from nature's moving picture and no isolation from my University of truth. I was both specimen and spectator, student and subject, teacher and text. I was not a machine or a descendant of a sinful, fallen angel from the Garden of Eden. My kinship to lower forms was inescapable.

I was different and fitter because I was freer. I was far freer to rove and think and plan with fewer limitations to my liberties

than the Indians in surrounding villages and the wonderful but
still less free subhuman kinfolk of the jungle.

4. *Reason's Ethics in Action in the Field*

We finally beached our canoe on the shore of the island in
the endless everglades, where I was to see the real-life drama
of Dr. Binder's religion of reason at work in a Shepibo Indian
village.

It was also to be for me a test-tube-sized neolithic community
in which the theories of Genesis, deterministic Communism, and
Dr. Schweitzer's religion of reason could be evaluated at the
primitive human level.

Our invasion was at first treated with cool, sullen, unsmiling
reserve by the small, statuesque, bronze-colored Indians. My
mind was crawling with ugly rumors about these ex-head-hunters
and head-shrinkers. While I sensed the lack of "Southern hospitality," I noticed that curiosity tempered with shyness marked
the deportment of these neolithic children.

Without an invitation, we sat down with a large family. The
beginning of the thaw was slow because I was a total stranger.
Before long the doctor and his son, familiar to the group, were
conversing quite normally with these old friends and their "stair-
case" assorted children. My strangeness was forgotten or forgiven.
The doctor's jests and obvious affection warmed the atmosphere.

Already I sensed that these people could be, like all other
groups I knew, kind, proud, vain, sensitive, suspicious, fun-loving,
and murderous within the web of their ethical or religious convictions that made them half free and half slave.

My second observation remained my biggest discovery. Dr.
Binder really loved these people. I gathered this from the overtones of comments of concern and jests, but also from observing
his approval of his adored, fine-looking son while the boy talked
independently with Indian youngsters his own age in their language. Dr. Binder practices the brotherhood of man on the

strength of his ethical conviction derived exclusively from personal free reason.

As we were walking from one family to another, Dr. Binder
said to me, "You know, animals are driven by impulses. Only
man can free himself from animal impulses. This is the unique
point in man. Man can meet injustice with forgiveness, hatred
with forbearance, thoughtlessness with understanding, hostility
with kindness, and misery with compassion. Every individual
here is precious to me. Love is a manifestation of human
freedom."

Before long, the inhabitants were exposing their many ills to
Dr. Binder as usual—partly, it seemed, as a gesture to please him.
They borrowed heavily on the doctor's capital of Western medical
know-how. He dipped into his limited portable dispensary for
remedies that brought liberation from pain and anguish to some
of the sufferers.

One girl, who was stricken with acute abdominal pains, was
stretched out on a grass mat for a cursory diagnostic examination.
The doctor instructed her parents in their own language. He
produced a sort of spiritual comfort but also specific pills for
the patient, aimed at a known though unseen parasitic target
in the girl's alimentary tract.

Dr. Binder turned to me, saying, "Goodness to me consists of
lessening misery while adding beauty to the world. I think a
pain-free smile is beautiful."

As we passed on to other families, we saw other maladies and
all varieties of sores and skin abrasions. There were marks of
malnutrition. Bellies were distended with worms. Gross signs
of leprosy, tuberculosis, yaws, and venereal diseases were observed
on the nude frames of some of the fly-covered children.

Dr. Binder said that intestinal parasites and anemia are almost
universal in the tribes, and malaria is widespread. Because these
people are cut off from responsible medical aid, the chronic,
world-wide diseases and tropical supplements plague them un-

mercifully, shortening their lives by adding extra health problems to an existence overburdened with suffering.

I cannot say that these diseased people appeared unhappy. They were enjoying what they conceived to be the pursuit of tribal virtue.

Like other creatures in this paradoxical universe of luxuriant beauty and horror, they stalked and were stalked. Only those freest in body and mind survived the rigors of childhood. They all learned to feed on life—sometimes on diseased or decaying carcasses—and life fed on them inside and out.

*   *   *   *   *

Being professionally curious about the condition of the dentition in this domain, I persuaded the doctor to cajole the inhabitants into the mental and physical posture that would make them willing and accessible to a mouth examination by a foreign stranger. We had more refusals than acceptances. Our silly suggestion provoked much shy giggling. Finally some adventuresome children surmounted their fear and started a mass movement. There was not one chair in the whole village, but I managed fleeting glances into the cavernous mouths by bending low over my clients, who sat motionless on the messy ground distractingly alive with ants.

To my horror, I found that my Western profession had in a few instances made its way to the jungle frontier towns like Pucallpa. Here vendors who sold oral health care for private gain had taken payment for cosmetic services. A few front teeth in a handful of the grandest elders in the Indian village were ornamented with shining gold crowns, whereas large, carious lesions and large, chronically abscessed residual roots had been left without care. As in Lambaréné, pus oozed from gums inflamed with untreated pyorrhea. The swindle of capping good teeth with gold ranks among the black marks of guilt in the balance sheet against the West in dealing with so-called primitive peoples.

As we walked from family to family, I could see the marked contrasts between the usual professional exclusiveness and commercialism and Dr. Binder's quality of compassion. He invited all the sick to come to his temporary hospital in Pucallpa for free treatment, no strings attached.

In a tiny incident I saw the more inclusive aspects of his missionary message implemented. As we passed one Indian family, Dr. Binder noticed some young boys teasing newly hatched baby birds. They enjoyed their chirping, animated, fluffy toys. The perishable playthings were not destined to survive the frolic long. Gently but firmly the doctor admonished the boys and spoke of the kinship of all life and the duty of universal compassion.

I am sure the birds died, but mercy to humans and subhumans was shown to be indivisible. More important, the great principle of evolution and the interrelationship of species was taught by Dr. Binder's example. For in this village, a reasonable friend with real powers to heal is a master teacher. He teaches kinship by serving as a veterinary when he has the opportunity to relieve the pain of subhuman kith or pets.

Dr. Binder said, "I do not believe as Dr. Schweitzer does in reverence for all life, but I agree with him that compassion must be all-embracing."

Dr. Binder's singular, personal, consistent moral motive is as clear as the sun in a cloudless sky. He is using his medical skill in the service of his ethic as a merciful teaching-example of his religion of reason.

*   *   *   *   *

We were stopped in our clinical walk through the village that should have been a ward by what I thought at first was an apparition, or perhaps an Albino Indian. Soon the mystery was solved. The man hailing us was a white American missionary.

The evangelist greeted us warmly, took us to his primitive, pathetic, makeshift church. This done, he invited us to his relatively comfortable little hut apart from the village to meet his wife. After a prayer, we were invited to join our host and hostess in a cup of tea and the luxury of a piece of canned cake.

After I made bold to explain my lack of orthodox faith and my detachment from all denominations, I asked the fundamentalist missionary in a friendly, jocular way if the soul-saving business had been brisk. He smiled sadly but tolerantly and said no, the natives did not seem to care.

Though not a physician, our dedicated missionary friend told of trying in despair to cope with some of the baffling diseases. For example, two days before he had heroically helped give an enema to the chief's oldest very sick wife. When last seen, the woman was failing fast from the still undiagnosed affliction. The missionary said despondently that he thought the woman's husband had taken her away, perhaps to die.

Our hospitable proselytizer for the Biblical God and Genesis, speaking paternalistically for his flock, thanked Dr. Binder generously for the treatment and medication given to the heathen jungle dwellers. He expressed embarrassed gratitude for the free medical service Dr. Binder had given him personally.

The missionary, quite fit now after Dr. Binder's treatment, like a good neighbor and a debtor with genuine gratitude, gave the doctor some fresh eggs to take home.

My observations in the Shepibo Indian village did more than confirm Dr. Schweitzer's concept of will-to-live, for these creatures were obviously "endowed with freedom and capable of reflective, purposive action." More than this, like the ultimate quanta of action described by Heisenberg, each individual had immaterial uniqueness, non-mechanical singularity, degrees of freedom, and uncertainty, indeterminacy, probability, and an indivisible wholeness. The personality of each acted like a field force working on others at a distance.

At any rate, though these people owned property in common, they did not follow the Marxian notions of historical and economic determinacy. Nor did the men appear in this tropical setting like creatures specially created from a void, nor did the women seem the products of a male rib. These forest dwellers

show the kinship of all life on the one hand and the indivisibility
of the human family on the other.

Dr. Schweitzer's theory of will-to-live and his religion of reason
seemed to fit this community perfectly.

Though the inhabitants in Lambaréné humored me and kept
me talking, I had the distinct feeling that my story lacked a vital
link. Science is a giant and until many in its ranks endorse the
plausibility of universal freedom and picture Dr. Schweitzer's
role in it, the ferment will work too slowly to clarify our world
of chaos and confusion. I did not have to wait long for support
from a world-famous scientist, which supplied the missing link
I missed so much.

5. Climax on the Scientific Summit

As I flew from Lambaréné to Europe I planned to call on
Dr. Werner Heisenberg as a final adventure in my safari of
discovery.

By now the reader should know how vital I considered Dr.
Heisenberg's testimony on Dr. Schweitzer's theory of the universe.
At any rate, I hope the reader can share vicariously the feeling of
expectancy that enveloped me when I picked up the phone in
Zurich to ask the long-distance operator to call the great theo-
retical physicist at Gottingen, Germany.

Soon I heard a jovial voice at the other end of the wire
saying, "If you are not a newspaper reporter, come to my home
at five o'clock tomorrow."

When the door opened at the Heisenberg residence, I was
greeted by a round-faced, ruddy, jovial, vivacious, well-tailored
man in his middle fifties.

My genial host said, "And how was my good friend, Albert
Schweitzer, when you left him at Lambaréné?"

After my report on Dr. Schweitzer's well-being, Dr. Heisenberg continued, "When I was with Dr. Schweitzer last, he told
me he was becoming famous. He proved it by saying that five

of his autographs for trading purposes among children were already equal in value to one Max Schmeling signature."

Responding to the genuine hospitality, I answered, "Dr. Heisenberg, you are in Dr. Schweitzer's thoughts very often. Your name is mentioned frequently in Lambaréné and always with the warmest affection. Dr. Schweitzer has great joy in your most successful and most recent penetration into the unknown."

I added, "I found Dr. Schweitzer's otherwise austere monastic room a collection depot for scientific treatises, tracts, and theses from prize-winning scientists the world over. Dr. Schweitzer will certainly devour your new ideas with great relish and understanding."

After the amenities, when I finally composed myself in a comfortable chair across the study from Werner Heisenberg, I felt as if fate had given me a reporter's pass to a choice seat in the theater of contemporary history at a moment of great climax.

The stature of my host, long ago a Nobel Prize-winning philosopher-physicist, had recently grown larger and more significant in the world press. I had read reports of his current successes as I moved through South America and Africa and Europe.

Reports in journals with world-wide distribution announced that Dr. Heisenberg had finally managed the Titanic task of completing the mathematical formulation of the continuous field theory that Albert Einstein had sought in vain.

The same journals acclaimed Dr. Werner Heisenberg as Dr. Albert Einstein's successor. In one sense I knew this to be a serious mistake.

Dr. Heisenberg has been a banner-bearer for a system of physical reality and philosophical thought which opposes the system of physics and philosophy that Einstein championed with integrity, charm, and incredible brilliance.

While Einstein was modernizing and unifying the mechanistic edifice of classical physics, Heisenberg was succeeding in exposing the false tenets of this rigid system by founding the indeterminacy principles on the new solid grounds of physical reality.

Besides being Einstein's antagonist and adversary, rival and opponent, in the realm of physical reality, Dr. Heisenberg carried his new views of "indeterminacy" founded in physics into the heart of the marketplace of world-shaping philosophical ideas. He clearly demonstrated how modern non-classical, non-Newtonian science challenged Western Christianity as well as Marxian dialectics and determinism.

The purpose of my visit was to find out whether Heisenberg could confirm or deny Dr. Schweitzer's theory of the universe and philosophy of will and freedom by virtue of his new insights into physical reality.

I had long suspected that Heisenberg's break-through was as important to our age as the discoveries of Newton and Darwin had been to the nineteenth century. Heisenberg's concept could be the vital and final link needed to assure the success of Dr. Schweitzer's role as a prophet of freedom, particularly if Heisenberg's indeterminacy principle provided the latitude for liberty denied by classical physics.

The truth is, Marx composed his philosophy from the principles of materialism in which matter was the final determinant of all that happens or ever will happen.

The new physics and philosophy championed by Dr. Heisenberg not only challenges Marxian determinism but it prepares the way for new affirmative philosophies such as the one given to the world by Dr. Schweitzer.

Whereas Dr. Heisenberg's theory of "indeterminacy" is not as yet a specific, definitive, affirmative principle of freedom—and certainly Dr. Heisenberg has not yet offered the world a philosophy of systematic thought founded on the demonstrable reality of freedom in physics—nevertheless his "indeterminacy principle" focuses world-wide attention on the reality of immaterial, irreducible probability packets as causal factors in events and as an ultimate truth about the nature of the universe.

I was aware of these facts before I met Dr. Heisenberg. I must now report two more cataclysmic break-throughs that I unearthed in my personal interview.

*   *   *   *   *

The two pronouncements, which I venture to call culture-shaking, represent the summit climax of my own circuitous safari of discovery.

The first momentous generalization that grew out of our conference is this: Every single proposition in Dr. Schweitzer's philosophy of the universe is, in Dr. Heisenberg's opinion, "consonant with every aspect of the new developments in the field of physics."

The great scientific scholar-specialist, whose regular "beat" is the opposite end of the knowledge spectrum, confirmed as scientifically reasonable the philosophical truths achieved by the conscious rational method of inquiry exemplified by Dr. Albert Schweitzer.

The second proclamation ranks equally with the first and is a logical consequence of its philosophical projection. Dr. Heisenberg told me that whereas the scientific socialism of Karl Marx was founded on classical physics, "there is not at this moment in history one shred of scientific evidence left to support the catechism derived from the so-called scientific cosmology of Communism."

Dr. Heisenberg, in speaking of the contemporaries of Marx (1818-1883) said, "We cannot possibly expect that those thinkers who a century ago introduced dialectical materialism would have foreseen the development of quantum theory."

In the case of Russia's more recent revolutionary leader, Nikolai Lenin (1870-1924), the story was somewhat different. Dr. Heisenberg had a verbatim quotation proving that Lenin was aware of some evidence of immaterialism and indeterminacy in physics. In this quotation Lenin dismissed the factual data with the popish, authoritarian assertion that "all this is but another *confirmation* of dialectical materialism."

In my judgment, the consonance claimed between the new science and Dr. Schweitzer's ethical structure and its simultaneous impact on Communism is the most transcendent kind of harmonious musicality in the history of human thought.

I do not want it thought that I gloat over this anti-Marxian, anti-Lenin scientific bombshell. The new scientific blast was not directed against the Reds. The new evidence is equally devastating to parallel materialistic and dogmatic tendencies in the West. But Western dogma was already doomed by earlier scientists.

Heisenberg's ethical message is essentially anti-hate. Antipathy between East and West has accentuated relatively insignificant differences. Hate has hidden the dangerous broad-band affinities of the two materialistic religions now in perilous but unnecessary collision.

The theme of Dr. Heisenberg's book, *Physics and Philosophy*, may be epitomized in his simple sentence, "The openness of modern physics may help to some extent to reconcile older traditions with new trends in thought."

*   *   *   *   *

After my visit with Dr. Heisenberg I concluded with more fervor than before that Albert Schweitzer's theory of Reverence for Will is the highest, widest spiritual achievement of the human mind, serving as it does the essence of freedom in the universe.

Dr. Schweitzer discovered and described the importance of the half of the universe ignored by classical science. This half is nevertheless real but invisible, certain but immeasurable, perceivable but not palpable, spiritual and supra-personal but not supernatural, creative but not separate in its sublimity from man at his highest.

Albert Schweitzer is the catalyst of great goodness in a world in search of a cosmic basis for its quest of freedom and the laws of responsible, inclusive love. He is unique among prophets, for his views fuse the scientific experience of the universe with the reflected truths about the cosmos. His cosmology and behavior are indivisible.

In our hour of crisis Dr. Schweitzer offers us a theory of the universe. It involves reasoned reverence for responsible freedom. It is the religion of individual reason.

Dr. Schweitzer has lived according to the canons of his religion of reason for more than half a century. He has done so to reflect its power and to exemplify the inherent perfection of his compelling message. He has beamed the living dream as an example to the sick West first, but he has also radiated his curative idealism to the East and indeed to the whole ailing world.

I would like to urge contenders for Christianity and contenders for Communism to consider jointly and explore together this new scientific and rational cosmology. This vision could prevent masses of men from destroying one another over differences in two obsolete cosmologies whose essential truths are preserved in the new cosmology that Dr. Schweitzer offers the world.

The religion of reason affirms that goodness must have wholeness. Goodness is not won by obedience to ancient dogma or to the modern State.

Goodness is conformity to informed, individual reason. It is good and reasonable to protect, foster, and create higher and higher forms of personal freedom through deeper and wider visions of limitless personal human responsibility.

The single key to education and success is self-perfection in the service of universal individual freedom.

In the dawn hours of the Space Age we need less learned ignorance and less irresponsible science. We need, rather, a crash program in free thinking, in reason, in ethics, and in responsible freedom, perhaps under the new banner of Dialectical Immaterialism.

Until education is re-evaluated, re-thought, and renovated, more arbitrary schooling will only advance our peril. We need primary schools, high schools, colleges, and universities dedicated to objective free inquiry in the realm of values before we destroy ourselves over provincialisms, ancient taboos, and obsolete cosmologies.

There must be established schools free from nationalism, where global scholars with cosmic-sized ideas can be nurtured preparatory for the day when the growing human family on our shrinking planet will establish one common government.

Until the kinship of life and the oneness of the human family are basic to the concepts of justice and government, until the liberty of every individual is represented by laws established by the consent of all, the fragments of freedom achieved by personal sacrifices in the past will be imperiled, with or without war.

In the meantime, Dr. Schweitzer's individual-to-individual plan of service might be taught so that increasing numbers of creative individuals in the field of industry, agriculture, health, and education will, like Dr. Mellon and Dr. Percy in Haiti and Dr. Binder in Peru, carry Western skills to the peoples who need them most. This spiritual offensive is part of the moral dynamism of freedom.

If the Albert Schweitzer Education Foundation receives financial support to foster common idealism through the channels of free scholarship represented by scholars like Dr. Schweitzer, it may become one of the people's instruments to achieve peace with freedom based on a world-wide religion of reason.

Whether or not the Albert Schweitzer Education Foundation becomes great and aids in this cause, I am convinced that reverence for reasoned individual freedom is the only complete, composite theory of the universe that beckons the human family forward with hope.

My foremost discovery affirms one point above all others: The sole issue that challenges every whole scholar and every true educator on the face of the earth is to find a unifying theory of the universe.

With these global suggestions of purpose for the Albert Schweitzer Education Foundation and for other spontaneous educational efforts as one answer, my personal safari of discovery comes full circle to Albert Schweitzer's original prophetic challenge cited at the beginning of this book:

> For there must indeed arise a philosophy profounder and more living than our own and endowed with greater spiritual and ethical force. In this terrible period through which mankind is passing, from the East and from the West we must all keep a look-out for the coming of this more perfect and more powerful form of thought, which will conquer the hearts of individuals and compel whole peoples to acknowledge its sway. It is for this that we must strive.

Index

[267]

Philosophy, 153, 182; *see also* Ethics; Will
Philosophy of Civilization, The (Schweitzer), 6, 68, 180
Physics, 156, 245, 261
Physics and Philosophy (Heisenberg), 262
Planck, Max, 248
Princeton University, 86, 95
Prophets, 97-98, 99; Hebrew, 107
Prophet in the Wilderness (Hagedorn), 6
Protestantism, 146

Quakers, 97
Quantum Theory, 248, 249, 261
Quest of the Historical Jesus (Schweitzer), 68, 91, 121-140

Reality, 247, 248
Reason, 103ff, 109, 110-111, 116, 126, 127, 128, 140, 145, 159, 160, 163, 168, 170, 182-189, 242, 246ff
Reformation, 149
Religion: and philosophy, 182; Communism as, 222-223; in history, 61, 117; modern, 114, 191; personal, 49; *see also* Christianity
Renaissance, 110
Reverence for Life, 30, 45, 76, 80, 102, 112, 116-117, 119, 121, 140, 165, 180-181, 192, 193
Rice, Howard C., 10
Rockefeller, Nelson, 93
Rogers, Mrs. Julian, 10, 75
Roosevelt, Franklin D., 53
Roosevelt University, 86
Ross, Emory, 10, 84, 89
Rousseau, Jean Jacques, 111, 197
Russell, Bertrand, 88
Russell, C. E., Mrs., 5
Russia, 63-64, 67

Saturday Review, 7
Schilpp, Paul, Dr., 10
Schopenhauer, Arthur, 111, 157
Schrodinger, Erwin, 247
Schweitzer, Albert: and Einstein, 72; and Heisenberg, 261; as a prophet, 97-98, 99-100; at Lambaréné, 19, 24-25, 27, 30-33, 42, 43, 45; attacks on,

17-18, 60, 90; authors evaluation of, 230, 232, 262-263; "being manifested in phenomena", 249; compared to Gandhi, 68, 77; compared to Marx, 221-225; compared to Jesus, 32-33, 49, 50, 92, 97, 120, 121, 135; ethics of, 49, 102ff, 117-118, 119-120, 165, 175, 192, 206, 216, 217, 234, 263-265; honors accorded, 96; *Indian Thought and Its Development*, 56, 57; *Mysticism of the Apostle Paul*, 144; on aesthetics, 173-174; on atomic weapons, 18, 234-235; on Christianity, 198, 199, 219; on education, 180-188, 207, 210; on Essenes, 91, 92; on freedom, 159, 163-164, 165, 166-170; on God, 127-129, 134; on Goethe, 149-154; on Hegel, 220; on Jesus, 121-127, 129-141, 144; on Paul, 144-149, 150; on rationalism, 202; on Adam Smith, 213-214; *Out of My Life and Thought*, 68, 101; *Paul and His Interpreters*, 144; personality, 52, 96, 117; personal religion, 49-50; *Philosophy of Civilization*, 6, 68, 180; preparation for Lambaréné, 16, 45, 46-47; *Quest of the Historical Jesus*, 68, 91, 121ff; Reverence for Life, 30, 45, 76, 80, 102 112, 116-117, 119, 121, 140, 165, 180-181, 192, 193; will-to-live, 29, 32, 49, 102, 110, 116, 128, 140, 141, 159, 165, 180-181, 247, 251
Schweitzer, Mme., 33-34
Science, 114-115, 157, 161, 183
Seaver, George, 7, 121, 236-237
Segregation, 17, 24-25
Sermon on the Mount, 133, 136
Shaw, George Bernard, 157
Silver, Ali, 10, 27
Smith, Adam, 213
Spinoza, Baruch, 111, 150, 151, 157
Spirit, 137; *see also* Will
Stalin, Joseph, 152
Stanford University, 86
Stassen, Harold, 11, 84
Steere, Douglas, 10, 84
Stevenson, Adlai, 10, 79, 86-88, 236
Stocks, Dr. and Mrs. J. W., 9
Stoics, 107